Barkley's wealth of scientific knowledge about the effects of adult ADHD, not to mention his personal wisdom, make this a "must read." Anyone suspecting that someone in their life suffers from adult ADHD will benefit from Barkley's uncompromising description of this insidious disorder, advice for managing it, and his compassion for the plight of the loved ones who desperately want to be helpful.

—**J. Russell Ramsay, PhD,** Associate Professor of Clinical Psychology, University of Pennsylvania Perelman School of Medicine; author of *The Adult ADHD Tool Kit: Using CBT to Facilitate Coping Inside and Out*

Barkley has devoted his career to the scientific study of ADHD, and also has firsthand knowledge of how disruptive and sometimes devastating it can be to patients, families, and loved ones. In a most genuine and heartfelt way—and in simple straightforward language—he bares his soul in an effort to help others understand and successfully manage this often misunderstood disorder. Full of hope, compassion, personal experiences, and sophisticated knowledge and advice, this book will forever change how you view this disorder.

—**Kevin Murphy, PhD,** President, Adult ADHD Clinic of Central MA and former Chief of the Adult ADHD Clinic at UMASS Medical Center, Worcester, MA

A foremost internationally recognized ADHD expert, Barkley offers 40 years of insight from scientific research and clinical experience enhanced by his compassionate understanding derived from personal family experiences. A highly recommended book for anyone who is touched by ADHD.

—**David W. Goodman, MD, FAPA,** Director, Suburban Psychiatric Associates, LLC; Director, Adult Attention Deficit Disorder Center of Maryland; Assistant Professor, Department of Psychiatry and Behavioral Sciences, Johns Hopkins University School of Medicine, Baltimore, MD

Caring for someone with ADHD is difficult, and this book is an invaluable source of support. It is packed with explanations, stories, advice, and encouragement. Barkley combines years of research and clinical experience in this engaging account of how to understand and help someone with ADHD.

—**Frances Prevatt, PhD,** Professor of Educational Psychology, Florida State University, Tallahassee; author of *Succeeding With Adult ADHD* and *ADHD Coaching: A Guide for Mental Health Professionals*

This is a wonderful, easy-to-read book specifically for the spouse/partner or family member of an adult with ADHD. It provides important background information for recognizing the condition and understanding its diagnosis and treatment. Barkley insightfully discusses the panoply of feelings such as frustration, guilt, or discouragement that may be evoked by ADHD in a loved one. He goes on to address practical matters such as how to talk to a loved one about getting professional help for ADHD, helping the loved one understand and accept ADHD, and advice for living with an adult with ADHD.

—**Mary V. Solanto, PhD,** Associate Professor, New York University (NYU), Department of Psychiatry; NYU Child Study Center, New York, NY

When an Adult You Love Has ADHD

When an Adult You Love Has ADHD

Professional Advice for Parents, Partners, and Siblings

Russell A. Barkley, PhD

American Psychological Association • *Washington, DC*

Published by
APA LifeTools
750 First Street, NE
Washington, DC 20002
www.apa.org

To order
APA Order Department
P.O. Box 92984
Washington, DC 20090-2984
Tel: (800) 374-2721;
Direct: (202) 336-5510
Fax: (202) 336-5502;
TDD/TTY: (202) 336-6123
Online: www.apa.org/pubs/books
E-mail: order@apa.org

In the U.K., Europe, Africa, and the Middle East, copies may be ordered from
American Psychological Association
3 Henrietta Street
Covent Garden, London
WC2E 8LU England

Typeset in Sabon by Circle Graphics, Inc., Columbia, MD

Printer: United Book Press, Baltimore, MD
Cover Designer: Naylor Design, Washington, DC

Library of Congress Cataloging-in-Publication Data

Names: Barkley, Russell A., 1949- author.
Title: When an adult you love has ADHD : professional advice for parents, partners, and siblings / Russell A. Barkley, PhD.
Description: Washington, DC : American Psychological Association, [2017] | Includes bibliographical references and index.
Identifiers: LCCN 2016012286 | ISBN 9781433823084 | ISBN 143382308X
Subjects: LCSH: Attention-deficit disorder in adults—Popular works.
Classification: LCC RC394.A85 .B386 2017 | DDC 616.85/89—dc23 LC record available at https://lccn.loc.gov/2016012286

British Library Cataloguing-in-Publication Data
A CIP record is available from the British Library.

Printed in the United States of America
First Edition

http://dx.doi.org/10.1037/15963-000

CONTENTS

PREFACE

This book is the culmination of a lifetime of experience with attention-deficit/hyperactivity disorder (ADHD) in children and adults. That experience constitutes my professional career as a clinical neuropsychologist. For more than 40 years I've been engaged in clinical work, research, consulting, and teaching concerning ADHD. But just as important to the purpose of this book are all of my experiences growing up within a family in which ADHD was present both in my immediate family and in a number of relatives. In particular, ADHD greatly affected my fraternal twin brother, Ron, whose life was tragically ended at the age of 56 in no small part due to his disorder (among other disorders). Compounding this tragedy for our family was the more recent suicide of my nephew, Ethan, who was Ron's son. Ethan impulsively took his own life in August of 2013, just before his 30th birthday. Ethan also had ADHD, among other psychological difficulties. The preparation of this book was therefore not just a professional project but a personal one for me as well. That lifetime of personal family experiences lends a landscape-sized background of tone and coloring to the information presented here, more than in any other book that I have written. I want to share that professional and personal knowledge about ADHD with others who are parents, siblings, partners, or close friends to a loved one experiencing adult ADHD.

PREFACE

I

WHAT YOU NEED TO KNOW ABOUT ADULT ADHD

CHAPTER 1

HOW TO TELL IF A LOVED ONE HAS ADHD

Do you know an adult loved one who you feel has serious and persistent problems with their attention, concentration, distractibility, impulsiveness, forgetfulness, self-control, or all of these symptoms? Do you have an adult child, partner or spouse, brother, or sister with these problems? If so, do you want to know more about attention-deficit/hyperactivity disorder (ADHD) and especially how you can best help them? Then this book is for you.

Why should you trust what I have to say about ADHD? Because I know ADHD inside and out, personally and professionally, like very few others do. I have conducted research on ADHD since 1973 and have published nearly 300 scientific studies and book chapters on ADHD and related disorders. And every week, I follow every research article newly published in the world's scientific journals to stay abreast of key developments in this field and to summarize those key findings in my newsletter, *The ADHD Report.* So ADHD is my professional specialty.

But it is not just a professional focus for me. Members of my own family also have ADHD. They include not only various extended relatives but also a fraternal twin brother, Ron, whose ADHD indirectly cost him his life in a car crash in the summer of 2006. I share more of his story later in the book. Just as tragic was what happened 7 years later when Ron's son with ADHD impulsively committed suicide after an argument with a girlfriend. So I have a personal stake in understanding ADHD and how it affects those of us who deeply care about someone with adult ADHD.

You want to know what ADHD is all about. You want to know how you can tell if a loved one may have it. If they do, you want the facts about it straight up, not sugar coated. You also want to know all the risks ADHD imposes on those who have it, and indirectly on those, like you, who care about them. You also want to know what helps treat adult ADHD and what you can personally do to help your loved one. By effectively treating your loved one with ADHD, he or she can have a happier, more successful, and more effective life and a stronger, closer relationship with you and others. You need to know what doesn't help ADHD so that you don't waste valuable resources on sham treatments. And you likely want to know what you can still do if your loved one does not yet want your help or anyone else's. You want to know all these answers directly and quickly so that you don't waste your time. I will do just that.

I won't tell you how great ADHD is, because it isn't. I won't tell you what a gift it is for those who have it, because it's not. It is a serious disorder that your loved one would give up in a heartbeat if that were possible. Yes, people with ADHD can be incredibly successful; I discuss some of them. But their success is not due to their ADHD. It is the result of how they and the loved ones around them helped that person to master and manage it and then to pursue paths in life, often nontraditional ones, in which ADHD might not pose such a big problem.

WHAT ADHD LOOKS LIKE

The signs of adult ADHD are many but can be initially classified as difficulties with attention, inhibition, and excess activity level. Those all have something larger in common—they all reflect a substantial problem with self-control, as I discuss in the next chapter. Here I want to explain what signs and symptoms have to be present for someone to be diagnosed as having ADHD. Before I do so, you need to understand that ADHD falls along a spectrum or dimension of symptoms in the human population. Most people have no symptoms or just a few that occur only occasionally. Others have more frequent symptoms but those do not interfere much, if at all, with their daily life activities. Think of them as having an ADHD-like personality: talkative, outgoing, occasionally impulsive, sometimes distracted, and active. But when the degree of those symptoms reaches a level of severity and frequency where they interfere with effectively engaging in major life activities, such as work and education, the person now can be considered to have the disorder of ADHD. Yet even among those with the disorder, their symptoms and impairments can also vary in severity from mild to severe. So ADHD isn't like pregnancy, that you have or don't; it is like language ability in which people range from gifted to typical to severely deficient or completely unable to talk.

In this book, I focus on adults with ADHD who have been impaired enough to qualify for a clinical diagnosis of the disorder. But understand that milder forms of the condition can exist in some adults and not be very impairing, if at all. I chose this focus of necessity because the majority of adults likely to read this book have loved ones who are substantially impaired from their ADHD or they probably wouldn't bother with reading it. In explaining ADHD, I won't talk down to you or oversimplify it. Instead I explain the science of ADHD to you like any educated person would want it explained, professional terms and all, as if you were sitting before me in my office.

To help you understand how ADHD symptoms can affect people differently, I give you quotes from real people and real-life case stories across a wide range of adults and their situations. These range from people who are highly successful in their work (although often not in certain domains of life outside of work) to people who struggle to sustain their employment at all and from those with just a few focused problem areas to those with many issues. I do all this to show the broad diversity of how ADHD adversely affects adults and their lives. But realize that although ADHD can be a very impairing disorder in adulthood, it is among the most treatable disorders in psychiatry, with many effective treatments for its management. I discuss those in the later chapters of this book.

Dreams, Interrupted: A Partner's Story of Adult ADHD

My current boyfriend with whom I live is 26 years old and we are living in New England. His mother has told me that he displayed symptoms of ADHD very early in life. But his parents decided not to medicate him because of personal beliefs against drugs and not wanting to stamp him with the stigma often associated with the label in school. I've recently come to realize that his ADHD is still present and has largely been what's hindered him from accomplishing many of his goals up until this point. Yes, he has had some small successes, but as a whole, he does not feel like he is on the same level as his peers, either when he was at school or now in his line of work. I can see all the symptoms of ADHD I read about on the Internet. I wish his parents had taken them more seriously when he was a child. Maybe then he would have been treated earlier and so might not be having so many difficulties.

As a child, he paced endlessly about, his mother told me, and as far as I can tell he still does. She said that through his middle and high school years and even into college, his grades never matched his potential or high intelligence. He has friends to whom he has even taught grammar, English, and vocabulary because he is so smart. I know that some people don't have the amount of knowledge he does yet they have finished their master's degrees, while he is kind of stuck in limbo, having yet to finish his undergraduate degree. His father told me that my boyfriend never had "low"

Dreams, Interrupted: A Partner's Story of Adult ADHD (*Continued*)

grades when he actually completed his work. But he didn't complete a lot of it. And so he got a lot of 0's due to not turning in homework or projects. In college he was able to get a number of A's, but that was offset by the fact that he also got a number of W's (withdrawals) or "Incompletes" that resulted from not turning in final papers and from missing final exams.

We have had a number of financial problems and debt since we have been together because I often find that he has made bad decisions with money. A prime example: We now have just one car but we used to have two. Up until 2 years ago or so when I first met him and we were both working full time, we both had cars. He had a really nice sports car. Then it broke down. Of course, he had no savings and we got completely overwhelmed, with no money to fix it. When he finally got the money to fix his car from his tax return a few months later, he decided that he wanted to show me some appreciation for being so helpful during some hard times. He knows that he shouldn't have, but he wound up on a whim taking me to Las Vegas for a long holiday weekend. He ended up spending $1,100 of the $2,000 he needed to purchase a new engine for his car. The car was later repossessed because he couldn't pay for everything he needed to fix it in time. He spends so much time wondering why he makes these horrible and impulsive financial decisions. . . . This wasn't the first time he has done things like this.

Another problem—he can't seem to stay with an occupation very long. After he left his initial job in sales, he decided to focus on his music full time because he has always had a love of music and is a great musician. He has now had some pretty good successes with music. Yet one time he was working with a major writer who's written many popular songs. Here they are giving him instrumentals to write for them so they can add lyrics and pitch their songs to well-known artists. But when he is under the gun like this with a deadline he can't seem to make himself sit down and write, even though it's what he has done since he was a kid and what he says he has always wanted to do. When the time came, he knew he had to sit down and work and just get one song placed with a major artist

(continues)

Dreams, Interrupted: A Partner's Story of Adult ADHD (*Continued*)

to get his foot in the door in that highly competitive business. But he was unable to stick with it. So he failed to meet their demands and the song promoters dropped him. Now we are living in an unorganized, somewhat dirty, one bedroom . . . shack. . . . He keeps telling me that we deserve so much more. I am younger than he is by 3 years, already finished with school and college, and now want nice things in life. I really think that he should be able to motivate himself to work better and give us so much more. But he can be so unfocused and he just doesn't seem to be able to plan for the future or think things through.

While he considers himself to be a songwriter, and it's always been his passion and what he excelled at, he has also tried lots of other activities, none of which he sticks with for very long. His mother told me that in school he played baseball, basketball, tennis, and clarinet, and he still plays piano. He then transferred to a high school for the arts and focused mainly on both ballet and vocal music; he even danced in a ballet company for a few years while in school. There he was in student council and even thought about pursuing law for a while before he decided he wanted to go to college for art (which he did at first). Along the way he has taught himself computer programming and even spent a few months making an app for a major Internet company. But he also pursued videography, has been a DJ, has toured with bands on the weekends, has done some video editing for others, and occasionally does some song mixing, and music producing. Despite all those different career potentials, he is currently doing wedding photography just trying to make a living before we lose more than we have. In short, he starts a million things, yet he doesn't finish much at all.

I've also found that he is unable to mute emotions at times. With me he does his best to avoid arguments because he considers us both to be generally positive people. However, if I push him about an issue in our relationship or about his projects too much, he ends up yelling and goes on a whole rant in which he keeps asking me why I have to go and ruin everything. He wants to know why we can't just be happy the way we are. Eventually, he does start calming down, maybe even faster than most people would who get so upset.

Dreams, Interrupted: A Partner's Story of Adult ADHD (*Continued*)

One thing that annoys me is that he constantly interrupts me while I am working at home or at my office. It's because he can't deal with it being too quiet in our home or being alone for very long. Another thing he does that can be irritating is that he is always pacing, shaking his leg, and literally pulling out his hair.

A few years ago before he met me he was dating a girl who had just finished her PhD in sociology. He told me that he would never forget what she told him when they broke up. She said, "I just finished my Ph.D, I'm going to want to settle down soon, start a family, buy a house, and you're not ready for any of those things. You're fun and I enjoy spending time with you but this is just right now. I'm not looking at you as a long-term option." I am starting to see her point. Yet he can be so sweet and kind to others, tutoring people who need help, answering questions, and volunteering to do things for others. We need to get him some professional help, or I may also have to move on from this relationship.

Note. All cases in this book are real but have all identifying information disguised so as to protect the identity of these individuals. In some cases they may be an amalgamation of several different people I have known.

It's About Being Very Inattentive

When an adult has ADHD, inattentiveness may take different forms. It may mean the person cannot pay attention for long periods of time. Or, it may mean the person is easily distracted. I describe some common behavior patterns in the remainder of this chapter.

Can't Concentrate or Sustain Attention

I am 50, female, well educated, and I even made it through law school. Yet I was diagnosed with ADHD 3 months ago because

> I cannot persist at doing things I find to be dull or boring. But much of legal work is just that. So I have floundered professionally and personally all my life. Everyone missed it while I was growing up and even through college because I was bright enough to learn things quickly. But the more I progressed in college and then in my career, the more I had to process, the more work I had to do that I found uninteresting, and the more trouble I ran into in school and later on the job. Now, with the diagnosis and treatment, everything has changed and I have hope that I can live up to what I expect of myself personally and professionally.[1]

This symptom is especially likely to occur if the work to be done is dull or tedious. As a result, adults with ADHD often do not finish the projects they start, may not even begin the projects they know must be done, and/or they put off doing boring projects until the absolute last minute. Even if they[2] start the work, people with ADHD are not able to sustain the focus of their attention on the task for as long as others are able to. Also, while doing work, they may daydream, talk to passersby, jot down notes on unrelated projects or ideas, doodle on a notepad, interrupt the work frequently to get beverages, use the bathroom, visit with others, check e-mail, surf the Internet, or find anything else to do

---

[1]All personalized statements are either (a) from actual comments by clients seen in my clinic or research projects made to me, (b) from e-mails written to me by adults with ADHD, (c) comments or e-mails their loved ones said to me, or (d) paraphrases or amalgamations of such statements. In all instances, all identifying information has been altered to protect identities and confidentiality.

[2]To avoid using just one gender, I will alternate the use of *he/him* or *she/her* throughout the text or use the gender neutral term *they/them*.

that requires less effort than the work they are faced with needing to get done. They may often report not being able to think about work or other boring but necessary ideas for very long before more interesting ideas pop up and cause them to divert their thoughts to other, more pleasant ideas.

Easily Distracted

> My wife will be talking to me, but she can get so easily distracted, even by other thoughts, that in the middle of our conversation on one topic I can see her mind go "pffitt" as her thinking jumps the rails and off she goes on to some other track or tangent.

When work or some other boring activity must get done right away, the adult with ADHD often finds other things around them to be highly distracting. These are usually events, sounds, or even the actions of others, or anything else that is "off-task" and not relevant to the goal or project at hand. But the adult with ADHD can't ignore them like you can do. Adults with ADHD find it hard not to think about, react to, or otherwise interact with this distracting event. The interruption or distractor may cause them to think about ideas that have nothing to do with the work needing to get done. It can also cause them to start talking about the distraction when it has absolutely nothing to do with the project at hand. And it may even lead them to change their behavior so they leave the task or situation, and shift to interacting with the distracting person or event. All this leads the adult with ADHD to be "off-task" a lot of the time.

If it is a solitary activity that has to get done, it causes him to take far longer to accomplish it than others typically require. At other times, he simply doesn't finish the work at all. His powers of sustained attention are so weak and fragile that many interruptions or distractions that others would find easy to ignore will overpower his weak concentration so that things just don't get done. In short, more interesting but irrelevant events around him are like magnets or flashy neon lights to his restless mind. These distractions cause your loved one to get sidetracked easily from the business at hand.

It's About Poor Inhibition (Impulsiveness)

> My adult son has made many impulsive choices about money. On one occasion with a girlfriend, he impulsively spent $450 a night on a 3-day "romantic" weekend in an expensive hotel in New York City when he knew his rent was due the next week and this money was needed for that expense.

Adults with ADHD are often impulsive—they typically show a rather stunning quickness or "rush to judgment" when making decisions. They give short shrift to thinking through their ideas for the best ways to do something. And they don't think about any later problems their plan of action may create. Acting on impulse, adults with ADHD think, say, and do things with far less regard for the consequences that may be associated with those actions, both now and later, than would others.

The adult with ADHD is just responding on autopilot at the moment to his initial feelings about the choice, conflict, or other decision to be made. Her behavior is reactive, usually based on some whim, not thoughtful action based on deliberation. Sometimes this impulsiveness can seem exciting and fun, such as making spur of the moment decisions while on vacation about fun things to do next. Yet most of life is not spent on vacation! The consequences for making a too-quick decision about more weighty matters in life than mere entertainment can result in far more serious consequences.

Adults with ADHD are usually not monitoring themselves and what they are doing but instead, like the Nike slogan, they "Just Do It." They sometimes realize after the fact that what they have said or done was a huge mistake, one they are likely to regret. So they may eventually say they are sorry, wished they had not said or done what they did, and hope to try to do things better the next time. Yet that is little consolation to others when the adult with ADHD keeps doing or saying such impulsive things repeatedly.

It May Also Involve Being Hyperactive

People with ADHD are often far more active and restless than others, especially if they are in a boring situation. This is certainly even more true for children with ADHD, who are described as "constantly on the go" or "acting as if driven by a motor." But it is also true of some adults with the disorder.

More Fidgety, Restless, or Active

> I married my best friend last April. He is a builder, so I didn't think anything about how active he always seemed to be. We had never lived together, and being as each of us had always rented a room in homes there wasn't any opportunity to hang out except in the general community. We didn't find a house to rent till May, so we didn't really live together till then. By mid-June I was almost out of my mind with my husband's over-the-top behaviors. He is so active when we are home, cannot sit still for long to read or watch television, and always has to be doing something, even though he rarely finishes the projects he has started. Help!

As children with ADHD grow up, their outward hyperactivity diminishes substantially. The climbing on things, running about, pacing, and generally moving more than others becomes far less of a problem by adulthood. Instead, it becomes a problem of feeling more internally restless. This leads to feeling as if he needs to stay busy in various activities. Minor fidgeting may be especially apparent when he is bored, like when he has to stay seated or confined to a classroom or meeting room. He feels a need to stay busy with lots of activities to do, such as sports and physical pursuits. Adults with ADHD may also like more active work, such as the trades, travel, sales, videography, physical education, sports, the military, police work, driving for a living, emergency medical technician or physician, or even trial lawyer.

Often Talk Excessively

> I am 51 years old and a saleswoman. I was diagnosed with ADHD as a child. I can't stop talking or thinking or changing from project to project, or keep a job, or stick with anything I say I'm going to do.

Although this is not always the case, adults with ADHD often cannot stop talking in the presence of others (or even when alone). Some can speak so much that it seems their mouth is just a vehicle for expressing the constant stream of thought in their consciousness. Yet what she may be saying is often pointless. Or it is only tangential to the topic at hand, if there even is one, instead of making a direct, brief, coherent, and compelling point.

Along with their striking talkativeness, adults with ADHD show an apparent disregard for what anyone else may have to say in a conversation. Thus they come off as verbally domineering, self-interested, and insensitive to the views of others. They emit just a one-way stream of verbalizations. The give-and-take, that important mutual inquiring of each other in typical conversations, is rarely respected. Sharing and turn taking occur far less often in the verbal exchanges or social behavior of an adult with ADHD. Instead, one typically hears just a one-sided barrage of pointless verbiage. One can literally not get a word in edgewise. The minute one tries to utter even a single syllable, the adult with ADHD is "off to the races," reacting to it with her own incessant chatter.

The adult with ADHD frequently interrupts others or intrudes on others who are having a conversation. This is often seen as an unwelcomed hijacking of the discussion. In response, others start peeling off from the conversation to find different people with whom to have a mature and truly reciprocal talk. Or they simply try to get away from the verbal "stickiness" of the adult with ADHD.

Surprisingly, in contrast to this excessive speech, the adult with ADHD will suddenly be at a loss for words and ideas when she is put on the spot with an immediate question or demand that must be answered. In a classroom situation, for example, instead of giving a clear, logical, and brief explanation of the key ideas on a topic, an adult student with ADHD gives a smattering of spontaneous reactions containing only the most concrete and obvious contents of the assigned reading, if that. His explanation is often halting, and involves lots of delaying tactics or other ploys, such as "uhs" and "likes," to buy time for thinking. And he often misses the plot, crux, or deeper meaning of the reading material. Moreover, what explanations that may be given are often out of sequence relative to what occurred in the actual material he read. His comments also contain a lot of "beating-around-the-bush" types of statements before even getting to any of those key points.

An adult with ADHD may also get easily distracted during this broken narrative. He then goes off on tangents that have little to do with the story. He might even end this long and winding narrative with a "lost" look on his face, and say, "What did you ask me?" He has quickly forgotten the original question.

DECIDING WHETHER YOUR LOVED ONE MAY HAVE ADULT ADHD

The symptoms are just some of the major problems adults with ADHD can have with inattention, impulsive behavior, and even activity level. Now that you know them, let's do a quick check to see if your loved one might well have ADHD. Think about your loved one's behavior over the past 6 months. Then answer the following questions about their behavior. Simply answer *yes* or *no* to each of the items listed.

The Symptoms of ADHD

	Yes	No
(1) Inattention		
(a) Often fails to give close attention to details or makes careless mistakes in schoolwork, at work, or during other activities (e.g., overlooks or misses details, work is inaccurate).		
(b) Often has difficulty sustaining attention in tasks or play activities (e.g., has difficulty remaining focused during lectures, conversations, or lengthy reading).		
(c) Often does not seem to listen when spoken to directly (e.g., mind seems elsewhere, even in the absence of any obvious distraction).		

The Symptoms of ADHD (*Continued*)

	Yes	No
(d) Often does not follow through on instructions and fails to finish schoolwork, chores, or duties in the workplace (e.g., starts tasks but quickly loses focus and is easily sidetracked).		
(e) Often has difficulty organizing tasks and activities (e.g., difficulty managing sequential tasks; difficulty keeping materials and belongings in order; messy, disorganized work; has poor time management; fails to meet deadlines).		
(f) Often avoids, dislikes, or is reluctant to engage in tasks that require sustained mental effort (e.g., schoolwork or homework; for older adolescents and adults, preparing reports, completing forms, reviewing lengthy papers).		
(g) Often loses things necessary for tasks or activities (e.g., school materials, pencils, books, tools, wallets, keys, paperwork, eyeglasses, mobile telephones).		
(h) Is often easily distracted by extraneous stimuli (for older adolescents and adults, may include unrelated thoughts).		
(i) Is often forgetful in daily activities (e.g., doing chores, running errands; for older adolescents and adults, returning calls paying bills, keeping appointments).		

(continues)

The Symptoms of ADHD (*Continued*)

	Yes	No
(2) Hyperactivity and Impulsivity		
(a) Often fidgets with or taps hands or feet or squirms in seat.		
(b) Often leaves seat situations when remaining seated is expected (e.g., leaves his or her place in the classroom, in the office or other workplace, or in other situations that require remaining in place).		
(c) Often runs about or climbs in situations where it is inappropriate. (Note: In adolescents or adults, may be limited to feeling restless).		
(d) Often unable to play or engage in leisure activities quietly.		
(e) Is often "on the go," acting as if "driven by a motor" (e.g., is unable or uncomfortable being still for extended time, as in restaurants, meetings; may be observed by others as being restless or difficult to keep up with).		
(f) Often talks excessively (in social situations).		
(g) Often blurts out an answer before a question has been completed (e.g., completes people's sentences; cannot wait for turn in conversation).		
(h) Often has difficulty awaiting his or her turn (e.g., while waiting in line).		

The Symptoms of ADHD (*Continued*)

	Yes	No
(i) Often interrupts or intrudes on others (e.g., butts into conversations, games, or activities; may start using other people's things without asking or receiving permission; for adolescents and adults, may intrude into or take over what others are doing).		

Did you answer *yes* to 4 of the 9 symptoms under Inattention?[3] Or did you say *yes* to 4 of the 9 symptoms of Hyperactive–Impulsive behavior? Or did you answer *yes* to a total of 7 out of all 18 items in this list? If you did, then your loved one has symptoms of ADHD that are far in excess of what exists in typical adults.

Note. These 18 symptoms are from the diagnostic criteria for ADHD contained in the *Diagnostic and Statistical Manual of Mental Disorders* (5th ed.; *DSM–5*), by the American Psychiatric Association, 2013, Washington, DC: Author. Copyright 2013 by the American Psychiatric Association. Reprinted with permission. As of October 15, 2015, for billing purposes, mental health providers are required to use the latest version of the World Health Organization's diagnostic coding guidelines laid out in the *International Classification of Diseases* (10th ed.; *ICD–10*). Geneva, Switzerland: World Health Organization, 2015.

Now, answer these three additional questions.

- *Have any of these current symptoms lasted at least 6 months or longer?*
- *As far as you can tell, did they first begin anytime during childhood or adolescence?*

[3]The official *DSM–5* criteria for ADHD in the Appendix require that five symptoms be present on either symptom list to diagnose it. But research routinely shows that four symptoms is a better threshold for determining if the symptoms are deviant from typical adults.

- *Do any of these symptoms produce impairment in your loved one?* That is to say, do these symptoms lead to significant adverse consequences for the person in major life activities, such as home life, education, work, social relationships, and so on? A critical part of diagnosis is making sure that those symptoms are leading to impairment (harm or adverse consequences). *Both* symptoms and impairment must be present to make a diagnosis of ADHD.

If your answers were *yes* to all three of these questions, then your loved one may well have adult ADHD. The full diagnostic criteria for making the diagnosis of ADHD by a professional are contained in the appendix at the end of this book.

TAKING ACTION

When the time seems right, try to discuss your concerns with your loved one. This can be when your loved one complains yet again about the problems she is having in her family, work, school, or social life. When that happens, you should tell her you understand, that you think these problems might be related to adult ADHD. Then encourage her to get a professional evaluation for the disorder if you believe that she would be open to doing so. In Chapter 9, you can find more tips for starting this kind of conversation.

Even if your loved one has already been diagnosed, this review of the symptoms of ADHD may give you a better understanding of what the problem behaviors are that your loved one may be experiencing. Reading this book can certainly help you better understand and assist that loved one as well. And even if the adult you believe may have ADHD is not (yet) open to getting an appropriate evaluation and treatment, this book can still help you understand ADHD. It can teach you its causes, the impairments it leads to, and the appropriate treatments. It can also show you what you can still do to be of help even if your loved one does not want professional assistance just now.

CHAPTER 2

LOOKING BELOW THE SURFACE OF ADULT ADHD

In Chapter 1, I reviewed the most obvious symptoms in someone who may be manifesting attention-deficit/hyperactivity disorder (ADHD). But symptoms by themselves do not explain what is going wrong in their mental functioning. Once you understand that underlying disorder, you can then use that deeper knowledge to understand how to help someone with adult ADHD. In this chapter, I explain how ADHD affects the brain's normal processing and management of our behavior.

The symptoms of ADHD arise from a set of mental abilities or brain functions called the *executive functions*. There are at least six such executive functions. They occur mostly in the frontal part of the brain, behind your forehead. Like an executive in a business, this part of the brain contemplates the future and how best to run things at the moment to ensure both its current and later success. This frontal part of the brain is where goals get invented and plans to achieve those goals are formulated. It also sees to it that the plan is put into action and that the action is monitored for conformance to the plan and is readjusted as needed to accomplish the goal. These executive abilities permit a person to contemplate their future and then control their behavior so as to accomplish their goals and see to their longer-term welfare. In doing so, these functions let us become independent, self-determining people.

"A Tornado in Her Brain at All Times": A Mother's Story of Adult ADHD

I am a mother of a beautiful 24-year-old girl, who because of her choices last night, forced me to have the police at my house filing a missing persons report. She finally made it home at 5:30 a.m. She told us she forgot to put her cell phone next to her and fell asleep, so she didn't get the 30 missed phone calls or texts. It was a third date with a new guy we didn't know much about, and she was supposed to be home at 2:00 a.m.

She has had problems since she was a toddler, and we have taken her all over the U.S. trying to find out why she had learning problems. We flew to a neuroimaging clinic when she was 16 to see what was going on inside her brain. It showed us that she had severe problems with the front of her brain; basically, it showed like a tornado is going through it at all times.

I used to have the hardest time coming up with consequences for her behavior because I couldn't tell half of the time if she was being lazy or defiant. Now I know it's her executive dysfunction/ADHD thing.

She has been on an ADHD medication since she turned 16, and it seems to help her to some extent. But she has already totaled one car. We kept her from getting her license until she was 18. She appears to never ever learn from her mistakes. I see her going now into depression. She just doesn't handle advice. And she refuses to put any kind of "alarms" on her phone to help remind her of anything. I need to get her medications right. I'm in fear all the time that I am going to get a call that she is dead.

She is gifted and so sweet. She says she wants to help women who are coming out of abused situations or help people who are sick and make them feel beautiful through her cosmetology training. She is great at this but fails every test at her technical school. I am always looking and always searching to help find the keys to unlock my daughter from the prison she is in.

EXECUTIVE FUNCTION 1: SELF-AWARENESS

You can't begin to control yourself if you are not aware of yourself and what you are doing. So the first executive ability is one that permits you to become a spectator on your own behavior—to monitor yourself and what you think, say, and do. A person with no self-awareness has nothing to control. You must attend to yourself to be aware of yourself and your actions; then you can control them.

Much of what we do each day is rather automatic, and we deal with routine life using previously learned patterns of behavior. But some of the time, new things happen, our priorities may change, or the unexpected can occur. We must then override our automatic behavior to think about and act upon what is best to do in those situations. Like a business, much of what happens each day is the same. But the executive must be able to monitor that daily routine so that when problems arise or priorities change, the work being done can be shifted, flexibly, to deal effectively with those issues. Like a business executive, the executive brain must monitor much of what is going on in everyday behavior while that behavior is occurring. It can then override it if circumstances change. It can even change the course of actions that are being pursued if they are unable to achieve goals or are inconsistent with them. It can also invent new goals and plans and initiate the actions that are needed to accomplish them. All the while, the executive brain is monitoring our actions to see how well we are doing at getting to our goals (or those assigned to us by others).

Adults with ADHD are more limited in their self-awareness in that they are less able to watch over what they are thinking, saying, feeling, and doing. And so they are not as aware of how well or poorly they are doing in getting to their goals and long-term welfare. They are running on automatic pilot too much, like a car without a driver, or a business without a chief executive—no one is minding the store. You can get away with that for a while. But as you can imagine, it won't work out very well in the long run. This makes an adult with ADHD more reactive to events playing out inside and around them rather than being more proactive, thoughtful, and deliberate. Like the driverless car, they careen around life bouncing off guardrails, speeding recklessly, and running through the warning lights and stop signs because they are not paying much attention to what they are doing.

In our social world, self-control and thoughtful, deliberate action are prized because they are effective at promoting actions that are best for our own long-term welfare. To run on automatic pilot much of the time can be a recipe for social, educational, financial, and occupational disaster. Acting on impulse, going with the flow of life events around you, living moment to moment with utter disregard for your future, and going full throttle are exciting ways to act while on vacation, if then. But they are no way to run your daily life if you expect to succeed at being happy, effective, and productive. The executive brain is in trouble in ADHD. One reason is because the first executive function, self-awareness, is not working very well. And that leads to the next "system failure"—the incapacity to inhibit impulses—to stop the automatic brain when necessary. Your mother was right to admonish you to "stop and think before you act!" and you can't do that thinking without that first word—*stop!*

EXECUTIVE FUNCTION 2: INHIBITION OR SELF-RESTRAINT

Being able to inhibit your automatic behavior is crucial when faced with novel situations, unexpected events, or a change in your priorities. It creates that all-important pause between what happens in the environment and your response to it. That pause gives you time to think. And that thinking makes you be proactive rather than always being reactive to events. Inhibition sets the stage for being able to consider your options about whether, when, and how to respond to some event. Such deliberation gives you free will—which is basically the ability to choose among various courses of action. A major symptom of adult ADHD is poor impulse control or inhibition.

Self-control is not possible without first inhibiting your self. Self-control means any action that we direct at ourselves that leads to a change in our behavior from what we might otherwise have done automatically. Doing so allows us to improve the likelihood of something better happening for us later—either getting a larger payoff or avoiding a greater harm. And that hopefully leads to a better future, whether that is tomorrow, the next week, the next month, and even the next years in life. When we use self-control, we are adjusting our behavior with an eye on that future. And in that future, many prizes are to be had and hazards to avoid if one is able to anticipate them, plan well for them, and thus maximize the outcomes. None of that can happen without impulse control.

Many adults with ADHD are very impulsive. They can't stop, and so they are less likely to think. If they don't think before they act, then they are not as likely to improve their future as others. Others see such impulsive behavior as thoughtless, heedless, ill advised, and even irrational or at least immature. That is because other people find it much easier to stop and think before they act. They can't understand why the adult with ADHD doesn't do that. They see the adult with ADHD as just making bad choices and being poor at self-discipline.

> My partner's mother told me her son with ADHD (my partner) often missed the school bus due to playing videogames for so long that he forgot to get ready for school. Even now, as an adult who works in website design, I often notice that he can't stop what he enjoys doing in order to get ready for work or get started on some important impending project.

This problem of not being able to stop a fun activity when it is time to do so and shift to doing something more important is related to the poor inhibition seen in adult ADHD. It is a symptom that often surprises people because others assume that if someone has a short attention span, he should be skipping across various incomplete activities. But there will be certain times and places where an adult with ADHD persists excessively in an activity beyond the point where they should have stopped and gone on to do other things that need to get done. The things an adult with ADHD excessively persists in doing are usually fun or immediately gratifying activities. So the adult with ADHD keeps playing the videogame he started when he woke up this morning instead of getting ready for work or shifting to a home task he agreed to do for his spouse. Or he keeps binge watching a series of an exciting TV show on Netflix, continues surfing the Internet, constantly engages in instant messaging or tweeting others, keeps reading and posting stuff on Facebook, or just continues spending face time with the various entertaining apps on his smartphone. He may be doing any or all of these things when there is work that must get done or deadlines or appointments that must now be met. When the time is up for putting that entertaining activity away, he doesn't.

Some professionals call this *hyperfocusing*, as if it were some benefit conveyed by the disorder. In fact, it has long been recognized as a sign of dysfunction in the executive system of the brain. Persisting at things when a person should have stopped doing them is not a gift but a problem. It can create inflexibility in a person's pattern of behavior. They persist in doing things they should have stopped doing by now and shifted their behavior to the next activity needing to get done.

EXECUTIVE FUNCTION 3: WORKING MEMORY

> My girlfriend must be a strong candidate for having ADHD as she has very poor short-term memory. If she doesn't write down what is being said to her, she will not remember what was just said. So she always takes notes when someone is talking to her about anything that she must remember later and use. She often

> forgets her four-digit credit card PIN right on the spot at the ATM or when we need it to purchase gas, for example, even though she has actually been using the card for months! Then a few hours later, after I have had to pay for her gas on my own credit card or loan her cash, she suddenly remembers the PIN!

This frequent forgetfulness has little to do with traditional ideas about memory (e.g., long-term memory for information). The problem resides in a special kind of memory known as *working memory*. Working memory involves actively holding in mind what you are supposed to be doing and any related details about your plans and goals. It consists of the mental information that is supposed to be guiding the person's actions toward their goals or assigned tasks. Basically, it is "remembering so as to do."

What the adult with ADHD is forgetting is what she is supposed to be doing—what goal or task she is supposed to be pursing at this time and place. For instance, she goes into a bank to cash a check, forgets to fill it out completely, then does so on prompting from the male teller, gets to flirting with him, and then leaves without taking both the cash she came in to get and her checkbook. Any distraction serves to derail her goal-directed actions. She is then "off to the races," skipping from one thing to another completing little if any of it. It is as if her working memory is so weak and fragile that it cannot hold ideas in mind that are needed to govern her behavior toward her intended goals. In part, the poor sustained attention you read about in Chapter 1 is really poor persistence toward goals or assigned tasks. That poor persistence arises in part from this dysfunction in working memory. She can't hold in mind what she is supposed to be doing in order to get it done.

An adult with ADHD seems to be governed by the environment around him rather than the ideas he had about what he was going to do. He may not remember why he went into the room or recall where he was in the sequence of his plans. Instead, little things around him are more distracting and that causes him to forget what he was doing. The setting around him takes over and controls his actions more than his original plans or ideas.

The external world captured his behavior, stringing along his actions from one thing to the next, with little mental control guiding those actions to their originally intended goal. The original goal gets disrupted and forgotten. He is then sidetracked from his goals altogether and starts doing something else based on what he saw.

> My wife doesn't work, has few if any friends, can't make it to doctor's appointments, or make any plans because she cannot follow through with any commitments. This is very hard when you have kids.

One way that this forgetfulness can show up is when adults with ADHD don't follow through on directives, rules, promises, instructions, or commitments the way others are able to do. Part of this is due to their inattention, mentioned in the last chapter. The adult with ADHD may not have been listening enough when the instruction or request was made to remember and do it later. So they can't be expected to remember to do what they never really heard. But this forgetfulness is not just an attention problem, nor is it a language problem: An adult with ADHD understands what has been said to them or what they agreed to do.

Instead, an adult with ADHD has very poor working memory, and working memory is where we hold in mind what we have been told to do or agreed to do. If working memory (remembering to do) is defective, then those with the disorder cannot hold in mind just what rules, instructions, or promises they are supposed to be doing. Instead, the physical world around them takes over and suggests that they do other things. This is not a willful choice to disobey someone or break a promise. Mental representations, like rules or instructions, are simply not powerful enough to guide behavior as they do in others.

Does the adult with ADHD understand what she was told or agreed to do? Yes, usually. Give her a quiz later and she can recognize she was given that information. But did it control her in the situation where it should have? No. That is working memory and working memory isn't working well in adult ADHD.

> My husband, a graphics designer, can't keep a train of thought and he can't seem to listen to someone who is talking to him without eventually being 1,000 miles away.

Related to the problems with attention, distraction, impulsiveness, and forgetfulness (working memory) is a problem of fully comprehending what one sees, hears, and reads. Young children can be expected to learn only the most obvious and concrete bits of information from what they see, hear, and eventually read. But as we grow up, we are expected to process larger amounts of information. We do that by holding it in mind for further study—we use our working memory to do that. By doing so, we can grasp the deeper meanings of things. We can get the gist of a story that has been told to us; the meaning of what has been seen, such as in a movie or educational video; and the crux, plot, and major points of a book we have read. All of these require that we are able not only to understand things but also to hold multiple pieces of related information in our mind (our working memory), which lets us connect the dots. By doing so, we can see the larger meaning of things, the plot that is unfolding in the story, the various characters that may be involved, the sequence over which that plot is taking place, and the larger context in which all this is occurring.

In other words, the deeper meanings of complex things require that we keep all the relevant bits of information we have seen, heard, or read about something in our mind to try to fully understand it. If you cannot concentrate as long as others, and your working memory is poor, and you can't hold things in mind well, and distractions shatter even this limited ability to hold things in mind, then you are not going to get as much information as others out of what you see, hear, and read. Adults with ADHD just don't get what other people do out of complex information that is heard, read, or viewed.

Perhaps for this reason, an adult with ADHD is less likely than ordinary people to read much for pleasure, watch lengthy movies like documentaries or educational TV, or listen to lengthy stories or lectures spoken or read to them. The longer it takes to do so, the more trouble they have with getting all the right information out of the activity, and so the less likely they are to voluntarily do it again.

You can well imagine that over time, these problems with attention and working memory are going to take a toll on what your loved one is able to learn (knowledge), such as in her academic achievement or how much information she got out of school. This problem creates a higher likelihood of educational problems for the adult with ADHD and a lower likelihood of getting as much education as she should have for her level of intelligence and family background. And the more that her occupation demands such sustained attention, working memory, and deeper comprehension, the more trouble she also may have in her job.

EXECUTIVE FUNCTION 4: TIME MANAGEMENT

> Time escapes me and I don't know how to deal with this invisible but important part of my life.

Adults with ADHD seem to be oblivious to time. They can't seem to sense and prepare for impending deadlines, to understand how long it may take to do things or how much time they need to get somewhere they need to go. They also seem oblivious to the future more generally. As I mentioned earlier, all that seems to matter to an adult with ADHD is the now; whatever is taking place around them and in their minds at any particular point in time. So they are typically late for work, appointments, deadlines, classes, and meetings. The adult with ADHD seems blind to time. They often do not meet the time commitments they make with others, and bills are paid late or go unpaid. Adults with ADHD are therefore ill prepared for when deadlines finally do arrive. They seem to be adrift in time, unanchored from any sense of time and how they should have been guided by it in determining what they should have been doing to get ready for the impending future. Anything that is supposed to be done by a later time is essentially out of sight, out of mind. It has little or no influence in determining what they should be doing now to get ready for the arrival of that event. Once it does arrive, they are often caught off guard, ill prepared, and now must scurry about trying to accomplish at the last minute what any ordinary person would have gotten done earlier in anticipation of this particular deadline.

The life of an adult with ADHD is filled with many avoidable crises. That is because many things are being left to the 11th hour before any effort is put in to getting them done. But then she discovers that it is too late to do what is needed for the deadline. The deadline is now here, the appropriate work is not done or done acceptably, and the appropriate materials are not here or not organized. An adult with ADHD is now stressed out and scrambling like crazy to cobble anything together that may be just enough to get by. But such scrambling rarely suffices. It is too little, too late, and often poorly done.

This is a very serious deficit because, as we all know, the further we progress in our life stages, the more time sensitive life becomes—at least up until retirement. Everyday things must get done so we are ready for our immediate and longer term futures. This is why we have clocks, calendars, to-do lists, day planners, smart technology, computers, and many other products that help us get things done on time. After adolescence, as social and employment responsibilities increase, the more we are expected to do things in time, over time, on time so as to prepare for both the futures that are coming at us and the commitments we have made to others. Any deficit in the timeliness of human action can have far-reaching consequences. Those consequences can range from not completing courses and degrees in education to lost jobs, lost friendships, lost intimate relationships and marriages, lost property, poor credit, and just lost opportunities more generally. All of it is simply because the person with ADHD cannot deal with time—she cannot be ready on time, in time, over time for things that lie in her future. In short, she is blind to time, suffering a nearsightedness (a myopia) to the future.

EXECUTIVE FUNCTION 5: EMOTIONAL SELF-CONTROL

> I get irritated easily (ever since I was a kid) and I have a very short fuse! I have lost all my best friends throughout the last 6 to 7 years over my explosive behavior, and feel that I am the least liked person by everyone around me. I always felt as if I were the least liked child by my parents and even relatives due to my short temper . . .

Not only are adults with ADHD impulsive in their words and behavior but they are also impulsive in their initial emotional reactions to events. Many of the things we do across the day typically do not provoke much emotion from us. But occasionally, a few things each day strongly provoke our emotions, such as events that are frustrating or anger inducing. When such emotionally charged events occur, an adult with ADHD is likely to react quickly with his primary initial emotions rather than showing some emotional restraint. He fails to think through the situation more carefully, doesn't moderate his strong emotions, and doesn't try to substitute a more socially acceptable emotional reaction that is good for him in the long run. Instead, an adult with ADHD seems to wear his emotions on his sleeve for all to see when he is provoked by events or others around him.

This can occur as well with humor, joy, affection, and fun, or other positively arousing events. But the social costs for such excess joking, fun, or affection are nowhere near as devastating to their social reputations as are the negative reactions—those of impatience, frustration, hostility, anger, or even reactive aggression that spew out so impulsively in many adults with ADHD. Others will not stay in relationships with an adult with ADHD for very long or will even avoid that adult entirely when the adult with ADHD acts like an emotional hot head, blowing her cork easily over the slightest frustrations, social slights, or provocations. Also people won't long tolerate someone who unhesitatingly and repeatedly whines about small matters throughout the day. People with ADHD are therefore seen sometimes as being high maintenance, needing to be actively managed, or even drama queens. This is because they overreact, are emotionally immature, are quick to anger, or become impatient too easily. This means they have to be actively dealt with, calmed, and managed emotionally by others due to their limited emotional self-regulation.

When, as adults, we inhibit our initial emotional reactions, we can use this waiting period to modify, moderate, and otherwise alter our own emotional reactions to events. The internal deliberations we engage in about how we feel, why we feel that way, and what we should do about it can result in our modifying our eventual emotional response to the event. We can tone it down if that would be best. We can verbally reason with ourselves and thus reappraise and often downgrade the importance of the situation. We can use our visual imagery and self-speech to imagine other, more positive, peaceful, or joyous situations that can help us to more quickly calm down. This can help make our emotional reactions to things more socially acceptable than had we just impulsively displayed the initial, raw primary emotional response to an event. If we are angry, we can count to 10 and go to our happy place, as some say. By using images of positive past experiences and talking ourselves into calming down before we finally react to some emotionally charged event, we get emotional self-control.

Adults with ADHD struggle mightily with poor emotional control because they have less of the executive capacities just discussed that can be used for emotional self-control. Emotional self-control is essential if you want to make or keep friends or intimate partners, much less your job. The problem with showing strong or exaggerated emotional expressions often occurs in adults with ADHD, and is even more obvious in children with ADHD. They tend to react to frustrating, provocative, or stressful situations with poorly moderated emotions. Others would have dampened or quelled those feelings entirely considering the consequences at stake for their social acceptance by others, but not adults with ADHD. They show excessive displays of emotion, or relatively raw and impulsive feelings, that can lead to significant social conflicts with and eventual rejection by others.

It is not that their initial feelings are abnormal or irrational for the place or setting, as might be seen in bipolar disorder, schizophrenia, or autism. In many situations, we might feel just as they do. But those emotions are shown too quickly and strongly. The emotions are less moderated (mature) than what others would have shown in that circumstance. In short, we can understand why an adult with ADHD felt the way he did—we would likely feel that way too in that situation. What we don't understand so well is why he showed that emotion without some self-restraint, reflection, and down regulation of the initial strong feelings in that situation. He can't seem to get a grip over his emotions, chill, or otherwise calm down as well as or as quickly as others.

EXECUTIVE FUNCTION 6: SELF-MOTIVATION

> My adult son is 21 years old and is an undergraduate student studying engineering at a major university—one of the best in our country. But he gets so bored with his studies that he feels he is wasting his life and potential as he barely studies and his grades are terrible. I know he is smart, but his propensity to get bored so easily drives him crazy. He knows that if he could just concentrate on his studies he could contribute to the world and really unlock his gifted potential. Is there something we can do for him?

When faced with routine or uninteresting work or other activities, the person with ADHD often lacks the motivation he needs to get things done. Instead, he searches for more interesting things to do, such as any other activities that may offer the promise of a short-term reward. He often gets side tracked by more stimulating but irrelevant things rather than plow through the less interesting work that must get done.

Many adults with ADHD are sensation seekers. They are looking for anything to do that gives them some short-term excitement or entertainment even though that often conflicts with the tasks or other responsibilities they need to get done now. It is common to hear that adults with ADHD speed excessively while driving a motor vehicle far more than do others. They also participate more often in dangerous activities like extreme sports (speed skiing, sky diving, extreme snowboarding, car racing, motorcycle use or racing, etc.). Adults with ADHD sometimes overfocus on, and may even become addicted to, playing sensational videogames, or they spend far too much time viewing social media on the Internet or text messaging on their smartphone. But even things that are initially interesting to them may lose their appeal over time and do so much faster than it might for others. This leads adults with ADHD to move on, looking for the next more interesting or entertaining thing to do. Their life is filled with projects or tasks half-completed that seemed like good ideas to do at the time but that lost their appeal very quickly, rarely getting finished.

The problems with time management lead to another major problem for adults with ADHD. They show a greater disregard for or a devaluing of future consequences. If you cannot anticipate the future as well as others using the power of forethought, as in adult ADHD, then the future won't matter as much to you. The larger, later, and more important consequences in life will not be appreciated or valued as much as the smaller, more obvious ones in the moment. If, like an adult with ADHD, you don't think about and value those later, larger consequences as much as others are able to do, you won't care as much about them. And that means you won't work as long and as hard to get those rewards as other typical adults are able to do. You will repeatedly opt out of the extended work these later rewards may require. Instead, you will choose the easier, shorter course of getting the more immediate, though smaller, rewards or avoiding the immediate smaller things you don't like. In short, if you are an adult who has ADHD, you won't be able to delay gratification as well as others.

An adult with ADHD is often noted to work less hard, apply less effort, work less time, and more frequently take the short cuts in work, education, and life than do others of her age. Others will describe her as having less self-motivation, determination, drive, stick-to-it-iveness, and self-discipline than she should have for her age. Those people will see this as a choice, or as a personal or moral failing and often blame it on poor upbringing. They will not view it as a neurological deficit in the brain's executive system.

Perhaps you have fallen prey to just such moral judgments about your loved one with adult ADHD. At least now you can reframe that perspective. You can see these problems of self-control as the neurological symptoms of a deficient executive system in the brain and not as some deliberate choice the person is making to behave less maturely or irresponsibly. What you can now understand is the difference between *won't* and *can't.* The former implies that an adult with ADHD could change if he wished to but is choosing not to so. The latter means that he cannot change such deficits so easily because of an inherent biological limitation in an important brain system—the executive system.

There are many social skills and rules of etiquette that are based on our capacities for self-restraint, self-awareness, foresight, and deferred gratification—they are based on the idea that we keep an eye out for our future. Being able to share, cooperate, and reciprocate with others are examples. We do all these things because we know that in the future we are likely to meet these people again. If so, our cooperative actions make those others more likely to do the same for us. We all know that these important social skills are the basis for many social relationships—with family members, friends, colleagues, or even just occasional acquaintances, as well as strangers. Using these social skills improves our life and long-term welfare, and reduces the risk of unnecessary conflicts with others.

The deficiencies in the executive system of the brain in ADHD can help us to understand why an adult with ADHD may be having more problems in their family, social, and occupational life than others. It is because she struggles with these important social skills, such as sharing, cooperation, turn taking, and repaying the favors of others or fulfilling the promises she has made to others.

This inability to wait and delay gratification, in fact, is often what we mean when we say that someone is *impulsive.* Impulsive people seem to reduce the value of the future and overvalue the moment and the small things they can get now with little effort. He may be offered a chance to earn interest on their spare income by saving or investing it rather than spending what he has now on immediate pleasures. But he goes ahead and likely spends the money now. This is not just true of money, saving, using credit, and paying bills but of other consequences in their family, social, and occupational lives. It is far more difficult to advance one's position in social, educational, and occupational status by being an immediate gratifier like an adult with ADHD.

EXECUTIVE FUNCTION 7: SELF-ORGANIZATION

> My older brother with ADHD is very disorganized, despite being a successful entrepreneur. He never knows where things are that he now needs to complete some task. And he makes lots of careless errors whenever he tries to complete work or daily tasks. If it wasn't for his administrative assistants—he calls them his Radar O'Reillys—who anticipate what he will need, and keep him organized and supplied with the things he needs in the immediate situation, he would not be nearly so successful.

Because adults with ADHD are so easily distracted by events around them, more easily bored, and are less able to sustain their attention to what they planned to do or should be doing, they leave a trail of disorganization in their wake. Adults with ADHD often drop things where they were last used rather than consciously putting them back where they belong, such as placing their car keys on a hook by the backdoor, leaving dirty dishes and coffee cups throughout the house, misplacing money or other valuables (smartphones, for example). And because they cannot sustain their actions toward goals so that the goals are completed, they wind up filling their life spaces with lots of unfinished projects that can readily annoy more organized, goal-directed people with whom they live or work. All this makes for a messy, cluttered, and disorganized home and workplace.

The clutter in the life of an adult with ADHD is not of the type seen in hoarders, who continuously collect worthless things that they cannot bring themselves to discard. Instead, it is the debris from a life of partially completed projects. It is the materials often left out because adults with ADHD intend to get back to doing them but somehow never do.

Related to this problem with self-organization in adult ADHD is a difficulty with planning and problem solving. Planning and problem solving involve the ability to generate multiple ideas or options for how to respond to an immediate problem or an impending future event. It also involves thinking about how best to sequence the eventual steps we may choose to use. It is a type of mental play that comes from the ability to take apart and recombine information in our mind. This is much harder to do if your mind and life are poorly organized.

Adults with ADHD don't plan things out or problem solve very well. Consequently, we hear them complain not just that their mind is a jumbled mess, poorly organized, and less able to hold information (working memory) but also that they cannot manipulate that information quickly to plan out possible courses of action or to problem solve their way around obstacles as well as others can. This deficiency will have a substantial adverse effect on their work and educational activities, in particular where mental problem solving is so essential to success.

THE EXECUTIVE SYSTEM—PUTTING IT ALL TOGETHER

Let's briefly review what we have learned. A suite of executive mental abilities work together to give adults the ability to control their own behavior to be socially and occupationally effective and to improve their longer term welfare—to be as well prepared for the future as one can be. They are our Swiss army knife of mind tools to aim ourselves successfully at the future. Look at each of the executive abilities in the following list while thinking about your loved one with adult

ADHD. Ask yourself, does that person have significant difficulties in one or more of these mental abilities? Place a check mark next to each one you believe to be a problem. Which problems does he or she show?

- self-awareness ______
- inhibition and self-restraint ______
- working memory ______
- time management ______
- self-control of emotions ______
- self-motivation ______
- planning/problem-solving ______

Problems in the functioning of these mind tools are what are going wrong underneath the surface of adult ADHD. They are what give rise to the more obvious surface symptoms I discussed in Chapter 1. Understanding these deficits in executive functioning should help you to understand why ADHD is such an impairing disorder. The executive deficits underlying adult ADHD disrupt the ability to organize behavior over time to accomplish goals (and other work) so as to be well prepared for the future.

CHAPTER 3

THE FACTS ABOUT ADHD IN ADULTS

Loved ones of adults with attention-deficit/hyperactivity disorder (ADHD) often ask a variety of questions about the disorder, so I address the most common ones here.

HOW DO WE KNOW ADULT ADHD IS A REAL DISORDER?

When you discuss ADHD with others, do you ever hear something along the lines of, "I don't believe in ADHD. I think it's something people make up as an excuse for poor behavior"? A common assumption behind such claims is that there has to be some objective laboratory test of a disorder for it to be real or valid. This claim is absurd because no laboratory test can determine any mental disorders (or many medical ones for that matter, even for common complaints such as headache, backache, stomachache, not to mention the early stages of Alzheimer's, multiple sclerosis, lupus, and others). The absence of a test hardly means the absence of a disorder. Disorders are primarily discovered first by describing the symptoms that are believed to comprise that condition. Then scientists search for the causes that contribute to those symptoms. Only then, years or even decades later, is clinical science able to discover some essential objective means of testing for it.

Real disorders consist of a failure or serious deficiency (a) in the functioning of a mental ability that is universal across people (a mental adaptation) that (b) produces harm to the individual. It's that simple. We can show that ADHD meets both of these standards. Let's take the first one—evidence of a mental ability (or set of abilities) that is typical of adults is substantially impaired in people with ADHD. As I described in Chapter 1, overwhelming evidence indicates that ADHD involves a significant problem in both attention (poor sustained attention and distractibility) and inhibition (impulsivity and hyperactivity). These are universal traits or abilities in all people and are less well developed in those with ADHD. Thousands of scientific studies document this fact. But as you read in Chapter 2, there is more going on underneath these obvious problems with mental functioning in ADHD. There are difficulties in the brain's executive system or functions. All typical people have a prefrontal lobe, or executive brain, and it provides those executive mental abilities discussed in the previous chapter. Those mental abilities give us self-control. People with ADHD have less of those abilities. Just as some people have poorer eyesight; are not as good at sports, math, or art; are shorter in height than others; some people have less executive functioning. And when they fall substantially below others in that functioning, it can lead to impairment in effective functioning in many major life domains. That is when it becomes a disorder. As I show in the next chapter, indisputable evidence from hundreds of research studies now indicates that ADHD is routinely associated with maldevelopment and disturbed functioning in regions and networks of the executive brain, known as the prefrontal cortex. Thus, evidence supports the fact that adults with ADHD have less executive functioning than is common in all typical people.

Does ADHD meet the second standard for a valid disorder? Is it associated with harm to the individual? *Harm* here refers to an increased risk of mortality (death), morbidity (injury), personal suffering (a markedly reduced quality of life), or impairment in major domains of life activities essential to our survival and welfare. Those domains include family and social functioning; education; occupational functioning; financial management; sexual functioning; child rearing; and dating, marriage or intimate cohabiting, among other adult major life activities. Only one of these harms needs to be established scientifically. In the case of ADHD, all of them occur at a higher risk than would be expected in typical people. You can read more about these impairments in Chapter 5. They are the consequences of having adult ADHD. As you can see, ADHD handily meets both standards for being a valid mental disorder. ADHD is real.

HOW PREVALENT IS ADULT ADHD?

ADHD occurs in approximately 5% to 8% of children and 3% to 5% of adults. This refers to what percentage of the population would qualify for the diagnosis of ADHD, not what percentage of people actually get a clinical diagnosis of ADHD or treatment for it. Many people can have a mental disorder such as ADHD and not get diagnosed or treated for it. Getting diagnosed and treated can be difficult in parts of the United States, not to mention other countries around the world. States in the United States and other countries vary markedly in the access people have to expert professional services to get properly diagnosed with, and treated for, ADHD. In some places, many people can get such access, whereas in others, such as rural or impoverished areas, they may not have appropriate services and so never get diagnosed. For instance, in a 2006 study done at Harvard Medical School by Ron Kessler, along with myself and many other colleagues,[1] we surveyed a large representative sample of U.S. adults. We found that 90% of those adults who met the standards for a diagnosis of ADHD had never received a clinical diagnosis or been treated for it. At that time, adult ADHD was being markedly underdiagnosed by professionals. That is because many professionals did not know that adults could have ADHD. Also, there were very few clinics specializing in its diagnosis and treatment. Services have certainly improved since then. But it is still highly likely that a majority of adults who have ADHD are not being diagnosed and treated for it.

ARE THERE SEX DIFFERENCES IN ADHD?

ADHD is 3 times more common in boys than girls in childhood. By adulthood this sex difference nearly disappears, with nearly as many women having ADHD as men. It is not clear at this time why this difference in the sex ratio declines and becomes more equal by adulthood.

Is the disorder different in women than in men, as some trade books on women with ADHD may have suggested? Not really. The symptoms are the same in men and women. But men with ADHD are more likely to have problems with aggression, defiance, and risk-taking. And so they may be more likely to develop disorders related to such behavior (conduct disorder, oppositional defiant disorder, and antisocial personality disorder). They are also more likely to speed while driving, manifest road rage, and engage more often in

[1]Kessler, R. C., Adler, L., Barkley, R. A., Biederman, J., Conners, C. K., Demler, O., . . . Zaslavsky, A. M. (2006). The prevalence and correlates of adult ADHD in the United States: Results from the National Comorbidity Survey Replication. *American Journal of Psychiatry*, *163*, 716–723.

crime and possibly drug use than women with ADHD. Women with ADHD, in contrast, are not as likely to have these difficulties but may experience more problems with anxiety, depression, and eating pathology (binge eating, bulimia). But these are the same sex differences we see in the general population and so they are not specific to just men and women with ADHD. And those problems still occur more often in someone with ADHD than in someone of that sex in the typical population. For instance, men with ADHD may be more likely to speed with a car, use drugs, or be aggressive than women with ADHD but both sexes are more likely to do these things than would typical men and women. The same is true for anxiety and depression, which may occur more in women with ADHD than men with the disorder, but both of those disorders occur more often in both sexes than is seen in the typical population.

IS THE UNITED STATES THE ONLY COUNTRY THAT HAS ADULT ADHD?

No. The disorder is found in all countries and ethnic groups studied to date. So ADHD is clearly a worldwide disorder, even if it is not diagnosed and treated as readily in other countries as it is in the United States and other Western countries. ADHD is somewhat more common in urban and population-dense regions than in suburban or rural settings. It is found across all social classes but may be very slightly more common in blue collar or working classes.

ARE ADHD SYMPTOMS ALWAYS PRESENT?

Not necessarily. Some symptoms are usually evident most of the time in most situations but not in every situation. The symptoms of ADHD can also vary markedly from one situation to the next.

It all depends on the nature of the situation or context and what activities the individual is doing (or supposed to be doing). The symptoms of ADHD are often better or less obvious when an adult with ADHD

- is doing something new and interesting rather than something repetitive, very familiar, and boring;
- is allowed to move, fidget, squirm, or otherwise remain active during a task that requires some concentration and mental work;
- is engaged in an activity they enjoy or find very rewarding;
- can get an immediate reward or consequence, or there is an immediate deadline;
- works under supervision or in small groups rather than independently of others or away from supervision;
- is involved in an interaction that is one-to-one or has someone's undivided attention;
- doesn't have to wait for something to happen;
- can do work in small amounts with frequent short breaks and can self-pace the task;
- doesn't have to hold a lot of information in mind all at once;
- the steps in their work are written down and in front of them; and
- if the situation does not provoke strong emotions.

Knowing all this, you may find it useful to help your loved one with ADHD create situations in which the factors that make their ADHD worse are greatly reduced or eliminated and those factors that make the symptoms better are intentionally included in that situation.

ARE THERE DIFFERENT TYPES OF ATTENTION DIFFICULTIES?

Probably. Individuals who exhibit the attention problems in ADHD but do not display excessive activity levels or poor impulse control are being diagnosed with attention deficit disorder (ADD) by some clinicians. Or they might be called ADHD—inattentive type or presentation using the latest diagnostic manual. Yet new research is showing that many of these people may actually have an attention deficit distinct from that seen in typical ADHD. This other attention problem is not yet recognized officially as a disorder in the *DSM–5*[2] or other diagnostic manuals. But it was first recognized around 1985 (and possibly as early as 1789). It makes up as many as 15% to 30% or more of clinically referred cases being diagnosed as having ADHD, especially those being called inattentive type or presentation. On closer inspection, people with this syndrome have very little in common with people having classic ADHD. Researchers now refer to this new attention problem as "sluggish cognitive tempo" (SCT). I have recommended it should be called "concentration deficit disorder" (or "syndrome") because the name is not so demeaning. But that is just a name I suggested for this condition in 2014 and am encouraging other scientists to adopt. They have yet to do so. So for now, SCT is its name.

SCT cases often differ in many respects from people diagnosed with ADHD. These differences are why some researchers, including me, have argued that SCT may represent a separate attention problem from ADHD. However, it is one that can overlap with ADHD in about half of all cases of each. The differences observed

[2]American Psychiatric Association. (2013). *Diagnostic and statistical manual of mental disorders* (5th ed.). Arlington, VA: Author. http://dx.doi.org/10.1176/appi.books.9780890425596

so far between ADHD and SCT in research studies are outlined as follows—and they occur more often in SCT.

- *Having different attention symptoms.* Indeed, some of the symptoms of SCT appear to be opposites of those seen in ADHD. These include
  - daydreaming often;
  - often appearing spacey, mentally disconnected from the situation;
  - often staring;
  - often slow-moving, hypoactive, lethargic, sleepy, or sluggish;
  - often seeming easily confused or appearing to be mentally foggy;
  - having no significant symptoms of hyperactivity;
  - having no significant symptoms of impulsiveness or poor inhibition;
  - often being slow to react to events;
  - seeming to be often slow to process information and prone to making mistakes in doing so;
  - often having a poor focus of attention or being unable to select out what is important from what is not in the information around them;
  - possibly having more problems consistently remembering information that was previously learned (erratic retrieval from long-term memory);
  - having far less problems with self-control and executive functioning than do those with ADHD, and mostly having difficulties with poor organization; and
  - often being more socially reticent, shy, anxious, or withdrawn than others, and as a result they tend to be viewed as quiet and may even be overlooked or neglected by others in social situations, but they are not socially rejected outright as may be many people with ADHD.

- *Having a different pattern of risks for other disorders that sometimes coexist with ADHD.* These patterns include
  - rarely showing the social aggression associated with oppositional defiant disorder (which is very commonly linked in ADHD; 60%–80%);
  - being less likely to be antisocial or have conduct disorder (CD; includes frequent lying, stealing, fighting, law-breaking, etc.), as those with ADHD are more likely to have CD (25%–45%); and
  - being more likely to be anxious and depressed than typical people or even those who have ADHD.
- *Often being impaired in schoolwork but in a different way than those having ADHD.* This is probably due to SCT causing a tendency to make more errors in doing the work. In contrast, people with ADHD show more problems with productivity or the amount of work they complete in a given period of time.

If these and other differences from ADHD continue to accrue in the scientific literature, SCT might one day be given a separate official diagnosis. But for now, it seems to be another attention problem in adults worthy of more future research.

CAN SOMEONE OUTGROW ADHD?

Yes, they can. In my own follow-up study of children with ADHD into adulthood, my colleagues and I[3] found that at least 14% of those children by age 27 no longer exhibited symptoms compared with typical people, as reported by themselves and someone who knows them well. Just as important, they were no longer impaired by the symptoms in young adulthood. We found another 21% might

[3]Barkley, R. A., Murphy, K. R., & Fischer, M. (2008). *ADHD in adults: What the science says.* New York, NY: Guilford Press.

Pressure to Succeed With Sluggish Cognitive Tempo

After some research, I know with absolute certainty that I experience sluggish cognitive tempo, and as a result my entire life has been a struggle in motivation, finding purpose, escaping boredom, and thinking there's something wrong with me because I'm just so unable to knuckle down. I know deep down that I'm not lazy or stupid, but there has always been a "black hole" in my brain where motivation, purpose, and ambition should be. Somehow I'm not really able to access these things like other people do. It makes me sort of numb inside, as though I am imprisoned behind a big glass window, looking out, but unable to grasp things as I should. My parents and my friends often tell me I should "settle down," or "grow up," as though it's a choice I have to make. I would if I could. What they seem unable to understand is that I can't. It's not a choice. Sometimes it's just been easier to say I have fibromyalgia or chronic fatigue. They seem to understand that, and accept it. Only I know the fatigue is in my brain, NOT in my body!

It seems to be getting worse as I get older (40 this year), and it becomes apparent that while my friends are now all happily settled with families and mortgages, I'm the only one still scratching a living at short-time jobs and then spending all my savings by travelling. Travel is the only thing that offers me excitement, pleasure, and escape, and there is nowhere I haven't been. It's becoming apparent that I can't keep doing this my entire life, though I don't know what hope there is for me, in terms of recovery or treatment.

I'm really scared of becoming a drifter, of being penniless and homeless in my later years. It's a fear that reduces me to tears often, because I just don't seem to know what to do about it. I'm guessing it wouldn't have mattered back in the day of my mother's and grandmother's generations, when all that was expected of women was to be a good mother and housewife. Now that I'm expected to be a high-flying equal-status bread-winner, the pressure is really on. But it's just not in me. It's not there. How I wish things were different.

have remitted or outgrown the disorder if one based that conclusion on only the reports of one person, either themselves or that of their parents. So, 14% to 35% might remit in their ADHD. Even these adults remained toward the upper range of the typical population in their symptoms. But it was not enough to be impaired or to meet the standards for having a diagnosis of the disorder: About 40% to 45% of our participants met the criteria for a diagnosis of ADHD by young adulthood, and another 20% were quite symptomatic and impaired but didn't quite meet all the official criteria for having the diagnosis. Dr. Stephen Faraone and colleagues have reviewed other follow-up studies and reached very similar conclusions—some people can grow out of their ADHD, but many do not.[4]

Some research suggests that the symptoms of the disorder continue to decline throughout adulthood. But so few studies have followed children into middle or late life, so it is difficult to make any reliable conclusion. One recent study published by Rachel Klein and her colleagues[5] at New York University Medical School tracked children with ADHD for 33 years to an average age of 45. This study found that 22% to 32% of them still met the full diagnostic criteria for the disorder. Up to 60% of them had developed at least one other mental disorder during their adulthood, most often antisocial personality and drug use disorders. Only 32% did not have any mental disorder at this follow-up evaluation.

---

[4]Faraone, S. V., Asherson, P., Banaschewski, T., Biederman, J., Buitelaar, J. K., Ramos-Quiroga, J. A., . . . Franke, B. (2015). Attention-deficit/hyperactivity disorder. *Nature Reviews: Disease Primers*. Advance online publication. http://dx.doi.org/10.1038/nrdp.2015.20

[5]Klein, R. G., Mannuzza, S., Ramos Olazagasti, M. A., Roizen, E., Hutchinson, J. A., Lashua, E. C., & Castellanos, F. X. (2012). Clinical and functional outcome of childhood attention-deficit/hyperactivity disorder 33 years later. *Archives of General Psychiatry*, *69*, 1295–1303. http://dx.doi.org/10.1001/archgenpsychiatry.2012.271

A few very recent studies have suggested that changes in brain development and functioning may play an important role in who outgrows the disorder. Greater brain growth and improved functioning in certain regions of the frontal lobe (the executive brain) were found to be associated with outgrowing ADHD by adulthood.

CAN ADHD OCCUR WITH OTHER DISORDERS?

People with certain other mental disorders are more likely to have ADHD than are typical people. For instance, ADHD is more commonly seen in individuals with a history of oppositional defiant disorder, CD (aggression, delinquency, truancy, etc.), learning disabilities (delays in reading, spelling, math, writing, etc.), bipolar disorder, being a juvenile offender, adult antisocial personality, cigarette smoking, alcoholism and other substance use or abuse disorders, tic disorders or the more severe tic disorder called Tourette's syndrome (multiple motor and vocal tics), and autism spectrum disorder. Likewise, people who have ADHD are more likely to also have these other disorders. In fact, more than 80% of adults with ADHD have another disorder besides their ADHD. One reason for this is that some of the genes for these disorders may also be shared with those for ADHD. Getting those genes predisposes someone to a risk for both disorders. Another might be that the neurological problems that underlie some of these disorders can also affect parts of the brain that cause ADHD as well. You can read about the causes of ADHD in Chapter 4.

KEY POINTS TO REMEMBER

If your loved one has ADHD, remember that it is a valid neurodevelopmental disorder, not a choice. It involves a serious difficulty in a suite of mind-tools or mental abilities (attention, inhibition, and the executive functions) compared with typical people. And it can lead to harm, suffering, and impairment in major domains of life activities if it is not treated. ADHD is associated with significant adverse consequences across many, if not most, major domains of life activities, such as education, occupational functioning, and social relationships, among others. It may also increase the risk of early mortality or of a shortened life expectancy. And it is definitely associated with an increased risk of injury. Thus, we can see that ADHD in adults is a valid disorder. ADHD occurs in at least 5% to 8% of children and 4% to 5% of adults. It is more common in males than in females in childhood but the gender divide is far less in adulthood. It is found across all countries, social classes, and ethnic groups.

Another type of attention syndrome (SCT) may not be the same sort of attention problem as that seen in ADHD but can overlap with ADHD in half of all cases of each. It is characterized by frequent daydreaming, appearing spacey, staring, and being more absent-minded. The attention difficulties in those with SCT seem to be in focusing attention and rapidly processing important information. Those with SCT lack the problems with impulsiveness and distractibility that characterize the more common and classic type of ADHD. Socially, people with SCT are more passive and withdrawn and even shy. But far more research is needed on SCT to understand whether it is a disorder and how best to diagnose and treat it.

ACTION PLAN

Take some time to think about your loved one(s) with adult ADHD. If need be, try to reframe your view of them from someone choosing to behave badly or irresponsibly or just ineffectively to someone who is struggling with a valid mental disorder that is not of their choosing. See whether you can understand why they may be having difficulties in many different domains of life as a result of having ADHD. Ask

How I Correct People's Misconceptions About ADHD

I am a 33-year-old man and an emergency room physician in a New England hospital. I have never been as organized, productive, or successful as other people with my level of intelligence or education, especially other physicians. I get bored very easily with routine tasks. I love downhill skiing, racing cars and motorcycles, bobsledding, and I have even tried skydiving. So when it came time to specialize during my medical school training, I knew I would be terrible in primary care specialties like internal medicine, family practice, or pediatrics, seeing the usual parade of maladies that people are likely to show in outpatient clinics. I drifted toward being an ER doctor after my rotation in the ER in my residency, and I never looked back. I love it.

I think it's because emergencies that come through the door are crises that must be dealt with now as best as we can. We have to think on our feet in that moment or the person might die. And that adrenaline rush helps me to focus on what is necessary to do now. In a crisis, one doesn't need to contemplate and plan for the future to do well. You have to focus all your mental energies on what needs to be done to help this person right now. I thrive in that kind of environment.

Just don't ask me about how I drive (very fast in a Corvette) or how many speeding tickets I have gotten. I also don't handle money very well, and spend a lot on impulse buying, such as on fast cars and motorcycles, and sports betting. So I have a pretty mediocre credit score for someone in my income bracket. And my romantic relationships don't last as long as they seem to do for my friends because I get bored so easily once the relationship falls into any kind of routine.

I was diagnosed with ADHD a few years ago while in my residency training in ER medicine when I went and spoke to a psychiatrist at our hospital that specialized in it. The diagnosis really helped to explain why I struggle with self-control and personal organization so much, yet why I may not have as much trouble in my occupation. I knew there was something wrong with me that wasn't just a choice or mere lack of willpower.

(continues)

How I Correct People's Misconceptions About ADHD (*Continued*)

The problem is that many of my colleagues and friends scoff at the diagnosis of adult ADHD, claiming it is a myth or just a cop-out for excusing many of my difficulties, particularly those in my personal life. They think I use it to play the victim instead of just striving to do better. So when I hear that I teach them about the disorder. I confront them (diplomatically) with the fact that there are over 25,000 scientific papers in professional journals on ADHD, and that hundreds of those studies show it to be related to difficulties in brain structure, connectivity, and functioning. I explain to them that it was first described in a German medical textbook back in 1775! And that it is among the most genetically influenced psychological difficulties known to science. I even direct them to research papers showing this fact and also that genes for ADHD are being discovered and reported in respectable medical journals. Some myth! Because they are physicians too who respect science and published results in medical journals, saying all this and directing them to published research, such as using Google Scholar, helps them to "get it." Some people still don't want to believe this—It's just like some people won't ever believe in evolution. But other people do seem to change their minds about the disorder and about me. I love that one prominent clinical scientist who has a lecture on YouTube referred to ADHD as the "diabetes of psychiatry." It is a chronic medical condition that must be managed by a combination of life changes and medication to help people lead a more normal life. My colleagues and friends get that when I explain it to them that way: That it's not a choice, but a biological condition that I struggle against, and that it requires frequent management to contain it and prevent further damage to one's life. They would never scoff at a diabetic as having a deliberate moral failing or character flaw and they shouldn't be so dismissive of ADHD as being like that, because it really isn't. And that attitude gives me hope that, with my treatment, I can achieve more of the goals I have set for myself than I have been able to do previously.

yourself whether it is possible that many of the problems they have experienced in life come from their having a neurodevelopmental disorder of self-control—adult ADHD. Understanding that your loved one has adult ADHD can help you see their life, its problems, and any adverse consequences they have experienced in an entirely new light, like pieces of a puzzle falling into place to give a clearer view of the big picture. If you are going to help your loved one deal with their adult ADHD, you will need to understand this bigger picture that ADHD may help to explain. And you will need to approach them as someone struggling to cope with a mental disorder. That means not only being more understanding of their circumstances but also being less judgmental of them and more compassionate in willing to be of assistance to them. Luckily, you now know that adult ADHD is a very treatable disorder, and therefore you can see there is much hope that with proper treatment your loved one can lead a relatively typical, effective, happy, and successful life.

Now think about the situations that can make ADHD symptoms better or worse. Use that information to help both you and your loved one understand what can be done to help reduce their symptoms. Do that by finding ways to decrease their exposure to those situations that can make the disorder worse. You can also increase their exposure to settings that may help reduce their symptoms. Here are a few suggestions:

- *Establish boring or routine settings, with no immediate consequence for completing work.* Advise your loved one to try to arrange for more background stimulation in boring settings, such as soft music, more lighting, and more color. See whether some immediate reward or other positive consequence can be linked to getting the work done in this boring situation.
- *Places where he must remain seated or stay still.* Encourage your loved one to try to cut down on how many of these situ-

ations he must be in, if possible. When that is not possible, suggest that he try to remain standing in that situation so he can move around a bit. Maybe he can take in a rubber ball or some other small object to squeeze or manipulate to keep active while listening. Movement can be a key to helping him concentrate better!

- *Situations in which the work is long and tedious.* Suggest that your loved one break the work down into smaller amounts or quotas; take frequent short breaks; and periodically stand, stretch, or otherwise move around briefly. Suggest that they listen to soft music with no lyrics through ear buds using a smartphone, iPad, or MP3 player when they have to concentrate more than usual or read important material. Surprisingly, lightly sipping on a sports drink or other sugar containing beverage like lemonade periodically while doing demanding mental work can help sustain one's self-control and executive functioning. Why? It helps to keep blood sugar slightly elevated and blood sugar is the fuel of the executive brain. Don't gulp or chug it; just sip it lightly occasionally during the task.
- *Group situations that require being quiet and restrained.* See whether your loved one can reduce how many such situations she has to participate in for work, school, or social activities. See the prior suggestions for when she must be seated and sit still for other ideas to help with settings involving being quiet and restrained.
- *Tasks when work has to be done independent of supervision.* Suggest that your loved one try to work as much with others who can be supportive and help him focus on the work to be done. Suggest that he ask a coworker or supervisor to check in more often on what work he is supposed to be doing. During these situations, he can review what work he hopes to get done in the next hour or two so he makes a public commitment to

what he plans to do. He is more likely to do it if he has promised a supervisor it will get done.

- *Situations in which she must wait.* Try to avoid such situations when possible. When not possible, advise your loved one to always bring something along to do while waiting, such as squeezing a tennis ball, knitting, listening to music or a podcast on an interesting topic, streaming an episode of a TV series, or playing a game on a handheld device.
- *Occasions when strong emotions may be provoked.* Try to avoid social situations with others who have emotional control problems, can be socially aggressive or obnoxious, routinely have a chip on their shoulder, or in other ways are likely to say or do things to provoke your loved one to some strong emotional reactions. Advise your loved one to cut down on alcohol use in such social situations as it reduces impulse control. If you expect to be in that same situation with him, prearrange with your loved one that you will give him certain cues that he is getting excitable, riled up, or otherwise emotional to help him to self-monitor and so dampen his emotion. However, you must do this early in the sequence of the emotion if your loved one is to have much control in calming down.

Many, many more recommendations for how best to help your loved one with adult ADHD are in later chapters in this book, including formal professional therapies and medications. But by gaining a better understanding of the nature of your loved one's ADHD, you can already see how that leads to helpful recommendations you can make to them for dealing with their symptoms. Of course, your loved one has to recognize and accept that they have this disorder. So read Chapters 9 and 11 on how to talk with your loved one about adult ADHD if you think he or she has not yet come to fully accept that he or she has this disorder.

CHAPTER 4

WHAT CAUSES ADHD?

Substantial research now exists on the various and many causes of attention-deficit/hyperactivity disorder (ADHD). Scientific evidence points to neurological and genetic factors as the greatest contributors. That evidence is now unequivocal and why ADHD is referred to as a neurodevelopmental disorder in official diagnostic manuals. Our knowledge of the final common pathway in the brain through which those brain and genetic factors produce the symptoms has increased markedly in the past decade. Studies have used many different means to study the brains of children and adults with ADHD. The results show where in the brain ADHD arises and what is going wrong in brain development to create the symptoms of ADHD. Just as much, or more, research has also occurred on the genetics of ADHD, and the two disciplines are beginning to be combined in recent scientifically complex studies. That research examines the association of particular genes with the building and operating of particular brain structures, networks that connect them, and their functioning.

Just as important is the fact that in the past decade, no credible social explanation of ADHD has been developed. Sure, you will read in the trade media and on the Internet about ideas such as poor parenting, poor diet, excessive use of computers, smartphones, and the Internet itself possibly causing ADHD. But they don't. For instance, studies of twins and families have made it abundantly clear that the majority of differences among all people in the behavioral traits of ADHD are the result of genetics—differences in their genes. What little variation in the trait that is not explained by genetics is best explained by things called "unique events": Largely, biohazards, such as toxins or infections that were experienced by the individual during early development (often before birth). Those environmental poisons or infections can also lead to neurological injury or disrupted brain development. They include things such as maternal alcohol and tobacco use during that pregnancy and premature delivery that leads to hospitalization in a neonatal intensive care unit. They also involve lead poisoning before 3 years of age, stroke, and brain trauma, to name just a few hazards of life that can disrupt a developing brain.

This is not to say that such social factors are not important. They may well have some influence on people's adjustment in specific situations. They can also influence a person's life course risks, such as how much impairment they may experience in their home life, education, and work. Those are all partly influenced by the surrounding environment. And the social environment can certainly influence the risks someone may have for developing other mental disorders that do have contributions from social factors. Let's not forget as well that social factors determine how much access to care a person can get and the quality of that treatment. But in ADHD, social factors mainly influence the extent and diversity of impairments a child may experience or their risk for developing other (comorbid or coexisting) disorders, such as major depression, anxiety, or oppositional defiant and conduct disorders. Nevertheless, the prevailing evidence makes clear that those social factors do not create the ADHD itself.

ADULT ADHD IS NEUROLOGICAL

Throughout the last century, investigators have repeatedly noted the similarities between symptoms of ADHD and those produced by injuries to the frontal lobes of the human brain. Both children and adults experiencing injuries to the frontal region demonstrate deficits in sustained attention, inhibition, regulation of emotion and motivation, and the capacity to organize behavior across time so as to get ready for the future. You know now those are all symptoms of adult ADHD. Evidence continues to mount that ADHD arises from difficulties in the frontal lobes and their connections to other brain regions, such as the basal ganglia and cerebellum (see Figure 4.1). The networks involved in these brain regions involve important chemicals and their pathways. Those chemicals are called *neurotransmitters* and they work along certain pathways in the brain. Two of the most important of these chemicals in ADHD are dopamine and norepinephrine. Both are affected by ADHD medications that help to improve ADHD symptoms.

The brains of children and adults with ADHD show patterns of lower electrical activity, less blood flow, and less oxygen use in certain regions. Many studies of brain structure and functioning, such as magnetic resonance imaging (MRI), routinely find differences in the structure of selected brain regions—the areas are typically smaller than normal in children or adults with ADHD. More recent studies have found disturbances and abnormal development in the very small nerve fibers of the brain, known as "white matter microstructure." Those nerve fibers occur together in bundles in various white matter networks deep inside certain brain regions. They are like the fiber optic cables, containing lots of smaller lines of fibers, you see being buried underground in neighborhoods. These fiber bundles and their networks allow brain regions to communicate with each other. Overall, these brain regions in people with

FIGURE 4.1. Panel A: Diagram of the human brain regions involved in attention-deficit/hyperactivity disorder (ADHD). Panel B: The dopamine system of the brain—a neurotransmitter system influenced by certain ADHD medications. Panel C: The norepinephrine system of the brain—a neurotransmitter system affected by other ADHD medications.

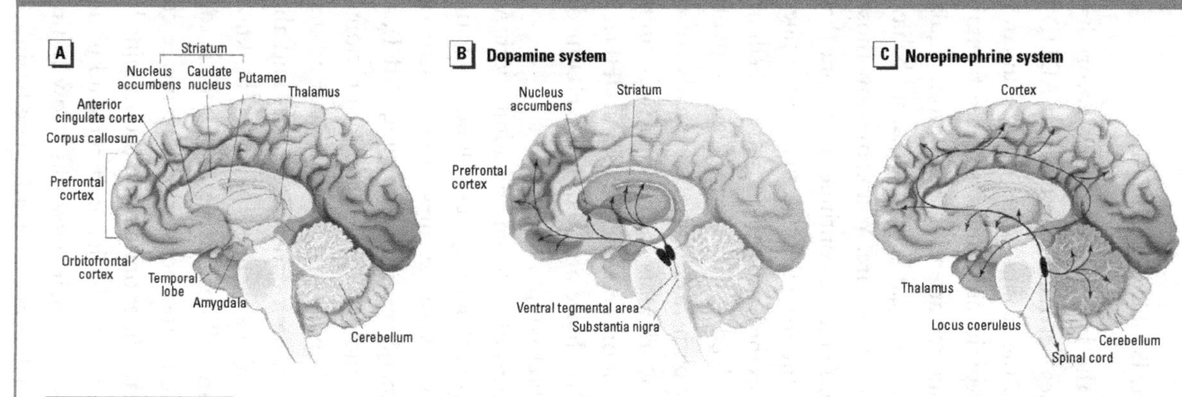

From *Neuroscience: Exploring the Brain* (2nd ed.), by M. F. Bear, B. W. Connors, and M. A. Paradiso, 2001, Baltimore, MD: Lippincott Williams & Wilkins. Copyright 2001 by Lippincott Williams & Wilkins. Adapted with permission.

ADHD are about 10% to 30% smaller and in children they are 2 or 3 years or more delayed in development. And the fiber bundles that connect them are smaller and less active, and may not properly connect up with other brain regions the way they do in a typical brain.

ADULT ADHD CAN BE ACQUIRED FROM CHILDHOOD BRAIN INJURIES

Although most cases of ADHD appear to have a genetic basis (see next section), in a smaller percentage of cases (25%–35%), ADHD may arise from early brain injuries or other disruptions to normal brain development. These include such things as being exposed to maternal alcohol consumption or smoking during pregnancy and greater pregnancy or birth complications. But ADHD can also arise from early high levels of lead poisoning and unusual autoimmune reactions to bacterial infections in the mother during pregnancy or in the child after birth. And such injury to the executive brain can certainly occur from head trauma, brain tumors, strokes, and so on. The list of such causes of early brain development problems is long because many things can adversely affect brain development. What they have in common is that they have the potential to damage or alter the development of the executive brain and then give rise to ADHD.

ADULT ADHD IS MAINLY GENETIC OR INHERITED

However, most cases of adult ADHD are not due to damage to the developing brain. So why are certain brain regions smaller, less well developed, and not functioning well in adults with ADHD who didn't experience brain injury? Most likely, that is because most of those adults have inherited the disorder. And what they inherited were different genes involved in brain development than occurs in typical adults. How do we know ADHD is mainly a genetic disorder? Evidence comes from many different sources.

For instance, many years ago, researchers noted the higher prevalence of mental disorders in the parents and other relatives of children with ADHD. Between 10% and 35% of the immediate family members of children with ADHD were also found to have ADHD. If a child has ADHD, nearly a third of their brothers and sisters will also have ADHD. A substantial percentage of the children's parents will also have ADHD, although often not diagnosed. One study found that 55% of families with an ADHD-diagnosed child had at least one parent affected by the disorder. If a parent has ADHD, 40% to 57% of their biological children will also have ADHD. Keep the last figure in mind if your loved one with ADHD is planning on having children, as this would be the risk that their children might eventually have ADHD also.

Studies of adopted children with ADHD find very much the same pattern. The adoptive parents and relatives have no more ADHD than would be expected from the base rate of the disorder in the population (3%–5% of adults). But the biological (genetic) relatives of the adopted children have significantly greater percentages with the disorder. Thus, ADHD occurs far more often among the genetic relatives of children or adults with the disorder, whether those relatives raised the child or not. This strongly supports a hereditary basis to this condition.

Studies of twins can also provide evidence for a genetic basis to a disorder. Twin studies provide data that can help to estimate the contribution of heredity (genetics) to various psychological traits and mental disorders. These studies can estimate the percentage of the differences among individuals in a trait, such as ADHD, that can be attributed to differences in the genes of people. For example, we know from twin studies that more than 90% of the differences among people in their height are the result of differences in their genetic makeup.

Twin studies focusing on ADHD estimate that between 70% and 80% of the differences among people in the degree of ADHD traits is the result of such genetic factors. Some studies even place this figure at over 90%. This is higher than the genetic contribution to differences among people in their personality traits, intelligence, and other mental disorders, such as anxiety and depression. But because the genetic contribution to ADHD is not a perfect 100%, these results mean that nongenetic factors cause some of the severity of ADHD symptoms in some people. I discussed some of those previously, concerning early brain injuries or pregnancy problems that adversely affected brain development. Those aren't genetic and cannot be inherited, but they can still cause ADHD in some cases.

More evidence that ADHD is genetic comes from studies finding particular versions of genes to be associated with the disorder that are less common in typical people. Scientists are now hunting for the specific genes that cause ADHD. They have focused on approximately 25 of them (and possibly as many as 45) that have appeared in prior studies as being more likely to be associated with ADHD. Most of the genes found to date are associated with regulating the neurotransmitters dopamine and norepinephrine in the brain (see Figure 4.1 for a diagram of these neurotransmitter pathways). Others may affect nerve cells in ways that help the cell increase the strength of a signal moving through the cell (e.g., Alpha2 receptors). More recently, genes have been identified that play a role in brain development. Those genes determine how and where nerve cells migrate to reach their normal destinations, and how well the nerve cell is supplied with nutrients, among other processes in brain development. Several recent studies have scanned the entire human genome searching for ADHD risk genes and have found at least 20 to 25 sites on chromosomes to be associated with ADHD. Important to understand is that these are genes that we all may possess, but these genes can vary in size (length) or the sequence of information coded in them. People with ADHD are more likely to have versions of these genes that are unusual in length or in their sequences. Those differences affect how the gene works in brain development, structure, and functioning.

ADHD therefore does not occur because of just a single gene. It arises from a combination of multiple risk genes. Each gene is contributing a small likelihood of risk for the disorder. The more risk genes one inherits, the greater the adverse effect these can have on the brain, and so that can result in a greater the number and severity of ADHD symptoms that a person may have.

As if the research in this area was not complicated enough for even clinical scientists to fully understand, the most recent research suggests a complex interaction between certain genes that pose an increased risk for ADHD and certain environmental toxins. For instance, if a mother is pregnant and her baby carries two of the major risk genes for ADHD, the odds that that child may have ADHD go up 2 to 3 times compared with that of a baby without the genes. We know that if a mother smokes during her pregnancy, even if her baby does not have these ADHD risk genes, the odds that her baby will have ADHD also go up 2 to 3 times over that of a baby whose mother did not smoke tobacco. But the really surprising finding was that if both risks were present (the baby had the risk genes and the mother smoked tobacco while pregnant) the risk that the baby would eventually develop ADHD was 8 times greater! This suggests that children with certain genes for ADHD may be more sensitive to certain environmental factors or hazards. If those hazards occur, then that greatly increases the child's risk for developing ADHD compared with just the risk associated with the ADHD genes alone or the risk from the hazardous event alone. Similar interactions between ADHD risk genes and other environmental factors have been found. These include such things as alcohol use by mothers during pregnancy, the number of infections the mother had while pregnant; how much stress the mother experienced during pregnancy; and how disrupted, abusive, neglectful, or chaotic the family life was during the child's early development. Therefore, the causes of ADHD may not only be multiple, but they may be even more complex than was initially believed to be the case.

Genetic testing may eventually contribute to more accurate diagnosis. It may even reveal genetic subtypes of the disorder that might differ in important ways in the nature of their ADHD or in their risks for certain kinds of impairment, as noted previously. Research on genetics also offers the promise that new and more specific drugs for ADHD may be developed that can better target the underlying neurological problems in adults with ADHD. Those drugs might prove even more effective and have fewer side effects than do current medications. But we are not there yet, so there is no need to get your loved one tested for their genes.

We now know that multiple genes can interact to create an increased risk for the disorder. If coupled with exposure to environmental hazards, as illustrated in my son's story, this combination could further increase the likelihood of someone having ADHD.

How Health Problems and Trauma in Infancy Can Contribute to ADHD

My son, age 27, has both hereditary and acquired ADHD. My brother (age 52; I'm 61), who is my only sibling, and my father had ADHD. My brother, a lawyer, still requires and takes daily medication (Ritalin) to function and manage his personal life and professional responsibilities. So it is quite clear that ADHD runs in my family. But my son also had a major medical crisis that began within 24 hours of his birth as a result of a Group B strep infection, which caused respiratory distress, sepsis, and pulmonary issues, where his lungs were unable to move from prenatal

(continues)

How Health Problems and Trauma in Infancy Can Contribute to ADHD (*Continued*)

function to postnatal, and so on. He was on a ventilator at 100% oxygen with blood gases well below normal. He was given Pavulon, which caused significant fluid retention. He reacted to any form of stimulation (voice, touch, etc.) with such a significant reaction that he coded (heart stopped) at least three times. During the fourth day in the NICU, we were told the chances of his surviving were very slim.

He was born 4 to 5 weeks early; however, he weighed 6 lb., 2 oz., and had an Apgar score of 8 to 9. Several events that occurred during labor caused him to go into distress: an overdose of the epidural anesthesia and the use of Pitocin. Also, the additional fact that he was not transferred to the NICU for over 12 hours after his condition became critical because of the transport team being in a distant location in the state and apparently there was no way to transfer him any other way considering his condition. The hospital where he was born was not a Level 3 trauma facility, and that prevented them from giving him dopamine, which was another major issue and prolonged the period of time he was not able to receive the necessary treatment for his life-threatening condition.

He miraculously survived, but at 18 months he suffered a mild concussion from a fall down a flight of stairs. He now has long-term effects from the trauma and the necessary therapeutic treatments that were used to save his life. But his greatest struggle and challenge has been his significant ADHD symptoms that have in turn caused major depression, with anxiety and panic issues.

KEY POINTS TO REMEMBER

A variety of genetic and neurological causes (pregnancy and birth complications, acquired brain damage, toxins, infections, genetic effects, etc.) can give rise to ADHD. This is likely to occur through some disturbance in brain development, structure, and functioning. A common pathway in the nervous system related to ADHD has been identified—the executive brain (frontal lobes) and its networks. These regions and their networks are less developed, function more poorly, and are disrupted in people with ADHD. The greater are the problems in these regions, the greater is the severity of someone's ADHD symptoms.

Heredity (genetics) plays the largest role in the occurrence of ADHD symptoms. The condition can also be caused or exacerbated by pregnancy complications, exposure to toxins, or neurological disease. Cases of ADHD can also arise without a genetic predisposition to the disorder. A person may be exposed to some biohazard, such as tobacco or alcohol during pregnancy, which can cause a significant disruption to this final common brain pathway. However, such acquired brain injuries account for only a small minority of ADHD children and adults. Most cases are genetically caused.

Social factors alone do not appear to be causing this disorder. However, such factors may contribute to the other disorders that may be associated with ADHD, such as defiance, social aggression, and antisocial behavior, not to mention depression and anxiety. That environment can also influence how impaired a person may be from their disability as well as how much treatment, and the quality of that treatment, they will receive.

In general, then, research conducted to date provides strong evidence for genetic and developmental neurological factors as causing ADHD. In many cases, these factors interact with each other to cause or worsen the predisposition to developing ADHD.

CHAPTER 5

WHAT ARE THE CONSEQUENCES OF UNTREATED ADHD?

Attention-deficit/hyperactivity disorder (ADHD) can lead to numerous adverse consequences in many areas of adult daily life. And not just for your adult loved one with ADHD but for you as well, if you are involved routinely in their life. Here I describe the various domains that research shows can be negatively impacted by adult ADHD. Not all adults experience impaired functioning in all of these areas. However, an adult with ADHD is more likely to have difficulties in these domains than would a typical adult. But with your help and with proper treatment, much improvement can usually be made in these domains for your loved one with adult ADHD. You will see that ADHD has a pervasive negative effect in someone's life if it is not properly treated. I will also mention how these problems may impact your own life.

You have every reason to be concerned about your loved one's ADHD—it can be a very impairing disorder. But don't get discouraged—ADHD in adults is also among the most treatment-responsive psychological disorders currently known. This review is not intended to make you depressed or cause you to give up hope. Instead, I am offering it to validate your concerns, to show that adult ADHD is a serious condition if not properly treated, and to help you motivate your loved one to get treatment.

SCHOOL

> How can I help my struggling son to find a way to be successful? He is 22 and has struggled with school all of his life. He is now attending a community college nearby but doing poorly. He says he wants to work in rock music and is frustrated because we do not have a local recording/production school in our small community. There is one several hundred miles away in Los Angeles that he would like to attend. But we are afraid he will fail there too and possibly get into alcohol and drugs, given what we have heard about the LA music scene. Living on campus in LA sounds like a potential for disaster for him.

Undoubtedly, the domain of education is the one most likely to be adversely affected by adult ADHD. In addition, it is affected more severely than other domains. This is especially so in childhood and adolescence because of the requirement to be in school during these years. But adult ADHD can also have an adverse impact during young adulthood if your loved one went beyond high school for any additional education. ADHD can also cause problems in her current life if she is participating in any adult continuing education programs, such as additional college, technical training, or work-related training. All this makes perfect sense when you consider the problems ADHD produces in inhibiting behavior, paying attention, remembering what she is told to do, resisting distractions, sitting still, and being quiet. It is even more obvious when you consider the executive deficits discussed in Chapter 2—difficulties with time management, self-organization, problem solving, emotional self-control, self-restraint, and self-motivation. All of those mental abilities are essential for functioning effectively in school or any other educational setting as an adult.

People with ADHD are more likely to have been held back in a grade (25%–50%), placed in special education (50%–80%), suspended for inappropriate conduct (20%–60%), or expelled

(10%–15%), or to have quit (10%–35%) before completing high school. They are therefore less likely to attend college. And if they do attend, they are less likely to complete that program (5%–10% vs. 35%–41% of adults). They have more days of unexcused absences from school; a lower class ranking in high school; a lower grade point average in high school; and if they attended college, more grades of D and F than adults in a general community sample. Individuals with ADHD therefore often have less education than do others their age. Obviously, those with high levels of intelligence are better able to achieve more years of education, and some may even complete advanced graduate degrees. Yet overall, the educational system was often a very difficult situation for adults with ADHD when they were growing up.

As we all know, if a person does not get a good education, this can have downstream negative effects. The amount of money a person is likely to earn both annually and across their lifetime is directly related to how much education they received. We should also not forget that the amount of education a person receives is likely to determine the types of occupations they will be able to pursue. Not graduating from high school, for instance, results in not getting access to many work opportunities and types of occupations. This results in a far more restricted range of work opportunities for such a person than for someone completing high school or someone who gets at least some college. So even after people with ADHD eventually leave school, their educational difficulties may have lasting detrimental effects on their adult lives.

WORK

> Learning that my wife, at age 49, had ADHD was such a surprise. But it provided the missing link in why she could get any job she tried (pharmaceutical rep, international importer, assistant to the head of a movie studio, associate producer of TV

documentaries, licensed stock broker, etc.), yet she was rarely able to keep it for more than a year before getting bored and moving on.

Another domain of adult life that is adversely affected by ADHD is work. Again, this makes perfect sense given the symptoms of the disorder and the deficits in self-control and executive functioning discussed in Chapters 1 and 2. If you are poorly inhibited, easily distracted, unable to sustain your attention as long as others, forgetful, and generally have less self-control or self-discipline than others because of your ADHD, work life can prove to be quite a struggle. Of course, this depends on the kind of work an adult chooses to do. Some jobs are more ADHD-friendly than others. For instance, an adult with ADHD might find being a salesperson or physical education teacher to be better suited to their ADHD-related symptoms and so be less impaired by them in such jobs. But he would find it difficult to deal with his symptoms if he worked at a desk job dealing mainly with paperwork or in which he had to manage a lot of time-sensitive logistics, such as if he were an event planner, builder, or factory plant manager. Yet, even when an adult with ADHD finds an occupation in which he is less affected by his ADHD, he may still have trouble with the organization and time management aspects of even these ADHD-friendly occupations.

As they enter the workforce, teens and adults with ADHD have more problems in performing their work as well as others. They start working earlier in life than others, which may sound like a good thing for them. But this is probably due to their being less likely to pursue further education after high school or to even graduate from high school. It also means they do not have the skills necessary to move up in such entry level jobs, like fast food worker, restaurant busboy or waitress, lawn care, farm field hand, or construction. Adults with ADHD change jobs more often out of boredom than do other adults. My own research[1] found that adults with ADHD were 2 to 3 times more likely to be dismissed from a job because of poor conduct and were fired from a greater percentage of the jobs they had held since leaving high school than were other adults. More than half of adults with ADHD have been fired from a job at least once and have quit jobs impulsively with no other job to go to when they quit. Perhaps this explains why a substantial number of adults with ADHD may go for several months or longer being unemployed.

Concerning behavior at work, adults with ADHD show more oppositional behavior, such as being hot tempered, argumentative, or defiant. More than half the adults with ADHD who participated in my study (see Footnote 1) had significant problems getting along with others. They were also less punctual for work, appeared to manage their time less efficiently, were more forgetful and disorganized, and so required more supervision than did other workers. Clearly, these problems can result in an adult with ADHD receiving lower ratings of her work performance from supervisors than do others without ADHD. All of this inevitably leads to a greater likelihood that an adult with ADHD will have formal disciplinary actions taken against her by her employers than would a typical adult. You can now see why an adult with ADHD spends significantly less time in any given job than do others. As a result, she winds up having held more jobs in her checkered work history than do other adults. All of these problems can lead to lower earnings, less opportunity for workplace advancement, and overall lower status jobs than adults without ADHD who persist far longer at the jobs they take.

---

[1]Barkley, R. A., Murphy, K. R., & Fischer, M. (2008). *ADHD in adults: What the science says.* New York, NY: Guilford Press.

Adults with ADHD also have more accidents at work, experience more injuries, make more claims for worker's compensation, and take more unexcused absences from work. They also may use more of their sick leave and spend more of their time at work not being especially productive than do adults in the general working population. Adults with ADHD are also more likely to file for disability claims or Social Security Disability Insurance. And if they drive a vehicle for a living or do so more often simply as part of their work, they show a greater risk for vehicular crashes. Just as was found with schooling, the workplace setting is likely to pose significant challenges to adults with ADHD more so than other adults, even those with other psychological disorders.

MONEY MANAGEMENT

> Our 24-year-old son with ADHD is still living with us at our home. He has purchased a lot of video recording and editing equipment so he can create movies, especially with special effects, that are so popular now, such as on YouTube. He likes to spend a lot of his time making short videos, watching other amateur videos on YouTube, and sharing his work with friends. But he always wants more equipment that he cannot afford. We have loaned him a lot of money for some of the equipment, and he has only paid off some of the debt. We recently found out that he secretly obtained a credit card through the mail and began using it to get more equipment. He has nearly reached his credit limit and is barely able to make the monthly minimum payments on it from the money he makes at odd jobs in our town. We have urged him to keep doing this as a hobby but to go back to school to learn a trade instead of working part-time as he does and focusing so much time on his videos. But he argues with us and insists that he can make it in the movie or advertising business if he can just get discovered by a talent scout, even though he has little idea of how to make that happen.

Adults with this disorder have a hard time managing their money, paying their bills, and handling credit. Impulsive people like those with adult ADHD find it hard to defer gratification, think about and plan for the future, and follow through on promises and commitments. And so they do not do very well handling their finances. Adults with ADHD are more likely to use their money unwisely, make purchases without thinking, and use their credit cards on impulse too much, resulting in overspending their budgets or income, and they are less organized and more forgetful when it comes to paying bills on time.

You may know all this because your loved one with adult ADHD may have shared such problems with you. Perhaps he asked you for advice or even financial assistance. Maybe he has already borrowed money from you and shown no sign of paying it back. He might even have taken funds from you without your knowing it at the time, only to result in a major confrontation once you realized what had happened. Perhaps you let him use one of your credit cards for a specific purpose only to find it had been used repeatedly for other reasons for which you did not give permission. Now you face a real double-bind: If you report it as fraud, he will be charged with a criminal offense, but if you don't, you are stuck with the bill and maybe even a lower credit rating. Even if this situation has not happened to you, you may find yourself living in a relationship with an adult with ADHD in which money, unpaid bills, and irresponsible use of credit cards have become frequent topics of arguments. If you are a parent of an adult with ADHD, these money problems may even have led your loved one to return to live in your home because he simply cannot make it financially on his own, at least not yet.

Adults with ADHD are less likely to save money and more likely to buy things on impulse or to go on shopping sprees. And so their credit card balances are higher than those of typical people of their age, and they often exceed their credit limits more than adults without ADHD. Many adults with ADHD have trouble sticking to a budget, if they have made one at all. As a consequence, they are more likely to have had their utilities turned off because of late or nonpayment of their accounts. Missing loan payments, such as for car loans, is also more common in the adults with ADHD than in other adults, which may explain why they are more likely to have their cars repossessed. It should be obvious why adults with ADHD have a poorer credit rating than typical adults.

When people have difficulty with handling money, they often borrow it from friends, family, or even coworkers. We found that adults with ADHD were more likely to borrow from relatives and friends than are other adults, thereby placing a greater burden on others to help them with their financial problems than is the case in adults who do not have the disorder. As I noted, this may be a situation with which you are all too familiar as someone with a close relationship with an adult with ADHD. After all, money matters have been reported to be one of the biggest sources of disputes among married couples or those living together, even when neither partner has ADHD. When one person does have ADHD, it probably makes these disagreements much more frequent and probably even more hostile. Trouble handling money, then, may be yet another reason you are so concerned about your loved one with adult ADHD. It also becomes another reason for him to get treatment.

FRIENDSHIPS

> Does an adult with ADHD have trouble accepting blame for something they did wrong? I find this likely to happen when they are called out on it by a non-ADHD friend. Does being wrong about something (even small routine items) make the

> adult with ADHD feel their self-worth is under attack and cause him an almost unbearable negative feeling? The negative feelings I see in my friend cause them to be excessively defensive. My friend can get so defensive that he will (a) not drop the complaint until he has been completely vindicated or, more likely, proven utterly wrong; (b) shift the complaint back on me or his other friends as our problem, and unrelentingly force them to take it back; (c) ignore or brush off the complaint; or (d) appear to have no empathy for our feelings during all of this denial and defensiveness.

It doesn't take a psychologist to appreciate just how the symptoms of ADHD and its underlying problems with self-regulation are likely to create numerous social difficulties for those with ADHD in adulthood. The list of 18 symptoms at the end of Chapter 1 alone reads like a scroll of impaired social behavior—cannot persist at things, is highly distractible, has poorly inhibited behavior, exhibits impulsive decision-making, talks excessively, interrupts others, intrudes on ongoing activities of others, has difficulties following instructions, blurts out responses in conversations, and cannot engage in leisure activities quietly. So it should come as no surprise that adults with ADHD often report significant impairment in their social relationships.

Studies of children with ADHD found that at least 50% had no close friends by the time they reached second or third grade. If the children also had trouble with anger and defiance, this number rises to 70%. As a result, children growing up with ADHD are far less likely to have been invited to play at the homes of other children, to be included in sleepovers with friends, to be asked to birthday parties, or even to be asked out on dates as they became teenagers. For those who are hyperactive and impulsive, their talkative, and generally outgoing and easily excitable nature may make them fun to have at a party or to be with in a short-term relationship.

But it can be stressful and overbearing over the longer term. Such social problems are likely to continue into adulthood, so you may hear that your loved one with ADHD might have memories of childhood that are filled with social problems.

The penchant of children and adults with ADHD to have more problems with emotional self-control alone guarantees more mercurial, conflict-ridden, and distressing relationships with others than is the case for typical people. Research shows that children and adults with ADHD have significant problems with anger and hostility. Those problems, not surprisingly, make them the ones most likely to be rejected by others. This negative effect on others does not take weeks or years to develop but can occur within minutes or a few hours of a child or adult with ADHD entering a new peer group.

Adults with ADHD often complain of significant problems with both initiating and maintaining social relationships. They may have unstable personal relationships, break off those relationships over trivial matters, or have difficulty with those social skills needed for maintaining friendships. This may result in their having fewer close friends, and some have even become social isolates or recluses by middle age. This is in part a consequence of a life-long course of social difficulties and in part to avoid any further such hazards. Their relationships are often described as being frequently punctuated with conflicts with those they considered to be friends or social acquaintances. One reason for this is that adults with ADHD can have trouble negotiating and resolving the everyday conflicts with others that anyone is likely to encounter. Those unresolved conflicts might add up over time, causing the friendship to end. The greater propensity to show strong emotions during social interactions with others among many, though not all, adults with ADHD is often one cause of this. The adult with ADHD is also more likely than others to be loud, boisterous, silly, or clownish.

A further difficulty is the adverse effect the disorder has in diminishing self-awareness or self-monitoring of ongoing behavior. Our adult patients have often told us that they simply did not realize just how poorly they were coming across to others during various social encounters. It is not surprising that such lack of awareness leads to social problems with close friends or acquaintances. Moreover, the difficulties of adults with ADHD might have with taking turns during conversations or social encounters, and their unguarded comments or insensitivity to the social etiquette appropriate at the moment cause harm in their social relations. An adult with ADHD often does not realize these social violations until it is too late: The social cost has been exacted, and others are likely to steer clear of further interactions with him.

Adults with ADHD are often described as being self-centered, demanding, intrusive, or insensitive to the feelings or needs of others. They are more likely to be unappreciative of assistance from others. And they can be socially "sticky," not knowing when to end the interaction and move on or let the other person do so. It is therefore not just the impulsiveness or inattentiveness of ADHD that tarnishes social encounters with others, it is also the poor emotional self-control, the more limited self-monitoring of social behavior, and the impaired ability to participate in the necessary give and take that makes for a successful social encounter.

Thus, adults with ADHD can be so demoralized at times about their situation in life not just their checkered educational histories or periodic failures in school or the workplace. It also can arise in many cases from this detrimental impact of their behavior on building supportive and lasting social relationships with others. No wonder adults with ADHD often have feelings of low self-worth. Perhaps you have firsthand experience with just these social problems with your loved one with adult ADHD.

DATING, MARRIAGE, OR COHABITING

> My boyfriend was diagnosed with ADHD as a child, and his family did not seek help at that point for fear that medication would change his personality. He has just now started on an ADHD medication (at age 34), and I have realized that the majority of our relationship issues are a result of symptoms related to both ADHD and proneness to be emotional, even angry. . . . I am at a crossroads between staying and leaving at this point because his behavior has become so intolerable for me and I feel so alone. He has been resistant to therapy up to this point but has now agreed to try because he wants his "old girlfriend back."

One of the most important domains of adult life is the relationship we have with people with whom we become intimate, such as in dating, marriage, or living with a partner. Because of the closeness and frequency of interactions in such relationships, not to mention the shared responsibilities they often involve, one should not be surprised that they can be negatively impacted by ADHD when it exists in one member of that relationship. Divorce rates are nearly 3 times higher among adults with ADHD by the time they are in their mid-40s. Adults with ADHD (especially women) may be less likely to be married than others of the same age who do not have ADHD because of their interpersonal difficulties. By mid- to late-life (60–94 years), adults with ADHD may also have fewer family members involved in their social network, and so may experience emotional loneliness. Even if they stay married, adults with ADHD are 4 to 5 times more likely than typical adults to report having fair- to poor-quality relationships. As many as 58% of adults with ADHD have maladjusted marriages and low levels of marital satisfaction compared with 25% of typical adults.

You can see in the following box the specific problem behaviors that occur in couples in which one had adult ADHD.

Problems Reported by Couples in Which One Person Has ADHD

These were identified as trouble spots by Drs. Robin and Payson in a survey conducted with these couples in which one of the adults had ADHD:

1. doesn't remember being told things,
2. says things without thinking,
3. zones out in conversations,
4. has trouble dealing with frustrations,
5. has trouble getting started on a task,
6. underestimates time needed to complete a task,
7. leaves a mess,
8. doesn't finish household projects,
9. doesn't respond when spoken to, and
10. doesn't plan ahead.

Note. Data from "The Impact of ADHD on Marriage," by A. L. Robin and E. Payson, 2002, *The ADHD Report*, *10*, pp. 9–11, 14. Copyright 2002 by Guilford Press. Adapted with permission. http://dx.doi.org/10.1521/adhd.10.3.9.20553

One factor that may be contributing to couples' relationship troubles and reduced satisfaction is that adults with ADHD report being markedly more likely than others to have engaged in extramarital affairs. Another is that adults with ADHD are often more emotionally impulsive and are especially quick to react to others with impatience, frustration, and anger. Such behavior can obviously generate more hostility in close relationships. Even young adults with ADHD who are in intimate relationships have been observed to engage in more negativity and less positivity during situations of conflict than do typical young couples. Perhaps as a consequence, adults with ADHD may be almost twice as likely to engage in violence in intimate relationships with loved ones with whom they are living.

Certainly, we all recognize that financial problems that occur within a marriage or intimate relationship can be a major source of distress. As I discussed, ADHD in an adult greatly increases the likelihood he will have such financial difficulties. These financial problems can be yet another reason for the poor marriage quality and lead to the higher divorce rates evident in adults with ADHD.

Recently, Gina Pera[2] wrote about the types of problems encountered in couples where one has adult ADHD. They include the following:

- disorganization, forgetfulness, and poor follow-through;
- combative communications and poor listening;
- problematic parenting style;
- poor decision making and cooperation;
- self-centeredness and insatiability (hard to please);
- "learned helplessness" (i.e., giving up on things when nothing seems to work);
- impulsive spending and acting without thinking of consequences;
- low intimacy;
- moodiness, temper, and low frustration tolerance;
- reactive aggression toward intimate partners;
- lack of interpersonal sensitivity and impaired empathy;
- mental rigidity and difficulty with transitions, compromise, and cooperation; and
- poor coping strategies developed over a lifetime of unrecognized or unaddressed ADHD.

[2]Pera, G. (2015). Counseling couples affected by adult ADHD. In R. A. Barkley (Ed.), *Attention-deficit hyperactivity disorder: A handbook for diagnosis and treatment* (4th ed., pp. 795–825). New York, NY: Guilford Press.

If you are in an intimate relationship with an adult with ADHD, perhaps you have witnessed just such problems in dealing with your loved one. Similar to some people I have met whose partners had ADHD, you may even experience resentment or anger, or feel overburdened. It can feel as if you are raising another child, given the amount of extra time, effort, and resources you may have had to invest in repairing the consequences caused by the ADHD in your partner. In some cases, you may even have experienced emotional or physical abuse stemming indirectly from the disorder in your loved one.

A Marriage Gone Bad From Adult ADHD

I was diagnosed with ADHD at age 9 and given Ritalin that I took faithfully for 9 years, finally stopping at the end of high school. It worked great in school, helped get me into a good college, and helped me have lots of normal personal relationships in high school. I stopped using medication when I was 18 and went away to college because I wanted to be "more normal." I found myself to be more charming off the medication, and so I decided in my infinite wisdom that I did not need a medicine. Even so, it took me longer to finish my sales and marketing degree than other students. Fast forward to age 26, where I had a relationship fall apart because of the following:

- frequent outbursts,
- impulsive behavior,
- manipulation,
- lying,
- displaced anger, and
- irrational behavior.

I then met the woman of my dreams, and after 5 years of dating, we married. However, when we started living together, she also noticed these problems in the relationship. We now have two children. She has

(*continues*)

A Marriage Gone Bad From Adult ADHD (*Continued*)

just asked for a divorce, citing those same complaints. I must admit I have not handled it well. As you can guess, my response has been all of the above behaviors as well as stalking behavior. This happened until very recently. She has now actually filed for divorce. I have been trying to find a diagnosis for all of my negative behaviors. I thought it was borderline personality disorder, bipolar, narcissistic. The fact is that it was just my ADHD that I was not treating. I went to my psychiatrist in May and he prescribed Adderall, which I decided wasn't for me. I figured I'd just self-medicate with coffee. Now I have given up. I have hired a divorce attorney to go up against my wife's attorney, and it is about to get ugly. This is the worst kind of brinksmanship. I am anticipating that this divorce will cost me $20,000 and a loss of $450,000 of net worth. It's going to be costly. I have been incredibly impulsive even now. However, I just started taking Adderall again, and I believe it will help me with 100% of my behavioral problems when combined with psychotherapy.

PARENTING

ADHD in a parent can make them less attentive to their children; less rewarding of their children; more inconsistent in using discipline; and more likely to respond with impulsive comments, directives, commands, or reprimands. In general, they can be more hostile toward their children than is seen in typical parents. Although this is not the case for every parent having ADHD, on average they are more likely than other parents to manifest these difficulties. Parents with ADHD also seem to be less adept at problem solving as it applies to dealing with child behavior problems. The home life that such parents organize around their children has also been noted to be less organized, more chaotic, and to have routines that are less structured and inconsistent than those in typical families. Thus, parents with high levels of ADHD symptoms clearly struggle with maintaining a consistent, calm, and organized approach to managing children.

Given that the children of adults with ADHD are also more likely to have ADHD as well as to be oppositional, the ADHD in both parent and child can greatly magnify the problems in family functioning. The impaired parental behavior created by adult ADHD can obviously result in higher levels of stress in the family lives of adults with ADHD. This is worsened when the child also has ADHD. It is also likely that the parenting problems in an adult with ADHD will contribute to a greater occurrence of child misbehavior, such as defiance, arguing, tantrums, and neglect of typical home and schoolwork assigned to that child. Again, if that child also has ADHD, the odds are even greater that these other difficulties with defiance and home and schoolwork will arise.

As noted, a parent with ADHD is less likely to monitor their children's activities than is a parent who does not have ADHD. Inadequate parental monitoring is one of several factors that can increase children's risk of accidental injuries. This may help to explain, in part, why children with ADHD have higher rates of such injuries of all types than do typical children. Not only are they more impulsive and risk-taking, but their parent with ADHD may be less attentive to their activities, monitoring them less often, and thus may be less able to detect and prevent behavior that can lead to accidents.

One might think that such problems would be a very good reason for the parent with ADHD to get additional professional help with child management, as is commonly done in standard training programs for parents of defiant children. But lack of treatment of a parent's ADHD can interfere with their success in such a training program. So I encourage the parent with untreated ADHD to get a professional evaluation and treatment first, to maximize the likelihood of their success in any additional programs.

Parental ADHD can be yet another factor that could potentially damage a person's marital harmony. It can do so by elevating the stress one or both parents may be experiencing in raising their children. Adults with ADHD are substantially more stressed in their roles as parents than are other adults. This stress stems partly from the parent's own symptoms of inattention, distractibility, and poor impulse control, and is also related to their difficulties with controlling their emotions and to the other executive function difficulties discussed in Chapter 2 (time management, organization, etc.). It can also arise from the fact that adults with ADHD are 8 times more likely to have children with ADHD than typical adults because of the strong genetic contribution to this disorder (see Chapter 4). Research suggests that 30% to 54% of the children of adults with ADHD will also have ADHD, thus creating an even more ADHD-filled family environment. Also, the children of adults with ADHD may be more oppositional and defiant even if they do not have ADHD. Children who argue, defy, throw tantrums, and otherwise refuse to obey can place a great deal of stress even on typical parents, but such behavior can overwhelm adults who have ADHD and their own emotion regulation problems. Having a child with ADHD, regardless of whether the parent has the disorder, can significantly increase the risk of divorce.

RISKY SEXUAL BEHAVIOR

ADHD is not associated with any higher incidence of sexual disorders, thankfully. However, my own research with Mariellen Fischer and other colleagues[3] in Milwaukee found some other problems

---

[3]Barkley, R. A., Fischer, M., Smallish, L., & Fletcher, K. (2006). Young adult follow-up of hyperactive children: Adaptive functioning in major life activities. *Journal of the American Academy of Child and Adolescent Psychiatry*, *45*, 192–202. http://dx.doi.org/10.1097/01.chi.0000189134.97436.e2

with sexual behavior. We found a pattern of early initiation of sexual intercourse during adolescence (1 year earlier on average) and an overall riskier pattern to their sexual activity as teens or young adults (more partners, less use of contraception). This riskier pattern of conduct led to a nearly 10 times greater risk for having been involved in a teen pregnancy either as the father or the mother (38% for the ADHD group vs. 4% for the control group). We also found a 4 times greater risk for having had any sexually transmitted diseases in the ADHD group than in the control group (17% vs. 4%) by age 20. These patterns of sexual risk taking and even early parenthood continued into the young adult years in the group with ADHD. Young adults with ADHD become parents far earlier than do others, sometimes as teenagers, when they are not prepared to be parents to a baby. Kate Flory[4] and her colleagues found similar risks in their own follow-up study in Pittsburgh, further confirming this increased problem with risky sexual behavior. For this reason, teens and young adults with ADHD seem more likely to place their children up for adoption or have the children be raised by their own parents (the baby's grandparents) than might other teens or young adults.

HEALTH AND MEDICAL PROBLEMS

A small but growing amount of scientific evidence indicates that children and adults with ADHD are more prone to certain health problems than are others. For several decades, we have known that

[4]Flory, K., Molina, B. S., Pelham, W. E., Jr., Gnagy, E., & Smith, B. (2006). Childhood ADHD predicts risky sexual behavior in young adulthood. *Journal of Clinical Child and Adolescent Psychology, 35*, 571–577. http://dx.doi.org/10.1207/s15374424jccp3504_8

adults with ADHD voice more complaints about bodily symptoms, such as headaches, stomachaches, and vague bodily concerns that may have little if any medical origins. These are known as "psychosomatic" or "somatoform" symptoms.

SLEEPING PROBLEMS

More adults with ADHD have sleeping problems (40%), as do children with the disorder. These are not the result of taking stimulant medication for their ADHD, although sometimes those drugs can result in more insomnia than usual. Even off medication, adults with ADHD report more insomnia or trouble getting to sleep, more restlessness while sleeping, and more waking during the night. Those adults also have a greater chance of having restless leg syndrome, a condition in which they feel that their legs have to be moving for them to be comfortable. An adult with ADHD also may have less efficient sleep, experience more breathing problems during sleep, and report being more tired the next day. That inefficient sleep and greater tiredness can make his problems with attention worse, as you can imagine. Treating his ADHD symptoms with medication during the daytime can sometimes help reduce these sleeping problems. Some research suggests that taking melatonin at bedtime (delivered under the tongue) may help induce sleep earlier than usual. Otherwise, the sleeping problems may need to be directly treated with other medical and psychosocial interventions. Some adults with ADHD find it helpful to create a going-to-sleep routine in which they disengage from technology, social media, and other more exciting activities, especially those that involve focusing for extended periods on a lighted computer, smartphone, or iPad screen. Also, this can include taking a shower at night before bedtime rather than in the morning, reading or light conversation with a partner before falling asleep, and then turning on a sound generator that plays soft music without lyrics or even using a white-noise machine to provide a little background stimulation.

EXCESS WEIGHT, OBESITY, AND EATING DISORDERS

Another problem for adults with ADHD is an increased risk for being overweight or having obesity. Adults with ADHD, or those children who grew up with it, are twice as likely to be obese (have a body mass index over 30) than are typical adults. Likewise, adults who are obese are 6 to 8 times more likely to have adult ADHD. This relationship of ADHD to obesity arises as a result of the poor impulse control, specifically, and poor self-regulation (executive functioning), more generally, linked to ADHD. If you couple that with situations where junk food is readily available, it is no surprise that the adult with ADHD tends to consume more such food than others. But it is also the case that adults with ADHD do not exercise as often; pay less attention to maintaining a healthy lifestyle; smoke more tobacco and marijuana; drink more alcohol; and are more likely to interact with electronic media, such as TV, Internet video games, and so on. Teenage girls and women with ADHD may be 3 to 6 times more prone to binge eating or even the more extreme disorder of bulimia. This is especially so if they also have coexisting anxiety or depression. All of these factors may be contributing to the risk of being overweight that can be associated with adult ADHD. Some research now shows that treating ADHD with medication in such obese individuals is likely not only to improve their ADHD but also to result in reduced weight (a well-known side effect of ADHD stimulant medications).

HEART DISEASE

By adulthood, children growing up with ADHD may have significantly lower HDL cholesterol (high density lipids, or "good" cholesterol) than do typical adults. This gives the adults with ADHD a poorer HDL-to-total-cholesterol ratio, both of which are risk factors for future cardiovascular or coronary heart disease (CHD). Future risk of CHD has been repeatedly linked to several health and lifestyle characteristics, with the most frequently being smoking, blood pressure, serum cholesterol (and specifically HDL:LDL and HDL:total ratios), body mass index, diabetes, and frequency of exercise. In my study with Dr. Fischer et al. (see Footnote 1), we found that the risk of developing CHD was 26% higher for the next 5-year period and 33% greater for the next 10-year period of life if current lifestyles were to continue for our ADHD group. The point here is that growing up with ADHD that persists into adulthood is associated with an increasing risk for CHD in future years, even if at a small magnitude of risk at young adulthood. We also found that adults with ADHD that had persisted since childhood had a 40% greater risk for current and future atherosclerosis of the coronary vessels. Once again, if you think or already know that your loved one with ADHD may show such a high-risk profile for CHD, here is but one more reason to encourage her to get treatment for her ADHD (and CHD risk) if she has not done so already.

EXCESS SUBSTANCE USE AND ABUSE

ADHD in adults predisposes them to difficulties with substance use, dependence, and abuse, regardless of their sex. Those adults are more likely to smoke cigarettes and marijuana than other adults and to smoke more of these substances than do adults without ADHD who routinely use them. Once they begin smoking, adults with ADHD may increase their use more rapidly than others who experiment with tobacco. One reason for this may be that smoking serves to partially treat ADHD symptoms. Nicotine, the addictive compound in tobacco, is a stimulant that has been shown to improve symptoms of ADHD. So this might be an instance where some adults with ADHD are self-medicating (self-treating) their disorder with nicotine. Even where that is not the case, the poor impulse control associated with ADHD would make an adult more likely to use and less likely to be able to quit using tobacco or other potentially addictive drugs. Caffeine is also considered a stimulant. Not surprisingly, research has found that young adults with ADHD consumed more caffeinated drinks per week than did young adults in the control groups (see Footnote 1). Again, this might be an effort at self-medication—trying to treat the ADHD symptoms by increased use of readily available stimulants. But caffeine is not especially effective at doing so because it increases the wrong neurotransmitter in the brain (epinephrine) and in the wrong regions (brain stem) than those involved in adult ADHD. So I don't recommend you encourage your loved one to just drink more coffee or other caffeine-containing beverages to try to manage their symptoms.

Alcohol is another substance that adults with ADHD seem to use more often than typical adults, even though in this case it does not treat their symptoms. But it may give them a temporary sense of well-being, help reduce their focus on their problems, and even reduce any anxiety they may be experiencing over those problems. So perhaps this is why some of them drink more alcohol than is typical. Alcohol is known to temporarily constrict or reduce our awareness of or concerns about time, such as the past and future. For that reason, it may help reduce concerns about ongoing problems and conflicts. Interestingly, some of the genes that seem to be linked to ADHD are also known to convey an increased risk for substance use disorders, such as nicotine abuse and alcoholism.

ACCIDENTAL INJURIES

> I am an adult with ADHD who is the successful owner of several car washes. Ironically, when I was 8 years old, I was hit by a 4,000-lb car going 30 to 40 mph on a country road in the winter. You see, I was sliding down a hill on a plastic sled. It was a dead-end road with not a lot of traffic. I was with my brothers and neighborhood kids, but it was my turn to sled. Because of my ADHD, I wasn't paying attention to what was coming down the road, and so when it was my turn, I wound up sledding right into a car. I hit the steel wheel, steel hubcap, and tire. Some of my hair was found later between the tire and wheel rim. I was unconscious, foaming at the mouth. My neighbor's mom was an RN and she had to pull my tongue out as I had swallowed it. At this point those around me believed I was actually dead. I still have visions to this day of standing beside myself watching her work on me, and a vision of my oldest brother running up the road to get my mother. I was unconscious for 11 hours. When I came to, the doctor asked me to move my hand and I opened my mouth instead. I don't remember much of the next few years other than prominent things. When I went back to school a few days later, I started having even more troubles in school than I had before the accident, such as not remembering things, not paying attention, not being able to do my work, and getting into fights.

For more than 40 years, scientists have known that children with ADHD are considerably more likely to experience injuries due to accidents of all types than are children growing up without ADHD. Interviews with parents of these children find that[5]

- as many as 57% are described as accident prone;
- more than one in five are likely to have experienced at least one episode of accidental poisoning compared with a risk of just one in 12 for typical children;
- more than one in four will experience bone fractures compared with one in eight typical children;
- as many as one in six children with ADHD have had at least four or more serious accidental injuries, such as broken bones, lacerations, head injuries, burns, severe bruises, lost teeth, or accidental poisonings; and
- the injuries children with ADHD sustain are also more frequent and more severe.

Other studies have found that children with ADHD are more likely to be involved in either pedestrian–auto or bicyclist–auto accidents while they are out playing in their neighborhoods than are other children. Also, when someone with ADHD has an accident as a child, the accidents are more serious ones and the injuries they experience are likely to be more severe than is the case for children who do not have ADHD.

---

[5]Nigg, J. T. (2013). Attention-deficit/hyperactivity disorder and adverse health outcomes. *Clinical Psychology Review*, *33*, 215–228. http://dx.doi.org/10.1016/j.cpr.2012.11.005. Also, Barkley, R. A. (2015). Health problems and related impairments in children and adults with ADHD. In R. A. Barkley (Ed.), *Attention-deficit hyperactivity disorder: A handbook for diagnosis and treatment* (4th ed., pp. 267–313). New York, NY: Guilford Press.

If you have known your loved one with ADHD since he was a child, you probably are aware of these accident risks firsthand. As a result, that loved one was more likely to have been taken to a hospital emergency room for treatment of his injuries than were people you know who did not grow up with ADHD. Your loved one with ADHD continues to be at a higher risk for experiencing accidental injuries at home and at work. Because of these greater risks of accidental injuries and more such injuries, ADHD can be considered a life-threatening disorder. It is therefore not surprising to learn that children with ADHD (and other disruptive behavior problems) were more than twice as likely to die before the age of 46 than children without the disorder (2.8% vs. 1.3%). It is also possible that left untreated across adulthood, the disorder may shorten a person's life expectancy, as it did for my twin brother and my nephew, his son, that I describe in some detail in the following section and in the next chapter.

DRIVING

> Someone close to me has ADHD and is a very reckless driver! I live in fear that this person will kill himself and/or others when he is using his car. He is 26 years old and I am very, very, very concerned. How can I make things better in this situation? I have so much anxiety and I have shed so many tears; this young man had one accident a month ago and today got a speeding ticket—one of many he has received. Help!

One area of adult life that poses serious risks for someone with ADHD is driving a motor vehicle. After all, if inattention is the most common cause of accidents while driving, then ADHD (being a disorder of attention) would be highly likely to cause far more accidents than would be the case for a typical adult. Now let me get personal for a moment to talk about my twin brother, Ron, who had ADHD since early childhood. I want to tell you about the car crash that tragically ended his life in 2006. I am doing this to show you how his ADHD, untreated at that time, predisposed him to this end. As others have said, statistics are people with tears wiped away. This is one such story, with many tears (see the newspaper report in the following box).

Fatal One-Car Accident in Keene

By: Andrea VanValkenburg
Staff Writer, *Press Republican*, Plattsburgh, NY
July 26, 2006

KEENE—An Elizabethtown man died Monday night when his vehicle overturned after hitting an embankment. Ronald Barkley, 56, was traveling southbound on the Bartlett Road in Keene around 10:06 p.m. when he failed to negotiate a small bend in the road and veered off the shoulder of the right lane. According to Ray Brook-based State Police, the vehicle struck an embankment and overturned. Barkley was ejected from the GMC Safari minivan during the crash and was pinned underneath as the car overturned. A passerby noticed the accident shortly after it occurred and contacted area officials. Within minutes, State Police and volunteers from the Keene Fire Department responded to the accident, but Barkley was pronounced dead upon arrival. According to police, Barkley was traveling at an unsafe speed when the accident occurred. Investigators believe he was not wearing a seat belt at the time of the accident. An autopsy was conducted at the Adirondack Medical Center Tuesday, which determined Barkley died of head trauma. No further information was available Tuesday night. (page 1)

Much goes unsaid in this article about my twin, not the least of which is that Ron (my fraternal, or nonidentical, twin) had also been drinking alcohol before the accident. And he was speeding for the road conditions and not wearing a seatbelt. You could stop there and say, well, that's what caused the crash. But wait a second. Why would he take such risks? Because Ron also had moderate to serious ADHD as far back into his life as I can remember. He was also not currently being treated for his disorder, although he had gotten some treatment earlier in his life. That fatal accident was indirectly due to the long-standing impact of ADHD on his driving patterns and habits (speeding, risk-taking, distractibility while driving, use of alcohol, and rarely using a seatbelt) that conspired that fateful evening to prematurely end his life at age 56.

Irreparable harms can befall those with ADHD (and others!) in this relatively mundane domain of major life activity—driving. Just as clear is the fact that those driving problems are responsive to medication treatments—treatments my brother was always too reluctant or distracted to obtain or to sustain for very long.

Many studies have focused on ADHD and driving risks.[6] They have found that adults with ADHD, like my brother,

- have slower and more variable reaction times;
- make more impulsive errors;
- demonstrate more variable steering of their vehicles in the roadway;
- are far more inattentive and distractible while driving than other adults;

[6]Barkley, R. A. (2015). Health problems and related impairments in children and adults with ADHD. In R. A. Barkley (Ed.), *Attention-deficit hyperactivity disorder: A handbook for diagnosis and treatment* (4th ed., pp. 267–313). New York, NY: Guilford Press.

- are more likely to use unsafe driving practices, such as not wearing a seat belt, not keeping their attention on the roadway instead of twiddling with the stereo controls or radio stations, text messaging or talking on cell phones while driving, or just socializing too much with others in the vehicle; and
- are more prone to road rage, or driving related anger and aggressive use of a motor vehicle when angered.

Such poor driving habits can easily lead to various adverse consequences in the driving histories of adults with ADHD. Among these is a 3 to 5 times greater frequency of receiving traffic citations, especially for speeding, as well as for illegal parking. The latter problem arises from their impatience—they don't want to take the time it may require in a crowded traffic area to search for a parking space. So they just park anywhere they like, impulsively. My brother did all of these things. Look at the following list to see if your loved one with ADHD is like other adults with the disorder in terms of driving risks. That is, they

- are far more likely to have a vehicular crash;
- have more such crashes;
- have more severe crashes as measured by dollar damages and people injured;
- are more likely to have their license suspended or revoked as a result;
- are more likely to engage in reckless driving;
- drink alcohol and drive;
- are more impaired in driving from that alcohol than others;
- have an average of 3 times more license suspensions/revocations;
- experience 50% more crashes;
- acquire nearly 3 times more speeding citations;

- are involved in more than twice as many accidents in which they were held to be at fault;
- have more than twice as many speeding citations and total citations on their department of motor vehicle records; and
- are likely to have more accidents while using other vehicles, such as motorcycles, dirt bikes, all-terrain vehicles, snowmobiles, and so on.

Perhaps you, too, have witnessed these increased driving risks in your loved one with ADHD and have been as concerned about him as I (and other family members) were about my brother's driving and lifestyle more generally. Here is yet one more reason you should follow up on these concerns about ADHD to encourage your loved one, when appropriate, to seek professional help if he has not done so already. Fortunately, the driving-performance problems of teens and adults with ADHD can be improved with medications that hopefully reduce their risks for these adverse and even life-threatening driving outcomes.

EXCESS INTERNET USE AND ADDICTION

Research is only beginning to explore the relationship between ADHD and excess use of technology, such as computers, smartphones, and so on, for playing games and using social media. What little has been done so far suggests that young adults with ADHD are 2 to 3 times more prone to use the Internet more often, especially for gaming, and to even develop an Internet addiction. Internet or gaming addiction involves such symptoms as preoccupation with the Internet or video game, uncontrolled impulses to use it, usage more than intended, tolerance, withdrawal, impairment of control, excessive time and effort spent, and impairment in decision-making ability concerning the use of the Internet or video game. The more severe are someone's ADHD symptoms, the more likely they are to develop an Internet or gaming addiction. This risk is also increased if the adult with ADHD uses marijuana, alcohol, or tobacco. The risk is further heightened if they have coexisting social phobia and/or depression with their ADHD. Treating ADHD with medication might reduce excessive Internet or game use in young adults with the disorder.

KEY POINTS TO REMEMBER

You can now see that adult ADHD can have a wide array of negative effects on various major areas of adult life when untreated—school, work, money management, friendships, dating and marriage or cohabiting, risky sexual activity, parenting, and health and medical problems. The economic impact of these problems is substantial for the individual with the disorder, for their families, and for their community. The social and emotional consequences that flow from a life fraught with these adverse outcomes for those with adult ADHD are also as serious, substantial, numerous, and no doubt troubling not only for the person with the disorder but also for you and other loved ones. That all of these would arise in conjunction with ADHD is easily understood in view of the symptoms of ADHD and the problems with self-control from which they seem to arise. What is clear here is that ADHD in adults has substantial and varied adverse effects on numerous major life activities.

What is also clear is the tremendous impact that each of these domains of risk has on the loved ones of adults with ADHD, such as you, who may be involved their lives. Lost in this averaging about risks across people are the concerns, fears, disappointments, and grief of others embedded in the life of the adult with ADHD and the negative consequences for them as well. Adverse social consequences rarely occur in isolation. Like tapping a spider web or tossing a stone into a pond, the adversities experienced by adults with ADHD create a rippling of negative effects throughout that adult's family, social, educational, and occupational networks, among others, negatively affecting the people who love them.

No single domain of risk here affects the adult with ADHD alone. That is because, nearly always, someone else dear to them and to whom they are dear is being adversely affected by that potential risk when it has occurred. I know that personally, and so do you. Someone takes the adult with ADHD to the hospital when they are injured, comes to console and assist him at the scenes of his accidents, and gets him medical care when he has ignored a serious medical or dental complaint for too long. Usually, some loved ones also counsel the adult with ADHD when she experiences problems at work; takes her into their home when she loses a job and becomes homeless; and gives her money for the unpaid rent, utility bills, and other debts. Let's not forget that, usually, parents or other loved ones will help get the adult with ADHD into the substance abuse rehab program or vocational training course when the need arises. Parents may also help him to support and raise his own children when his marriage crumbles.

In short, loved ones such as yourself strive to assist the adult with ADHD in many ways when bad things have happened because of his disorder. You have probably been embedded in and deeply touched by these consequences—it's likely why you chose to read this book. As discouraging as these various risks may seem, they may also serve to motivate you to learn more, and, hopefully, spur your loved one with ADHD to get treatment. You will find a lot of recommendations in the second half of this book for how best to help your loved one with adult ADHD in dealing with the domains of life discussed here. Just remember not to get too discouraged by these problems. Adult ADHD is a highly treatable disorder; it is more treatable than most other psychiatric disorders. The problem we face is not one of lack of effective treatments. The real problems are a lack of awareness of people about this condition, the fact that adults with it often do not get referred and diagnosed, and that those adults may not get access to appropriate care. As if the risks outlined here were not enough, untreated ADHD can also lead to increases in the risks for other psychiatric disorders, antisocial or criminal behavior, and even suicide, as happened to my nephew. That is the topic of the next chapter.

CHAPTER 6

IS MY LOVED ONE AT RISK FOR OTHER PSYCHIATRIC DISORDERS?

Unfortunately, yes. This chapter provides a brief survey of those disorders that are more likely to occur when attention-deficit/hyperactivity disorder (ADHD) is left untreated. Again, I do this not so much to alarm or discourage you about your loved one. Instead, I review these disorders to better motivate your loved one, through you, to seek a diagnosis and treatment if they have not yet done so.

Of adults with ADHD who are seen by mental health professionals, 80% or more have at least one other psychiatric disorder. More than 50% have at least two other disorders.[1] This is quite typical for psychological disorders. They tend to cluster together. Perhaps that is because certain disorders share underlying causes, such as genes or genetic predispositions, as well as underlying common neurological networks (in the case of those disorders related to brain dysfunction, like ADHD). The most common of these other disorders to occur with ADHD are discussed in this chapter. Although having these disorders can make managing ADHD more difficult,

---

[1]Barkley, R. A., Murphy, K. R., & Fischer, M. (2008). *ADHD in adults: What the science says.* New York, NY: Guilford Press.

understand that even in cases where ADHD is the only problem, it can also pose significant difficulties for an adult, as I discussed in Chapter 5.

ANXIETY DISORDERS

> My husband has been diagnosed with ADHD (inattentive presentation) since being a child. After we got married, his symptoms seemed to get worse. This prompted him to go get help. He's had some success with treating some of his symptoms through an ADHD medication. However, he still struggles immensely with confusion and anxiety. He has seen a couple of therapists, but even though they state they are familiar with ADHD, it seems they do not understand his confusion and difficulty in making decisions he feels good about. He is always filled with doubts, and this creates an enormous amount of anxiety and vice versa. This is causing so much unhappiness for him, especially since he is trying so hard to get better.

Anxiety disorders consist of an inappropriately high level of fear, foreboding, worry, anxiety, or specific phobia(s). On average, 25% of children with ADHD will have one or more anxiety disorders. They have at least a 3 to 4 times greater risk for developing such disorders than do children in the general population. For adults with ADHD, however, the figure climbs to as high as 52% in some studies, averaging across the research to about a 35% risk overall (see Footnote 1). The longer ADHD persists into adulthood, the greater is the risk for developing some type of anxiety disorder along with it. More recent research shows that such anxiety problems may be even more common in adults who have that other attention disorder noted in Chapter 3, sluggish cognitive tempo (SCT), many of whom get diagnosed as ADHD (inattentive presentation). It is unclear at the moment why persistent ADHD (or SCT) predisposes to a higher risk for anxiety disorders. Perhaps a history of chronic failure in various domains of major life activity could predispose someone to develop anticipatory fear and concern about similar situations in the future. But there may also be some shared genetic risk between ADHD and anxiety disorders. Regardless of the cause, studies do show that treating ADHD symptoms can result in reduced anxiety if it is relatively mild. However, additional treatments may be needed to specifically address an anxiety disorder where it is more prominent or where an official clinical diagnosis of an anxiety disorder is present, such as social or generalized anxiety disorder.

DEPRESSION

> I am 26 years old. The last 3 years of my life, I have faced several periods of depression because I feel like I'm not advancing in life. I feel like I'm losing time. Even though I see and feel clearly these repetitive patterns of being motivated about something, setting a goal, and feeling all excited about it, I then end up losing complete focus (I don't even know where in the process) and start doing something else. I just don't know what to do; the pattern has just repeated itself too many times. It has resulted in me feeling really bad about myself because I often feel like I can't accomplish anything. And even when I do accomplish something, such as in my dancing (I am a professional dancer), I forget the success too fast. That is because by the time something good happens, I already have thousands of other things going on in my head and very often it is thoughts of how I could have done it better, how I could have achieved certain goals if I had only continued the work and stuck with it when I started a while ago.

Depression or its milder variant, dysthymia, may occur more often in adults with ADHD. Research suggests that 16% to 31% have a lifetime risk for depression and 17% to 37% have such a risk for dysthymia (see Footnote 1). Overall, the risk for some type of depression is more than 3 times greater in people with ADHD than in the general population. Even when clinical levels of depression are not present, feeling demoralized is commonly associated with clinical cases of ADHD.

My own follow-up research with Dr. Fischer (discussed in Chapter 5) showed an elevation in the risk for suicidal thinking (33%) and suicide attempts (16%) among adolescents with ADHD during their high school years (see Footnote 1). That is also when such events are more common even in the general population (22% and 3%, respectively). But these risks had declined substantially by age 27, thankfully. Although my research mainly followed boys with ADHD to adulthood, very recent research by Dr. Stephen Hinshaw and colleagues at the University of California at Berkeley shows that this risk for depression and suicidal thinking and attempts is also higher in girls with ADHD followed to young adulthood.[2] Those risks are increased further if the girls experienced maltreatment (abuse or neglect) anytime during childhood or adolescence.

Having depression, it is not surprising, was the best predictor of which teens and young adults with ADHD experienced such suicidal thinking. But the severity of their ADHD was also a risk factor. More important, the severity of the person's ADHD, especially their poor impulse control, predicted a 5 times greater likelihood that if they thought of suicide, they would make an attempt. And when they did so, the attempts were far worse in terms of the injuries they sustained.

[2]Hinshaw, S. P., Owens, E. B., Zalecki, C., Huggins, S. P., Montenegro-Nevado, A. J., Schrodek, E., & Swanson, E. N. (2012). Prospective follow-up of girls with attention-deficit/hyperactivity disorder into early adulthood: Continuing impairment includes elevated risk for suicide attempts and self-injury. *Journal of Consulting and Clinical Psychology, 80,* 1041–1051. http://dx.doi.org/10.1037/a0029451

ADHD, Impulsiveness, and Depression Can Be a Lethal Combination

This was certainly the case with my 29-year-old nephew, Ethan, who had severe ADHD and experienced periodic depression but had refused to pursue treatment for these problems as an adult. Late one afternoon in August 2013, following an argument with his girlfriend, Ethan impulsively hung himself in his bedroom. Just before he did so, he left his bedroom and went into the living room to ask his older stepbrother where their mother was, probably so he could talk to her about the incident. Ethan was clearly upset and agitated. When he learned she was working back in her home office (and did not like to be disturbed), he returned to his bedroom and hung himself with an electrical cord. He was found just 15 minutes later by his mother. But it was too late to save him. Evidence suggested that he had not planned to kill himself (he showed no prior signs pointing to suicide, had expressed no plans to do so, and had not left a note). I also don't think he intended for his act to be fatal. It was done on impulse, out of anger at his girlfriend, and likely was meant to be a gesture of self-harm—but one that just went too far. Shortly into the gesture he likely lost control of events that would end his life so quickly and tragically—you only need to cut off the blood supply to the brain for 10 seconds or so to lose your motor control. This case clearly shows how impulsiveness, poor emotional self-control, and depression can interact to create a much higher risk for attempting suicide if an adult with ADHD thinks of doing so.

The reasons for such a link between adult ADHD and depression are unclear. But research shows that there may be a shared genetic risk between the two disorders (having one disorder in your family predisposes to having the other among the biological relatives). In addition, ADHD includes a deficit in emotional self-control that leaves the person more prone to experiencing impulsive emotions and being less able to cope with them when they arise. Also, depression is often associated with a greater exposure to social turmoil, stress, disadvantage, and even being victimized or abused. Children and adults with ADHD are more likely than others to experience such social stressors in their development than are typical people. And as Dr. Hinshaw et al. showed, as just discussed, early maltreatment can increase the risk for depression and suicide beyond just that elevated risk associated with ADHD.

> I was majorly depressed one time in my life and it led to almost a successful suicide. Fortunately, I survived, but it was due to being so confused as to why my brain never turned off. It was not "racing thoughts" but more of a consistent hyperactivity of negative thoughts—much more than positive—internally in my brain all the time! This thinking probably was impossible for me to self-regulate.

Research shows that if the depression is relatively mild, such as in dysthymia or demoralization, and ADHD is the more prominent problem, then treatment for ADHD can result in improvements in these forms of depression. However, where the depression is more severe, then it will likely require separate treatment and should probably be the first disorder to be treated before or alongside the ADHD because it may be life threatening.

A more severe mood disorder is manic depression, or bipolar disorder (BD). Most studies, including my own, have not found higher rates of BD in adults with ADHD than in those without ADHD. But some others have found this, especially when relatives have BD. However, if your loved one already has a diagnosis of BD, she is much more likely to have ADHD along with it. And the risk for having ADHD increases the earlier the onset of her BD. For instance, people whose onset of BD occurred in adulthood had a 25% chance of also having adult ADHD. However, those whose BD developed in adolescence had twice this risk for ADHD—about 45% to 50%. But if the onset of BD occurred in childhood, the vast majority of such cases will also have ADHD—about 80% to 95% (see Footnote 1). Clearly, something about BD predisposes one toward also having ADHD. And the earlier the onset of BD, the greater that risk for ADHD becomes. When BD is associated with ADHD, clinicians recommend that BD be treated first, again because it is a more serious disorder that can be a life-threatening condition. Then medications and other treatments for the ADHD can be instituted, but care must be taken when using ADHD stimulants so as not to potentially provoke manic episodes in someone with both disorders.

OPPOSITIONAL DEFIANT DISORDER

Oppositional defiant disorder (ODD) is a pattern of defiant, stubborn, angry, irritable, hostile, and otherwise oppositional behavior that creates considerable conflict in the person's relationship with others. For children, this type of behavior is aimed at their parents especially; for adults, it is usually aimed toward authorities or loved ones. ODD is 11 times more likely to develop in people with ADHD. ADHD comes with an inherent problem with the self-control of emotion, as discussed in Chapters 1 and 2; that problem creates a major predisposition to problems with managing anger and frustration, both hallmarks of ODD. From 45% to 84% of children with ADHD develop ODD within 2 to 3 years of the onset of their ADHD. But it isn't just limited to children: From 24% to 35% of adults diagnosed with ADHD also have ODD, and 50% to 60% recall having had significant levels of ODD as children (see Footnote 1). That means that ODD persists into adulthood in nearly half or more of the cases where it developed in childhood.

When ODD exists in an adult with ADHD, it brings with it additional risks for impairment in life. For example, whereas ADHD may be the chief contributor to poor work performance ratings by employers, it is ODD that is more predictive of the likelihood of being fired from a job. That makes perfect sense. Employers can tolerate a certain degree of distractibility, restlessness, chattiness, and even poor organization in an employee without dismissing someone from a job. But employers are far less likely to tolerate displays of anger, hostility, reactive aggression, spitefulness, and defiance of their authority.

Does it sound like your loved one with ADHD might have ODD too? If so, you probably know firsthand the difficulties they have with being impatient, easily frustrated, irritable, and quick to anger. You may have found them quick to argue or even to refuse to do things they have been required to do for work or in fulfilling other obligations. Then you also know just how hard it is to tolerate or accept these emotional displays from your loved one. You know about the excess drama ODD brings to your relationship and the added stress you feel when you have to actively contain or help him to manage his upsets. Maybe you have even become estranged from your loved one with ADHD for a while just to have a cooling-off period. It is understandable that you might want to seek some normalcy in your own life when the emotional melodrama gets to be too much to bear. That's OK. Such reactions are common among the relatives, partners, and friends of those adults with ADHD, especially if they also have ODD.

I am not asking or encouraging you to hang in there with a loved one who has both ADHD and ODD so that you can be her emotional punching bag or constant therapist. You have your own feelings, too, and you are entitled to seek some peace in your own life. You also have a right to feel hurt or upset. Or you may even have taken offense to any excessive and undeserved hostility or even aggression that may have been aimed at you by your loved one with ADHD. All I ask is that you continue to be involved in a relationship with her, as I hope you will. And I ask that you understand that such frustration, anger, and temper are not life choices or willful misbehavior. ADHD is a neurodevelopmental disorder that afflicts your loved one not by choice but by fate. She can no more help having ADHD and the poor emotional regulation it conveys than you can help being yourself. But don't seek to excuse her misconduct or emotional outbursts—that is not my point here. Instead, do try to understand why these emotional problems like ODD occur so much more often in your loved one than in others. With that understanding, you can then encourage her to seek professional help if that seems possible. I discuss in depth several therapies for adult ADHD in Chapters 11 and 12, including ADHD medications, that can help reduce these symptoms of ODD.

CONDUCT DISORDER

Conduct disorder (CD) is a pattern of multiple types of antisocial behavior, including lying, stealing, fighting, carrying and using weapons, running away from home, being truant, committing curfew violations, setting intentional fires, and even sexual assaulting others. In general, those with CD have a greater propensity for violating the rights of others and social norms and laws. Children with ADHD have a higher risk for developing CD (25%–45%) as they grow up, especially if they have already developed ODD. CD occurs in 17% to 35% of adults with ADHD, either currently or when they were younger (see Footnote 1). Notice that the vast majority of adults with ADHD do not have CD, but a significant minority of them had these symptoms during childhood or adolescence and they are more likely to have CD currently than typical people.

The development of CD in cases of ADHD is thought to be partly the result of the problems adults with ADHD have with inhibition and self-regulation that go with ADHD. However, these deficits alone do not automatically make an adult at risk for CD. Indeed, in most cases, people with ADHD do not get CD. More likely, impulsiveness linked to ADHD is just one predisposing factor that must be combined with other events across time to culminate in the development of CD. Those other factors include a family genetic risk for CD and drug abuse disorders in the parents or in extended relatives. They also include a greater likelihood of having had a disruptive home life and experiencing social disadvantages, maltreatment, and reduced parental monitoring of activities outside of the home when the adult with ADHD was a teenager, being raised by a single parent, and having been affiliated with delinquent or drug using peers.

When this pattern of CD behavior exists in a loved one with ADHD, it can be very hard to accept. After all, frequent lying, stealing, and fighting violate standards of morality and, often, laws. It is easy to sit in moral judgment of teens and adults with ADHD, especially those who have CD along with it. It is also easy to feel that he deserves what he gets if his antisocial behavior gets him into trouble with others or the law. It can be hard to explain to others, especially authorities or the victims of his misconduct, when he has done such things and harmed others or their property as a consequence. It is also difficult to go to bat for him with the juvenile authorities or the adult legal system when he has gotten into trouble. It can be a real financial and emotional strain to try to get him bail if he has been put in jail, to get him appropriate legal assistance, or to try and make reparations to the victims of his criminal acts. I know this personally, given that my twin brother had both ADHD and some signs of CD.

The way I coped with all the circumstances surrounding my brother may be the way you have found to deal with your own loved one if he is having such problems. We came to see Ron as you would any other person with a serious mental disability who needed the concern, love, support and even protection of his family. He was someone who simply could not handle adult life and all its attendant responsibilities very well. Although his life ended in that car accident I described in Chapter 5, my wife and I like to think that we at least gave him a few more years of life or a better quality of life than he might otherwise have had if we had not been there along with my mother and sister to try and help him with his life. And we know that he derived some happiness from being near our mother, keeping her company, cooking for her on Sundays, caring for her home, playing music at various local festivals and taverns, and relishing the beauty of the Adirondacks he so loved. I return to this theme later in this book (Chapters 9 and 10): how to cope with and help a loved one with ADHD who does not accept their disorder, rarely cooperates with treatment for it, yet clearly cannot deal with life unassisted.

ANTISOCIAL PERSONALITY DISORDER

Antisocial personality disorder (ASPD) represents a more severe form of CD and its continuance into adulthood. ASPD is characterized by gross irresponsibility, along with the symptoms of aggression, hostility, lying, and other forms of antisocial behavior noted in the previous section for CD. Anywhere from 7% to as many as 44% of adults diagnosed with ADHD may qualify for a diagnosis of ASPD across the research studies, averaging to about 25%. This is especially true for those who had developed CD by adolescence.

Some adults with ASPD also may show a lack of guilt or remorse for their misconduct and an indifference or lack of empathy for the harm that they have caused to others; those adults may also be said to have psychopathic personality disorder. By "indifference," I mean that they often show reckless disregard for their own safety and that of others, and a repeated failure to sustain work or honor financial obligations. For instance, they may spend money that has been set aside for paying bills on themselves, on drugs, or on other impulsive or entertaining activities, such as gambling. Their disregard for the safety of others, for instance, might involve their failure to supervise their young children, for example, to leave them alone as the adults go out to have fun.

I hope that your loved one with ADHD does not also have this ASPD, especially combined with those psychopathic features noted. ASPD is associated with more numerous and more severe adverse events than are most of the other disorders listed here. It also can bring tremendous heartbreak, stress, and frustration to loved ones like you, who have had to watch this pattern of self-destructive, antisocial, and even criminal behavior play out over the early adult years. Although the propensity for such irresponsible behavior declines with age, it can leave a wake of destructive consequences for the adult with ASPD and others around them. And it can often culminate in periodic prison sentences or death for them and harm to others. Although few if any treatments are effective for dealing with ASPD, some research does suggest that if the ADHD that is associated with it is treated with medication, the propensity for antisocial and psychopathic behavior may decline. Frequently, adults with ASPD do not get treatment nor wish to do so, at least not until some severe consequences accrue to them, often repeatedly over many years. Perhaps that is when they finally realize that their adverse experiences have much to do with them and are not the fault of others.

ANTISOCIAL BEHAVIOR

Even if they don't qualify for a diagnosis of CD or ASPD, teens and young adults with ADHD are likely to engage in antisocial or criminal activities. When they do, they are also more likely to engage in drug use and abuse. The two conditions, antisocial behavior and drug use/abuse, seem to go hand in hand, and further intertwine and worsen each other over time. That is because each problem predisposes a person to engage in the other type of behavior, in this case substance use and abuse. Or the opposite can occur. For instance, if you have a drug abuse habit, say with cocaine, crack, methamphetamine, or illegal prescription drugs, you may be more likely to steal money or property to obtain the means to buy your drugs of abuse. Or if you drink alcohol excessively, you may be more likely to get into fights with others. And in both cases, you may be more inclined to carry and even use weapons than would other people who are not using these substances or doing these antisocial activities. Similarly, if you engage in certain criminal activities, such as stealing or fighting, you may be doing so with others who are also prone to antisocial behavior. And those people are more likely to be using drugs and may influence you to do so.

We also know that certain types of crimes cluster together. People inclined to steal or break into people's homes to do so are usually armed with weapons and are also inclined to fight with others if they are confronted while doing so. Or consider that if an adult engages in one type of crime, such as running away from home as a teenager, she is much more likely to commit other crimes, such as steal and even engage in prostitution as means of support than would others who do not run away. All of this simply means that one of the best predictors that a person with ADHD will engage in drug use and abuse is the person's tendency to engage in antisocial behavior.

At least four factors predict which adults with ADHD drift into crime and drug use and abuse:

1. *The degree of impulsiveness.* That makes perfect sense. The same appears to be true for predicting the likelihood of engaging in illegal activities (crime). The impulsive person,

by definition, is less likely to consider the consequences of their actions than others. They are therefore more likely to do something illegal on a whim or impulse.

2. *The kind of social group a person hangs around with in his spare time.* If he pals around with people who are likely to be doing illegal activities, he may be more influenced to do so by his companions. Gangs are an obvious example of this sort of deviant social influence. However, the peer group does not have to be an organized gang to have such a negative influence on the probability that someone with ADHD will engage in crime or drug use—just having a few antisocial and drug using friends is enough to create such a nudge in the direction of crime and drug use.
3. *Level of education.* People with ADHD who have less education, especially if they did not graduate from high school, such as my brother, are far more likely to be doing antisocial things than people with ADHD who graduated or went on after high school to further their education. This probably occurs because not graduating provides someone with fewer job opportunities and ways to support himself legally than is the case for those with more education.
4. *The severity of someone's ADHD and its persistence from childhood to adolescence.* The persistence of ADHD alone can be a factor increasing the risk for crime. The type of crime most associated with ADHD is using, possessing, and selling illegal drugs and stealing money to buy drugs, as did my brother.

About one in four people with ADHD, at a minimum, are likely to use or abuse drugs as adults. And the same appears to be true as to what percentage are likely to engage in such frequent and persistent antisocial behavior as to be called ASPD. Yet, even if people with

ADHD are unlikely to have these other psychiatric disorders or to engage in highly persistent antisocial activities, they are more likely to do so at least once in their life and to do so more frequently than adults who do not have ADHD.

The most common forms of antisocial behavior in which adults with ADHD are likely to have engaged in while growing up are shoplifting, stealing without confronting a victim, breaking and entering, assaulting someone with their fists, and carrying an illegal weapon. That ADHD in anyone at any age would make them more likely to shoplift, steal, or fight with others is understandable in view of the very nature of ADHD, as I discussed in Chapters 1 and 2—that person is more impulsive and so more prone to give in to temptations than others. And they are more emotional when provoked, especially to become frustrated and angry. Also, more adults with ADHD have sold drugs illegally than had adults in our control groups. Of course, this means that adults with ADHD are more likely to have been arrested and to have spent some time in jail.

Antisocial behavior, of course, is more likely to occur in men than women overall, regardless whether or not the person has ADHD. But men with ADHD are markedly more likely to do so than are men who do not have ADHD. If you have an adult loved one with ADHD, you may have firsthand knowledge of or even involvement in their history of antisocial activities, drug use, and legal problems.

None of this means that every adult with ADHD is destined to be antisocial or to use drugs. Treating the ADHD at any stage in life is likely to reduce a person's propensity for risk taking, for doing antisocial activities, or for engaging in illegal drug use. And so there is always reason for great hope that earlier patterns of antisocial behavior and drug use in those with ADHD can be improved by getting treatment from mental health professionals for their ADHD and any related antisocial or drug-using propensities.

BORDERLINE PERSONALITY DISORDER

Borderline personality disorder (BPD) can develop in 15% to 20% or more of children with ADHD followed to adulthood (see Footnote 1). BPD is essentially a pervasive pattern of unstable interpersonal relationships coupled with deficits and distortions in self-image and poorly regulated emotions. It is often associated with increased impulsivity. The interpersonal relationships of people with BPD fluctuate markedly in their intensity from extreme idealization of someone to complete devaluation of them, often over short periods of time. It is also composed of fear of, and frantic efforts to avoid, real or imagined abandonment by others. For instance, when a partner unexpectedly says they are going to the store for milk, the adult with BPD accuses her of actually planning to leave for good or meet someone for a casual sexual affair. Adults with BPD often cannot tolerate being alone. They seem to need reassurance from people around them far more than do other adults. The BPD symptoms may be coupled with frequent threats or gestures of suicide. Or the person engages in acts of self-mutilation, such as self-cutting or burning, excessive piercing, and even excessive tattooing. The moods of an adult with BPD can fluctuate markedly as well, going from irritability and anger to anxiety and on to depression over a matter of a few hours. In some instances, stress-related paranoia or even dissociative episodes may appear in which they seem to talk and act as if they were someone else, as one sees in adults with split personalities. If you recall the movie *Fatal Attraction*, Glenn Close played a character with such a personality disorder.

BPD is a serious personality disorder in terms of its consequences for the individual. It often results in social rejection and the very abandonment such adults fear. It can lead to frequent job losses, financial misery due to his impulsiveness with money, occasional inpatient hospitalizations, self-injury, and even suicide. Children with ADHD who are most likely to develop BPD by young adulthood were those who already had developed CD by adolescence or were exposed to serious and chronic stress and family disruption, and possibly recurrent emotional, physical, or sexual abuse or neglect.

KEY POINTS TO REMEMBER

Adults with ADHD are highly likely to have at least one or two other psychiatric disorders coexisting with their ADHD. The most common of these disorders are depression and anxiety disorders and even the more severe BD. The person with ADHD is even more likely to have ODD and, to a lesser extent, CD, ASPD, and sometimes BPD. They are also more prone to manifest antisocial behavior than other adults during their lifetime, even if they do not have a diagnosis of CD or ASPD, the two disorders that involve such antisocial behavior. The presence of a second disorder further complicates the lives of adults with ADHD, as well as the management of their disorders. It also brings with it additional risks beyond those I have discussed for ADHD concerning impairments in various major life activities. And it surely further complicates the lives of people such as yourself who has a loved one with ADHD. All of this is yet even more reason to not only learn about ADHD and its treatment but also to encourage your loved one with ADHD to get professional assistance if they have not done so as yet. If they had been in treatment and stopped, then these are good reasons to return.

CHAPTER 7

CAN ADULT ADHD BE A GOOD THING TO HAVE? SOME ADHD SUCCESS STORIES

Perhaps by this point in this book, you may have become quite discouraged about the chances your loved one may have for a decent quality of life and opportunities for success, given all the risks portrayed in the previous two chapters. Don't be. That discouragement would be a huge mistake. Although adult attention-deficit/hyperactivity disorder (ADHD) can certainly be a serious disorder, it does not have to prevent someone from leading a happy or successful life if it is appropriately treated. The risk in spelling out the adversities that can be associated with ADHD in adults, as I have done, is that one can overpathologize the condition and make people lose hope for their loved ones. That was not my intent, as I have said repeatedly. Instead, I am trying to thoroughly familiarize

---

For this chapter, I compiled biographical information from http://www.biography.com; Wikipedia; and lists of athletes and celebrities with ADHD from http://www.parenting.com, http://www.addadult.com, and news websites such as *The Guardian* and *Elite Daily.* Several subjects were also featured in the online magazine *ADDitude*, both individually and in lists.

For the information on ADHD-friendly jobs and careers I used lists found on http://www.healthline.com and http://www.everydayhealth.com, and user comments on the online forum *Totally ADD Connect.*

you with the risks linked to the disorder so that you see it, eyes wide open, as the serious problem it can often be for people afflicted with it. Doing so may help motivate you to try to help them with their struggle in coping with this disorder. And your encouragement may help motivate your loved one to get the help they may require to manage their disorder and reduce all the risks discussed earlier in this book. So look for an opportune time to suggest to them that they get professional assistance if they have not done so already.

Some authors of trade books on adult ADHD have represented it as a gift. They see it as something that brings advantages that those without the disorder would not possess. Portraying adult ADHD as a gift or advantage of some sort is a mistake in my expert opinion, as it not only misrepresents the scientific findings on this disorder but also can minimize the seriousness of the disorder and foster false hope. Calling adult ADHD a gift may even border on the promotion of delusional thinking if adopted too seriously by the adult with the disorder or their loved ones. It can also lead to people doing nothing to help loved ones cope with or manage their disorder. After all, if it is a gift or advantageous trait, then it doesn't need treatment. And if it is such a great thing to have, why should society provide special accommodations and services in the educational system or workplace for those who have it? Why should such a "gift" make one eligible for worker's compensation or Social Security Disability payments? Why should people with it be granted special protections against discrimination under the Americans With Disabilities Act?[1] Why should insurance companies help pay for visits to mental health professionals and treatments for ADHD? Why should *you* even bother to step up and help your loved one deal with it if it is

[1]Americans With Disabilities Act of 1990, Pub. L. No. 101-336, § 2, 104 Stat. 328 (1991).

such a great "gift"? You can see the problem here: ADHD cannot be both a gift and a disability deserving of our compassion and help in society.

> ADHD is not a gift. It has ruined my life. The good things I continue to get from it are compassion for all people and not judging and a lot of knowledge about mental health. My boss allows me to do master's level work because he trusts me and he signs off on this, of course. It took me 6 years to complete my undergraduate degree but that's because my mom pushed me. Once I started working at a medical health office, I found my niche. I will be going back to school in 2 weeks to begin my graduate program as a physician's assistant. As for hyperfocusing, I can say that when I do get onto a subject that grabs my interest, it consumes my whole brain. My poor husband refers to these bouts of obsession as pitbull-like behavior. I feel bad for him when I get in this state because it makes it very difficult for me to hear, see, or do anything else. Luckily it tends to be short lived.

Thousands of articles have been published on ADHD, and in none of them was the disorder found to convey some special advantage, talent, ability, or other trait in comparison with typical people. So, no, ADHD is no gift if by that one means that it conveys some special or unique abilities not seen in ordinary people.

Lately, some of the professionals asserting that ADHD is a gift have backpedaled from the strong form of this claim in the face of all of the research that consistently finds that it is a disadvantage. Those people then substitute a weaker version of this claim. They say that by having to struggle against a psychological disorder, the individual with adult ADHD is made emotionally stronger, better in character, and perhaps even a more resilient person. The adult with ADHD is made so because of what they have had to go through in dealing with the deficits created by the disorder and the impairments in life activities to which these deficits have led. Calvinism meets ADHD: Through suffering, we find redemption and stronger character.

Perhaps that is true for some. But that is like wishing that we should all have some serious affliction so we can rise to the challenge of having to deal with it. That people may rise to the challenges of and overcome or compensate for afflictions and adversities that fate has cast upon them is not a reason to celebrate such circumstances, much as we may praise them for doing so. By all means let us encourage adults whom fate has afflicted with adult ADHD to rise to, confront, and even overcome the challenges and adversities it may be posing for their quality of life. We, the loved ones of the adults with ADHD, should surely encourage them to do so. But let us not misconstrue this as some blessing or gift so as to make the adult with ADHD feel good about herself. Doing so could even backfire in leading her to give up getting treatment for the disorder lest it ruin her "gift." It could give her yet one more excuse why she should not believe you when you say she may need help. Or it could lead her to quit trying to deal with the problems ADHD is posing for her. Just as one should not overpathologize ADHD, one should not romanticize or aggrandize it either.

By all means, let us celebrate those who have coped successfully with their ADHD and even succeeded in some occupations well beyond what typical people might have done. Yet neither that coping nor that success can be attributed to their ADHD. Instead, as I show, it is due to some of the many hundreds of other traits the person possesses in which they may have been afforded some talent. People are not good artists, actresses, comedians, musicians, chefs, athletes, TV personalities, entrepreneurs, and so on, because of their ADHD—they are so in spite of it. They just happened to be blessed with exceptional talents unrelated to their ADHD that allowed them to excel even with their ADHD. My brother was not a gifted rock guitar player because he had ADHD but because he comes from a long line of very competent musicians in our extended family and ancestors. It is also because he dedicated countless hours to perfecting that talent. And it is surely because our mother realized that he had a talent for this nontraditional occupation and that it might just save him from the educational nightmare he was experiencing at school. So she backed his musical interests financially early in his career when he quit school yet needed to find some calling or vocation to support himself. She went against the grain of the times, as well as our military father, who called for condemning and punishing him for his school failures and pressuring him to do better. She knew in her heart and soul that he had a disorder and that he couldn't be like typical teens and succeed in that customary educational path. This was the 1950s and 1960s, after all, when almost no one knew anything about ADHD. Instead, school staff blamed my parents for moving too much or just coddling him.

People with ADHD are certainly less inhibited. And it is well known that one's creativity can be enhanced somewhat by being less inhibited than others. Somewhat lower levels of inhibition promote thinking about, or even trying, far-fetched ideas that others would suppress thinking about because they are unusual, impractical, or seemingly irrelevant. This does not make people with ADHD more creative in general. Their impulsiveness is usually far more severe than in people without ADHD who are creative. But it might lead to specific instances in which some already highly gifted, talented, or creative people who happen to have ADHD are more inventive in their ideas or are more likely to take risks in their business or specialty. Some of those far-fetched ideas just might pay off handsomely. Likewise, ADHD conveys to people a high level of energy and typically unfocused activity. This can be directed for good or bad. But if someone with ADHD is also blessed with high athletic or an entrepreneurial talent and is surrounded by loved ones who can channel that excess energy and utilize exceptional area resources (see this chapter's section on Michael Phelps), then good things may come of it. It is this interaction of talent with excess activity coupled with direction by loved ones and their recruiting of resources that can promote that talent that may well help that person to succeed where others with ADHD might not do so.

Also, lost in such discussions about success stories of those who may have adult ADHD is that the stories tend to focus on just one aspect of the person's life, such as their vocation, in which they are unusually successful. Those stories often ignore the other domains of the person's life in which they may be struggling, such as socially, financially, legally, in their intimate relationships, and in their substance abuse (such as Michael Phelps and Ty Pennington).

Let's also not forget that adults with ADHD may be doing better than other adults with ADHD or than typical adults because they learned about it and got treatment for it. But the real reason I am going to describe several adult ADHD success stories here is that I view the role of their loved ones as absolutely crucial to that success. Many of the people who have succeeded in certain professions despite having ADHD frequently have had supportive loved ones like you surrounding them. Those loved ones assist, buffer, protect, encourage, support, organize, divert, fund, and otherwise motivate an adult with ADHD to succeed. Those loved ones also open doors for an adult with ADHD so that they might have a chance at success despite their ADHD.

MICHAEL PHELPS—U.S. OLYMPIC GOLD MEDAL SWIMMER

According to Wikipedia, Michael Phelps (age 31 at the time of this publication) is the most decorated Olympic athlete of all time, having won 28 medals, 23 of which were gold, in various swimming competitions at the 2008, 2012, and 2016 Olympics. It was during his second

Olympics in 2008 that I first learned of Michael's history of ADHD; the U.S. TV coverage carried an in-depth profile of Michael and his mother, Deborah Sue, a middle school principal. In it, she stated that Michael struggled to succeed in school, was very hyperactive and impulsive, and needed to have those energies channeled in some constructive way. So she introduced him to swimming at the age of 7. She did so as an outlet for his excess energies and because two of his sisters were already in a local swim team. By sixth grade, Michael was diagnosed with ADHD. Michael's mother clearly devoted many hours to keeping Michael organized and directed, as apparently did his sisters. His mother arranged for his coaching and kept him involved in swimming. Important as well is that she literally organized his day into 15-minute blocks in a written schedule so as to structure the day of this otherwise frenetic but directionless young man. Indeed, from his biosketch, it appeared that most of what Michael did as a teenager outside of his schooling was train in swimming most free hours a day, and then just eat and sleep. Little free time was left for getting into any trouble. Since his introduction to competitive swimming as a child, Michael has gone on to countless accomplishments in various events, including, of course, the Olympics. Clearly he is an exceptionally talented, hard-working, and accomplished young man.

Is Michael such a gifted competitive swimmer because he has ADHD? No. In no research done to date has swimming or even athletics more generally shown up as a field in which adults with ADHD excel more than do others. Some evidence does suggest that those having ADHD may be more likely than others to choose physical education as a major or to participate in sports at various levels. Yet this can be attributed to the fact that people with ADHD may be more likely to function effectively (to be less impaired) in physical education or sports than might be the case in other educational majors. They are not better at it than others in those fields but may be less impaired from their disorder in such fields than in others. This is "niche-picking," and we all do it. Over time, we learn where we are likely to succeed and fail given our talents, deficiencies, proclivities, and interests. So we keep self-selecting into those pursuits where we seem to do OK or even excel while avoiding other pursuits in which we have no talent, no history of success, and probably some experience with failure.

Moreover, Michael's father (who divorced Deborah Sue in 1994) was also a talented athlete who even tried out to play professional football for the Washington Redskins. He eventually became a Maryland State Trooper. Michael's sisters also showed great promise at swimming, so Michael's family has a clear (genetic) predisposition to athletic talent. His sister, Whitney, for instance, was talented enough at competitive swimming that she, too, tried out for the U.S. Olympic team, but her career was adversely affected by injuries. We cannot overlook the possibilities here then of both a genetic predisposition to athletic talent and an early home life that encouraged and supported athletics generally and swimming specifically in Michael. One also needs to mention his career-long coaching by a former competitive swimmer, Bob Bowman: "Incredibly invested in the success of people he cares about."[2]

Phelps has also been said to have a fierce sense of competitiveness that would have nothing to do with his having ADHD but with other facets of his unique personality. He is also taller than most swimmers, has a larger wingspan (longer arms, wider shoulders), and has greater ankle flexibility than most swimmers, all of which might arguably give

[2]Van Valkenburg, K. (2008, August 3). Phelps' voyage. *The Baltimore Sun.* Retrieved from http://articles.baltimoresun.com/2008-08-03/sports/bal-te.sp.phelps03aug03_1_swimsuits-and-energy-bars-michael-phelps-teenager-outgrowing

him some slight advantage at swimming.[3] Moreover, it is now known that physical exercise is a helpful means of coping with and temporarily reducing the symptoms of ADHD in children and adults. It benefits those with this disorder more than it does people having other disorders. So I say good for his mother, Debbie, for doing what she did to get Michael into competitive swimming. And good for Michael to persist at this physical activity for which he was extraordinarily talented and to which he has dedicated countless hours of training.

Yet some trouble did come Michael's way nonetheless. In 2004, he was arrested at age 19 for driving under the influence of alcohol, fined $250, and sentenced to 18 months' probation, attendance at MADD meetings (Mothers Against Drunk Driving), and community service (speaking to high school students about drinking and driving). In 2009, the year after his incredible success at the 2008 Olympics, Michael was visiting the University of South Carolina when he was photographed using a bong, or water pipe (often used for smoking marijuana). His poor judgment in these circumstances resulted in his loss of a substantial contract with Kellogg to appear on their cereal boxes. It also led to his getting a 3-month suspension from USA Swimming. In 2014, Michael was arrested yet again for driving under the influence of alcohol.[4]

This focus on some of his problems is not to diminish in anyway Michael's singular accomplishments in his sport. These mistakes, however, do highlight the fact that people with ADHD may excel in some things, succeed at others, yet still have difficulties in

---

[3]Hadhazy, A. (2008, August 18). What makes Michael Phelps so good? *Scientific American.* Retrieved from http://www.scientificamerican.com/article/what-makes-michael-phelps-so-good/

[4]SI Wire. (2014, September 30). Michael Phelps arrested for DUI in Maryland. *Sports Illustrated.* Retrieved from http://www.si.com/more-sports/2014/09/30/michael-phelps-arrested-dui-maryland

other domains due to their symptoms (impulsiveness, inattention, etc.). I note Michael's problems as well to show that it is unlikely to be his ADHD alone that led to his remarkable success.

Pay attention here to the involvement of the people around Michael in helping to

- channel his energies;
- focus and develop his athletic talent;
- find area resources that could further develop his athletic gifts;
- buffer him from the difficulties he was having with school;
- support him financially and emotionally; and
- keep him so involved and organized that there simply was little, if any, time for him to get into trouble most days.

It undoubtedly helped Michael's schooling problems that his mother was an assistant principal and former teacher. She had taught school herself for several decades. And so when he was not doing so well she worked with Michael herself as well as got him extra attention in school to address his severe problems with concentration. She also hired a tutor for him in math when he struggled with it, used sports examples to help him learn to solve word problems in math, and got him a separate seat arrangement in school when he kept bothering other children. She also developed cuing strategies to help him control his emotions, especially his temper, when he did not do well in swim meets. In general, she advises parents to work as a team with their children and teens with ADHD to help them through their difficulties handling work and life challenges.

Michael has been very clear about how important his family, especially his mother, was to his success. He repeatedly and publicly acknowledges his gratitude to his mother, sisters, and coach for their involvement in his success. The loved ones around people with ADHD clearly can have a constructive influence upon them.

Also bear in mind that Michael may have had resources available to him to promote his training and success, resources that others with ADHD, even of equal athletic talent, might not have had. Besides his mother's assistance, he gained access to the Baltimore Swim Club, where he met his coach. Such resources are not available in rural areas of the United States. Or consider that his coach brought him to the University of Michigan athletic department when he moved there for a coaching position and brought Michael to be his assistant, to name just a few resources and opportunities afforded to Michael by others. Family and community resources can certainly be brought to bear to diminish or even preclude some of the adverse effects ADHD might have produced in other, less resource-rich environments. Undoubtedly Michael Phelps is an unbelievably talented and accomplished competitive swimmer, humanitarian, and role model for others, especially in the field of athletics. He deserves all of the success and riches that have come his way. Yet, the importance of his loved ones and the resources they made available to him in his success here should not be overlooked either.

Other athletes who have done quite well in their vocations despite having ADHD are golfers Bubba Watson and the late Payne Stewart; gymnast Louis Smith; judo competitor Ashley McKenzie; football star and commentator Terry Bradshaw; football players Andre Brown and Virgil Green; baseball stars Shane Victorino, Andres Torres, and Pete Rose; track star Justin Gatlin; hockey player Cammi Granato; competitive rower Adam Kreek; professional basketball players Michael Jordan and Chris Kaman; Olympic decathlon athlete Bruce (now Caitlyn) Jenner; cyclist and Tour de France winner Greg LeMond; professional wrestler Matt Morgan; and many others. Thus, although ADHD alone does not contribute to one's success in sports, it is not a barrier to such success, as these athletes can clearly attest.

ADAM LEVINE—SUCCESSFUL MUSICIAN AND TV STAR

Born in 1979, Adam Levine first came to widespread attention as the lead singer, musician, and songwriter for the band Maroon 5, whose multiplatinum album *Songs About Jane* (2002) made him a star. More recently, you may know him as one of the judges on the popular TV show *The Voice*. And perhaps you saw his acting debut in 2012 in the horror TV show *American Horror Story: Asylum* and the film *Begin Again*. He is the winner of multiple music awards during his career and is a multimillionaire. He has spoken openly about his being diagnosed with ADHD as a teenager and his treatment for it.

Adam's father, Fred, was the founder of a retail store chain, and his mother, Patsy, was an admissions counselor. His parents divorced when he was a child, and he was in counseling to help him cope with his feelings about it. Claiming to have been consumed by music since childhood, Adam (like my brother) was rebellious in school and "didn't want to do the things they were teaching me."[5] By adolescence, he was using illegal drugs, such as hallucinogens, but he claims to have quit using them after an adverse reaction to a sleeping medication, Ambien. His first band that he helped form while in high school was Kara's Flowers; they were eventually discovered and signed to a record contract with Reprise Records. But the album and its debut single did poorly commercially, with the contract being dropped and the band eventually breaking up. Although he enrolled in college (Five Towns College) to study music, Adam dropped out and reunited with some of his former band mates. On the advice of

[5]Stuart, E., & Effron, L. (2011, November 17). Maroon 5's Adam Levine's playlist: Top 5 songs that impacted rocker's style. *ABC News*. Retrieved from http://abcnews.go.com/Entertainment/maroon-5s-adam-levines-playlist-top-songs-impacted/story?id=14966693

recording executives, the band added a fifth member and changed their name to Maroon 5. Their debut album in 2002 became a hit, winning Grammys 2 years in a row. Adam Levine has gone on to also write for or perform with many other singers, such as Kanye West, Alicia Keys, 50 Cent, Eminem, and Christina Aguilera.

Unlike some other stars with ADHD, Adam has done much to promote public awareness of the disorder, including working with the Shire pharmaceutical company in their informational program, "Own It," as well as collaborating with the major charitable foundations for ADHD in the United States, Children and Adults With ADD (CHADD) and Attention Deficit Disorder Association (ADDA). He also wrote an article on his experiences with teen and adult ADHD for *ADDitude* magazine. In the article, Adam talks about how he has struggled with the symptoms of ADHD all his life, such as not being able to sit still or focus on getting his schoolwork done. He credits his parents for being patient with and helping him. He also thanks a physician for treating him for his ADHD. Later, when he was off his medication, he complained of difficulties focusing on his songwriting and studio music recording, organizing his thoughts, and getting things done. So he went back to see a physician and was told he continued to have ADHD now that he was an adult. He was put back on medication and responded well to it. He continues to use it as of this writing and speaks publicly and unabashedly about his ADHD when asked about it. So does another singer-composer-musician, Justin Timberlake.

TY PENNINGTON—TV STAR, MODEL, ACTOR, AND CARPENTER

Ty Pennington, age 40, first entered popular culture as a model for print ads for clothing, watch, and soda companies and then played the role of a carpenter on the TV show *Trading Spaces*. He subsequently starred as a popular and dynamic happy-go-lucky television host for nine seasons on ABC TV's *Extreme Makeover: Home Edition*, until the show ended in December 2012. He has since participated in various TV specials, such as HLNtv's *American Journey* (2013), and in 2015 donned an apron as a TV chef on the show *On the Menu*. Ty is not only an Emmy-award winning TV star (2005, 2007) but also an artist and accomplished carpenter. He even has his own line of furniture with the Howard Miller Company and his own furniture company. Ty is a consultant and celebrity endorser for Sears for his own line of home décor and furniture products. He has written books on home repair projects and had a partnership with a home remodeling show company, Marketplace Events. He also has done philanthropic work, such as with a charity in Hawaii that teaches disabled children surfing and other water sports. His other charitable work includes being a participant in celebrity sports events to raise funds for various charities, and assisting the Bayer pharmaceutical company with their campaign on cardiac health. More recently, he assisted Shire pharmaceutical company, the manufacturer of several ADHD medications, with their campaign to promote awareness of adult ADHD and has spoken publicly on TV shows about it.

Like Michael Phelps and Adam Levine, Ty is a multimillionaire. And like them both, he had considerable difficulties in school as a child. His mother, Yvonne Pennington, cited his serious problems focusing and paying attention in school. She claims that in first grade he would hoist his desk onto his shoulders and wear it while running around the class getting laughs from his classmates. Although said to be intelligent by his teachers, he could not sit still and made frequent trips to the principal's office for his misbehavior. Like many children with ADHD, Ty was incredibly hyperactive, according to his mother, jumping off roofs and running about in the street without looking out for traffic. He referred to himself in one interview as having been a disaster as a child and as being the poster child for ADHD.[6] He had a knack for taking things apart and building things, which likely led to his training and eventual work as a carpenter.

Yvonne was raising Ty and another child as a single mother, working as a waitress, and attending night school to eventually get her degree in clinical psychology. Her training helped her to understand what was going wrong with Ty in school. She got him diagnosed by a physician in the 1970s while he was in elementary school. She also learned how to use behavior modification strategies with Ty, such as token systems, to help him get his work done. Ty also received special educational services in his public school and his mother worked jointly with his teachers to establish behavior therapy programs with him in class. In the 1980s, she eventually spoke with Ty about his ADHD and advised that he return to see a doctor for further treatment. He was placed on a stimulant medication often used for ADHD that helped him concentrate better. He was able to return to art school, having dropped out earlier, and eventually graduated with honors. Ty then worked in various vocations, such as modeling, construction work, graphic design, and acting before getting his position on the TV show *Trading Spaces*.

In an article in *ADDitude* magazine,[7] Yvonne said that "even today, his spontaneity gives me heart attacks," recounting the time when she switched on the TV to see Ty zooming down a steep driveway using an ottoman for a skateboard. Still, if her experiences have

[6]ABC News (Producer). (2008). *Celebrities with ADHD: Ty Pennington.* Retrieved from http://www.youtube.com/watch?v=RKdfSqy4NOs

[7]Dutton, J. (2008, April/May). ADHD parenting advice from Michael Phelps' mom. *ADDitude.* Retrieved from http://www.additudemag.com/adhd/article/1998-2.html

taught her anything, it's that parents should learn to appreciate the unique features ADHD can offer. "The very traits that once held Ty back are now his biggest assets," she says. "Many parents in this situation focus on what their kids are doing wrong. I encourage them to focus on what they're doing right. Do that, and the possibilities are endless."

Ty says of his ADHD (in an interview with Glenn Beck, who also has ADHD[8]):

> I mean, the whole thing is like changing your mind constantly going, wait, wait, wait, wait, I got another [idea]. But they also can't focus on one thing. But, you know, usually in that situation you are not the first person someone's going to pick to get the job that's going to be the one that they say doesn't get it done. You are the one that doesn't finish the projects. You keep going down the line, down the line, down the line. And what happens is my confidence just kept waning and waning until it wasn't until I finally got treated literally in college that I realized, hold on a second, you know what, I actually do have a talent, I can put myself through school and I actually can make something of myself.

Of his getting treatment for ADHD, Ty said:

> Now, that personality doesn't go away because I got treatment, you know. I'm still that kind of guy but I can actually complete the tasks. I can actually finish a sentence and actually finish the projects that I've got on my to-do list.

[8]All direct quotations in this chapter from Ty Pennington's interview with Glenn Beck can be found on Beck's website (http://www.glennbeck.com/content/articles/article/196/12741/).

And as for the benefits of treatment, Ty said:

> Once I was put on lasting medications like Vyvanse, next thing you know, bam, it's like somebody gave me glasses and all of a sudden I could see, you know, not only what I couldn't see before but I could see the mistakes I made and how I could correct them and how, you know, like my grades are well, really focusing, my grades went from Ds to As, I'm putting myself through art school, instead of doing one project, I'm actually completing three, could show just how talented I am because I'm also very competitive. Next thing you know instead of having the idea, I'm actually completing it and saying, this is what I mean, you can see. They can actually see it instead of me trying to explain the thought. Until then people were just like, "huh? What are you saying?"

Unfortunately, as with Michael Phelps, Ty had his own arrests for driving while intoxicated. This mistake, along with other driving problems, are relatively common events in the lives of adults with ADHD, as I discussed in Chapter 5. Ty was given 3 years' probation, a 3-month suspended license to drive, and 3 months in an alcohol treatment program, as well as being required to attend meetings of MADD, just as was Michael.

Notice here that as with Michael Phelps and Adam Levine, an incredible interest in and talent for a particular activity, dedicated practice within that field, and the assistance of loved ones can combine to turn that talent into a successful life's vocation, even if it is not in the more routine channels of success that require advanced formal education, such as in the professions. And it doesn't hurt that all of these successful adults with ADHD were diagnosed with the disorder and received various treatments for it.

Other celebrities with ADHD include chef Jamie Oliver, dancer Karina Smirnoff (*Dancing With the Stars*), actor Will Smith, comedian-actor Jim Carrey, socialite/heiress/reality TV star Paris

Hilton, child star Christopher Knight (*The Brady Bunch*), TV and radio host and commentator Glenn Beck, comedian-TV host Howie Mandel, political consultant and commentator James Carville, TV star Michelle Rodriquez (*Lost*), actor-director-writer Ryan Gosling, actor Woody Harrelson, actress Marriette Hartley, singer-performer Britney Spears, singer-producer Will.I.Am, and singer Solange Knowles (also little sister to Beyoncé).

ADHD-FRIENDLY OCCUPATIONS

> I am a 24-year-old woman who has only recently discovered my ADHD. The most frustrating part of ADHD for me is the inability to find the proper career path. It would seem to me that many physicians seem reluctant to provide any insight into careers that are antithetical to this disorder. It seems to me adults with ADHD need to have someone tell them, "Listen, there are certain careers you are going to find to be an uphill battle and it would be in your best interest NOT to pursue this." I have recently dropped out of medical school due to lack of interest, quit my job in retail sales due to lack of interest, and quit just about every job I've ever had due to lack of interest, as a matter of fact. Living in [my] mother's basement forever is not what I want for my life, yet here I am. I'm not sure why it took so long for me to be diagnosed. Nevertheless, in your expert opinion, what are some of the best and worst careers for untreated ADHD?

You can gather from the biographical profiles that adults with ADHD can be successful. Noteworthy, however, is that their success often comes in unorthodox ways and often out of a checkered history of school difficulties and sometimes brushes with the law. Implied as well is that there may be certain professions or occupations, many nontraditional, that may be more conducive to success for someone with ADHD. Those professions involve great latitude for people who are inattentive, overactive, impulsive, unconventional, and at times more emotional than others. I am certainly not saying here that ADHD comes with a gift for the various talents shown by these accomplished people, such as in music, acting, the performing arts, athletics and sports, or being an entrepreneur. Those talents would have existed in these people whether they had ADHD or not. But these are professions in which, if one is so blessed with such talent, one may be able to succeed despite having ADHD. Even then, getting treated for it may further facilitate one's success, as the cases illustrated. These successful people are also working in vocations in which high energy and creativity may even be assets. But that may only be so if coupled with the right personality traits, intelligence, and native talent for some activity or vocation. And even then only when supported by loved ones that surround and nurture them, as well as by encouraging friends and colleagues.

If you are concerned about a teen or young adult with ADHD who has yet to find the right calling, or an older person with ADHD thinking of a career change, you might think about the various occupations that do not place a premium on sitting still. Or suggest that your loved one try vocations that don't require concentration or focusing for long periods on tedious material or tasks. Those potentially successful pursuits should also not emphasize protracted inhibition of one's ideas, social isolation, or great emotional restraint and passivity. You would also not encourage them to try jobs that require being exceedingly quiet for long spans of time, engaging in repetitive and uninteresting activities over extended time periods, or planning out and executing highly complex plans over weeks and even years of time.

I am sure you can think of alternative occupational features to these that are more forgiving of ADHD traits. Start first with a consideration of what talents and aptitudes the individual demonstrates.

If you are not sure, encourage your loved one to get a vocational/occupational evaluation. Pay for it if you need to and can afford it. Combine those aptitudes with what you learned about the abilities that are more limited in ADHD in Chapters 1 and 2. Then think of vocations that celebrate the former while minimizing the latter abilities.

Here are some vocations that patients I have known and other ADHD experts have found to be more compatible with an adult's symptoms of ADHD:

- sales and marketing, retail sales;
- office receptionist;
- physical education teacher, athletics and sports, physical or occupational therapist, health club manager, or personal trainer;
- outdoor adventures and recreation, camp counselor;
- fisherman, merchant marine, shipping industry;
- fishing, hunting, trail or other outdoor guide;
- park ranger, police, or fire department, airport security;
- the military;
- the manual trades, such as carpentry, plumbing, electrical, masonry, roofing, landscaping, construction, mechanic, and so on, and self-employment in these trades;
- delivery truck or taxi/Uber driver (not long-haul or bus driver, unless on medication);
- auto or motorcycle repair and racing;
- cable TV installer or repairperson;
- photography and videography, or other jobs in the film/video industry;
- sports commentator or journalism;
- acting or theater, comedy, other performing arts, entertainer, poet, dancer, singer, musician, music producer, musical director, and so on, or teaching any of these;
- florist;

- hairstylist, barber, or beautician;
- technology-related jobs, such as computer/smartphone sales, graphic artist, technology help desk in a large business;
- video game tester (yes, they exist);
- the crisis occupations, such as emergency medical technician, emergency room nurse or physician, combat medic, and so on;
- elementary education teacher;
- the culinary arts (chef, baker, kitchen manager), food service (but write down all orders), bartender, or food distribution, cookbook author, restaurant critic;
- pilot, flight attendant, airline gate service agent; baggage handler, or mechanic;
- life coach to adults with ADHD;
- entrepreneur; and
- lawyer (trial or other active subspecialty).

KEY POINTS TO REMEMBER

Adult ADHD is not a gift. It does not confer any benefits, blessings, unusual talents, or superior traits. But its symptoms may interact with other talents or gifts of the individual, high intelligence, a supportive family or social environment, and special resources so as to not preclude people from being successful. In the right mix of these factors, ADHD might even contribute something to their success. One key to most success stories among adults with ADHD was that they had found an aptitude or talent in which they were quite good and in which they had a strong interest. A second key feature was that they had loved ones who believed in them and supported those talents or aptitudes, even if those talents were in rather unorthodox talents or fields. These parents or other loved ones did not place a dogmatic emphasis on traditional educational success. Instead, they emphasized

- being educated or knowledgeable, especially in one's areas of aptitude or talent, and learning by whatever means was most suitable to the child, teen, or adult with ADHD;
- opening doors to possible occupations or further training;
- obtaining access to unusual resources;
- identifying mentors and coaches, and other resources that could help facilitate further development of that person's aptitudes and talents; and
- helping them to organize more external structure, greater accountability, closer supervision, and other ways of creating substitute "frontal lobes" or "executive brains" so as to help compensate for the ADHD person's weaknesses in these areas, including time management.

There you have the formula for possible success:

aptitude + loved ones + support + encouragement + structure + unconventional channels of further development + a belief in and acceptance of the person with ADHD.

Can you think of ways in which you might be able to contribute some of these success factors in the life of your loved one with adult ADHD?

CHAPTER 8

THE IMPACT OF AN ADULT WITH ADHD ON YOU

As a loved one of an adult who has attention-deficit/hyperactivity disorder (ADHD), you are undoubtedly affected in multiple ways by being a part of their life. If you have very frequent interaction or a close relationship with that loved one—for example, as a parent, spouse or partner, sibling, or close friend—you have surely seen the effects the disorder can have on their day-to-day life activities. Here, I discuss the possible effects your loved one's ADHD may be having on you.

> My family is at a critical juncture now. Our daughter is 21 and still exhibiting a combination of ADHD symptoms and spoiling (having picked our battles—that was part of the fallout!). She is my heart. But then—my husband is my life, going on 29 years. He has had it! He's done. I'm not and feel a bit like King Solomon having to choose which son gets to live. I have offered to move out with our daughter—who's a sweetheart, btw [by the way]—and help her manage the disorder before bringing her back home. He truly has given the last inch he had to give.

LIFE DISRUPTIONS AND SACRIFICES

It is difficult if not impossible to have a loved one with ADHD who is experiencing one or more of the adverse consequences I discussed in earlier chapters without the life of someone else close to them (you) being disrupted in some way. The difficulties he may have had or is having in continuing his education may affect you as a parent, spouse, or partner because you want and need him to succeed in becoming a fully self-sustaining adult. Perhaps you are also paying part or all of his tuition and it angers you to see your hard-earned funds going down the drain because of his poor school performance, excessive partying, or other irresponsible behavior that prevents him from benefiting from his educational opportunities. Your loved one may even have dropped out of school and has few if any prospects for a good job as a result.

If you are a parent, your son or daughter with ADHD may even have had to move back in with you after failing at school or having quit or been fired from yet another job. Perhaps, as with my brother, important bills have come due or important consequences are imminent and simply cannot be ignored any further without posing serious harm to your loved one. And so you have been forced to intercede on their behalf, perhaps yet again, to ward off those consequences. Maybe you paid an important bill for them, like a much-delinquent car payment so their car is not repossessed. Or, as I did with my brother, you paid the child support payments to prevent them from being incarcerated. You may even have arranged for medical or dental care to manage some condition that has been allowed to fester and go untreated for far too long so that it can no longer be ignored. For instance, like my brother and later his own son, perhaps your loved one developed a tooth abscess so advanced from neglect that they are at risk of a blood infection or fatal heart disease. So you intervene, pay the dental or medical bills, and get them back on the road to recovery, at least from this crisis.

But there is more to this than just the financial disruption and drain on your own resources that a loved one's ADHD can cause. There is also the disruption of your time, life, work, and other major activities you must sustain as a self-supporting adult. There is the extra time needed to talk her through her latest crises, maybe to take her places she needs to be, to make amends with others she may have offended or harmed, or intercede with others such as her employers in hopes of getting your loved one yet another "second chance."

That time had to come from somewhere in your own life, and most likely, it was time already planned or even committed for doing something else of importance or value to you. So you had to cancel your own plans, sacrificing your own interests, to deal with issues related to your loved one. Perhaps these or other crises in the life of a loved one with ADHD led you to have to take time off of work, maybe even jeopardizing the status of your own job. Or you had to take time away from other family commitments so as to help your loved one deal with yet one more problem situation. Whatever it was you had to do, it necessitated that you alter your own plans at the time so as to help her deal with the latest crisis. Besides your time, maybe you even had to give up your much-needed sleep, perhaps over an extended time, to deal with her latest crisis. This can occur not only from being directly involved in her nighttime problems but also from your fear and worry about her present circumstances. All of this and other things you have had to do for her meant that you had to drop everything you had planned or needed to do and assist her with her latest problem.

Let's also not forget the disruption and sacrifices these problems and crises pose for your relationships with others. For instance, if you are a spouse or partner to someone with adult ADHD, his impulsive, emotional, and even reckless behavior may adversely affect the relations you have with mutual friends, with coworkers, with supervisors or employers, with neighbors, and with your children and extended family. You don't just pay a financial price or one involving your time when you have a loved one with adult ADHD. You may also pay a social price. Have you lost friends because of the ADHD symptoms, impulsive emotions, and related executive deficits of your loved one with ADHD? Have you had to deal with spouses, relatives, friends, neighbors, or even strangers so as to repair the social damage that may have occurred due to his ADHD, such as his impulsive offensive comments, excessive displays of emotion, failures to keep promises and repay loans, self-centered and domineering social interactions, and so on? Have you had to make sacrifices in your marriage, your relations with your children, and your social or occupational networks that stemmed from having to deal with his ADHD-related actions and their consequences?

I am not asking you to have a "pity party." I am not focusing here on life disruptions due to a loved one's adult ADHD to have you wallow in the sacrifices you have made; to discourage you from helping him further; or to encourage you to criticize, attack, or abandon him, but to acknowledge the greater-than-normal sacrifices you may have made on his behalf. I know those sacrifices. I have been where you are now. I do this to recognize that those disruptions occur and that your sacrifices likely have gone unheralded. And I also do it to validate any feelings you may be having related to them, such as being grossly underappreciated or even taken for granted for such sacrifices that go beyond the call of usual duty to a loved one. I will talk more about such feelings. Yet those feelings cannot be fully understood or appreciated if we don't acknowledge that ADHD in an adult loved one can bring far more disruptions, unexpected adversities, and sacrifices to our lives that deserve recognition, credit, and respect.

Yes, we all provide such assistance from time to time to people we care about, because that is part of what it means to care about someone. Such acts of kindness and assistance are considered to be a traditional part of human life because they are only occasional. We know as well that those we assist would likely do the same for us, which is also what it means when such concern for another is mutual. Relationships have reciprocity of sacrifice. But when this disruption of your life occurs repeatedly, far more often than is typical for such a close, mutually caring relationship, then it is not reciprocal. It is lopsided, and when what is being demanded is more than just routine assistance, well, it becomes a rather one-sided self-sacrifice. That can wear on you sometimes, straining or even breaking that close bond with the your loved one with ADHD.

In the case of adults with ADHD, the number of times you have had to assist them and the greater magnitude of that assistance relative to the few, if any, times they have come to your own aid can be very disproportionate. My guess is that even when they occasionally reciprocated, it was likely with far smaller acts of assistance. This disproportionate assistance provided by you can be so exceptionally lopsided that you experience not just a sense of disruption of your own life but also a gross sense of unfairness. You may even feel like you are being used—as if they are taking undue advantage of you. If so, it is not only unjust, but such repeated dependency on you to rescue them from their poor judgments seems highly self-centered on their part and greatly inconsiderate of your own life, needs, responsibilities, and resources. You may even have concluded that "enough is enough," only to find yourself being pulled back into yet another new crisis or fiasco of their own doing from which they cannot extricate themselves without your help. Perhaps you feel trapped on a train heading for self-destruction, tied to a boulder that is hurtling down an infinite trail of never-ending crises, or caught up in the strong magnetic field of a black hole of unending needs and unpredictable drama.

If you are a parent to a son or daughter with adult ADHD, you might feel trapped in your moral commitment to your child and forced to undergo the repeated disruption of your life by the adverse events she is experiencing. If you are a spouse or partner to an adult with ADHD, you likewise may feel bound by the promises you have made to her, perhaps even through your wedding vows. But you may feel that you didn't really "sign up" for all this disruption and sacrifice. The need for your repeated assistance with her problems and the frequent disruptions of your life that all that entails may greatly strain or even break up this relationship. After all, there is only so much you can be expected to commit or endure as her parent, spouse, lover, or friend. Disruptions of your life automatically create sacrifices you must make to stabilize the life of your loved one in some important way. But that can occur so often that you may believe there is no end in sight to the withdrawals being made from this emotional bank account.

I appreciate that you have helped a fellow human being whom you love. I want to also credit you with stepping up and making all those sacrifices. It means you are a person of good moral character. And I want you to know you are not alone in having made such sacrifices, as many of us with loved ones with adult ADHD have done the same, sometimes with little or no recognition.

GREATER STRESS

> My eldest son, James (now 21), has severe ADHD, along with a handful of comorbid disorders. Naturally this has been a bumpy road for all of us, but for no one more so than for my younger son, Tim (now 18). He is 3 years younger, and the chronic chaos of life in our house has been wearing on him for years. He is completely fed up. He is tired of the drama, tired of being a target for aggression, tired of not getting equal attention. He has been dealing with anxiety, fear, and general turmoil for a long time. I am afraid he will soon become depressed. I suffer chronic depression, and I know how devastating it can be. Tim is becoming aggressive and angry in response to his brother's problems and he has become an emotional "eater." He laments at having a brother who is "just plain crazy" and has asked me to please "lock his brother up so we can be normal." The anger and lashing out between them is getting much worse, and his relationship with his brother may never be repaired if something does not change. I just don't know where to go next.

It virtually goes without saying that when you are being repeatedly involved in the adversities that your loved one with ADHD is experiencing and the fallout it has on other family members, it is incredibly stressful. You are being called upon to deal with the unexpected adverse event due to a loved one with ADHD, often at the last minute or 11th hour, and far more often than do other typical people with their typical loved ones.

You can experience such stress not only from the constant disruptions but also from watching your loved one struggle with life's demands. We are upset, bothered, and otherwise troubled by witnessing adverse events that happen to others and especially to our loved ones. That is because, in some sense, we reexperience those stress events ourselves, vicariously. We feel these emotions even at a distance from the crisis of a loved one with ADHD in which we may not (yet) be directly involved. We understand what it is like to undergo those adverse events and experience, in a small way, some of the same feelings as the person who is undergoing that actual negative or harmful event. The witnessed suffering of others bothers us even if we are not a party to that harmful event. Such empathy, especially for a loved one, can lead to a form of secondary stress that can have its own ill effects on our emotional well-being and our lives.

So you are being exposed to more serious and repeated stress events, both primary (involved) and secondary (witnessed), than are others who don't have a loved one with adult ADHD. With everything that has been written in the mainstream media about the adverse effects of stress in our lives, I don't have to tell you that you are going to be prone to stress-related illnesses, emotional problems, and other adversities. I address how to prepare yourself for such stress in more detail in Chapter 16. Here, I simply want to acknowledge that being a loved one to an adult with ADHD can bring with it far more stress-inducing scenarios and can do so far more frequently than others are likely to experience. You will need to take extra precautions to reduce such stress. You need to make yourself more resilient to stress when it occurs and less likely to suffer its ill effects.

THE EMOTIONAL IMPACT WHEN A LOVED ONE HAS ADHD

Besides the sacrifices and the stress, having a loved one that has adult ADHD can lead to other emotional consequences. I discuss these next.

Initial Excitement or Fun

Sometimes, when you first come to know and love an adult with ADHD, such as through dating, the initial reaction can be one of temporary excitement, fun, or thrill. That's because the person you are getting to know is talkative; engaging; and full of activity, adventure, with a devil-may-care personality that, briefly, can seem interesting and even boldly refreshing. They are not held in check by the usual social anxieties others experience. She may even be more easily excited, emotionally expressive, funny, and quick with affection or charm. Here is a person who abandons routine caution to try adventurous things others would hesitate to do. She may even appear to be courageous, brave, or tough, given the risks she seems willing to take.

It can be initially exciting to be with someone with ADHD because of the thrill seeking in which he is willing to indulge, such as extreme sports, impulsive travel, risky hobbies, or just a life that is unpredictable—a real swashbuckling personality. This can be great for a few weeks or a few months. But if the relationship grows closer, you are spending more time together, and especially if you move in to live together, then look out. This once thrilling lifestyle of impulsive, adventurous action can quickly become one of unnecessary risk taking and gross irresponsibility. Underneath that childlike joie de vivre in ADHD is often an impulsive, distractible, and unpredictable nature that fails to contemplate or deal with much of the mundane but important aspects of daily life and its responsibilities. Yet left unaddressed, the mundane can become the next crisis. Consider such mundane things as keeping promises, holding a job, being on time, managing money and paying bills, running a household, raising or even monitoring children, maintaining your health, seeing to your personal safety, caring for others, and even following the law. These routine responsibilities hold no inherent excitement, adventure, or thrill. Yet if they are not attended to routinely, trouble is surely brewing.

Irritation

It is little wonder then that a common emotional effect of having a loved one with ADHD is irritation, annoyance, or even outright anger at being asked repeatedly to step in and help correct for the consequences of his continued misconduct and impulsive decisions. This is especially the case where those consequences were likely foreseeable by others (who don't have ADHD). You rightly ask about your loved one, "How could he have done such a thing?!" "What was he thinking?!" "What in the world is wrong with him that he could find himself in such a fix?!"

For instance, consider the following scenarios from the lives of former patients of mine, participants in our research studies, and my own family members.

- Your adult sister with ADHD has just called to ask you for money after telling you she has left her second husband (and children) to run off with a former high school sweetheart she just met at a her 10th high school class reunion last night because she knows this is truly her first and only love. How could any sane person who is married and has kids do such an impulsive and ridiculous thing, you ask.

- Your brother with ADHD is calling from jail because he was picked up by the police, yet again, this time for selling marijuana outside a nightclub. He desperately (of course) needs you to get him an attorney and post his bail. What on earth was he thinking when he did this, you wonder, especially because it is not his first offense of this type.
- Your partner with adult ADHD has come home early from work saying that she has just quit her job over yet another argument with her supervisor about her long breaks or consistent tardiness. Never did she consider that she has no other job prospects lined up or that bills need to be paid. You ask yourself, rightly, "How could she do such a thing again?"

These are true stories. Any of them sound familiar? Such repeated, immature, and impulsive decision making can initially make you irritated and even angry toward your loved one. Yet your emotional reactions, reasoning, arguments, and even threats seem to change nothing in their behavior in the long run. You know that without some major change, these types of things are going to happen again—it's just a matter of time.

Frustration

You may also have experienced incredible frustration because, once again, the things you try to do, that typical people would try to do, to help your loved one learn not to do such things don't seem to be working toward that end. You find yourself frequently on the hook for the assistance they will need to extricate themselves from yet one more immature, irresponsible, or impulsive action that other adults of their age would simply know not to have done. When things we try to do to improve a situation fail, we experience incredible frustration (and anger). Because an adult's untreated ADHD is not simply cured by its consequences or by your frustration about them, their impulsive actions continue unabated. You want to scream at them, "Just grow up!" "Wake up and smell the coffee!" "Act like an adult!" and tell them to stop this chronically poor decision-making—but it does little or no good. Until your loved one is evaluated, diagnosed, and properly treated, little improvement is likely to be evident.

Humiliation and Shame

Although less common, let us not overlook a few other emotions that can occasionally occur when dealing with an adult with ADHD: social embarrassment, humiliation, or shame. This is especially the case if you are a close family member, such as a parent, spouse, or even adult child, of someone with ADHD. Your loved one is periodically acting in ways that embarrass you in social situations or rise to the level of humiliation because of her impulsive comments or behavior, risk taking, poor organization and time management, or poor emotional regulation. You are at times frankly ashamed of how she has behaved, especially in front of others when you were present (or even if you weren't but learn of it later). Perhaps in anger she threw a drink in someone's face at a bar when you were both out enjoying a night on the town and she got in an argument with someone. Maybe she got drunk at a dinner party and sexually groped the husband of your neighbor or close friend. Perhaps she "sexted" a far-too-revealing selfie to mere acquaintances, who were offended by this gesture of excessive intimacy and called you about it. Worse yet, maybe she left her toddler poorly monitored, resulting in the child's wandering off in a mall while she shopped for new clothes.

Or maybe you own your own business, and after giving your adult child or partner with ADHD a job because he had so much trouble holding down a job with others, you find that he has been embezzling funds from your petty cash. Or maybe you started hearing complaints that he was wasting time flirting with an attractive manager or was repeatedly failing to show up to do his job as part of a team and hence greatly burdening your other employees to finish that job on time. I could go on endlessly with actual examples from clinical practice or my own family. But the bottom line in all of these situations was the experience of embarrassment and humiliation arising from the poor judgment and inexcusable or just immature conduct of a loved one with ADHD in an important social context.

Discouragement

Eventually, there is just so much irritation, frustration, anger, or humiliation one can tolerate from the repeated impulsive or irresponsible actions of a loved one with ADHD until discouragement and demoralization set in. Try as you might, the emotional hits just keep on coming. Nothing you do to help seems to accomplish much beyond temporarily resolving the immediate crisis, only to have yet another problem, issue, or crisis arise. The crises come: frequent, unbidden, and unexpected. When people are exposed repeatedly to adverse events on which their actions seem to have had no effect, the emotions they often feel are discouragement, demoralization, helplessness, and even depression. They may also experience a grief reaction over all of the losses that can mount up in the life of a loved one with adult ADHD—all the opportunities squandered, potential successes missed, and other accomplishments they should have had given their talents, abilities, intelligence, and other qualities. We grieve what might have been for them had they not had adult ADHD. And we may even grieve over our own disruptions and sacrifices that had to be made in support of a loved one with adult ADHD. This is especially so when what we have done did not seem to change the larger course of our loved one's life or even keep them alive. I know those feelings personally. They hurt.

Some people who have loved ones with adult ADHD experience a state called "learned helplessness": They become emotionally numb and no longer try to ward off the chronic problems of their loved one or intercede to resolve the crisis. They can no longer emotionally afford to care or try. And so they stop doing so. Like an emotional punching bag, they get hit with the various adverse events of their loved one or with the impulsive emotions or even abuse from their loved one. They simply take it, without much of a reaction other than the appearance of being stunned or numb. Usually this happens when the relationship cannot be easily terminated, such as between a parent and their adult child with ADHD or vice versa. Or it can occur when a spouse or partner feels trapped in a marriage by economic circumstances or shared children. You simply can't walk out on your loved one as others could do. Abandonment or estrangement from them is not an option. Without an obvious escape from such adverse consequences, people become numb and succumb to a state of learned helplessness. They soldier on but have no further reactions and take no further steps to ward off the next problem, crisis, or emotional assault. This reaction is not common, because it is a very advanced stage of discouragement that arises from lack of any escape from repeated adversity. But it can and does happen. I hope you have not found yourself in this same situation of learned helplessness. You may not realize it, but there are very few circumstances in which you have no choices, including the ones I have detailed here.

Guilt

Of course, no survey of the emotional impact of having a loved one with ADHD would be complete if I did not mention guilt as a rather common reaction that you may have. This can be especially likely if you are a parent to an adult child who has ADHD. Society has a deep and profound belief that nearly goes without question that misbehavior, especially in children, is largely a result of poor parenting. By *bad parenting*, people often mean *bad mothering*, but both parents may bear some of society's condemnation for allowing a child to express such misbehavior. Our culture believes that self-regulation is largely learned and that the bulk of that learning comes from the manner in which our parents raised us. And so if children or adults display a lack of self-control, the immediate knee-jerk conclusion by others is that it is the result of a lousy upbringing by that person's parents. You may be as prone to such thinking as are others in society. If so, then you undoubtedly have felt the frequent pangs of guilt that can accompany raising a child with ADHD to adulthood. And you bear that guilt throughout their adult years whenever your adult offspring behaves in inappropriate, impulsive, or irresponsible ways. You may blame yourself as much or more than society may be blaming you, even if no one directly accuses you of creating this problem.

When our adult children behave badly, it reflects on us, even if it shouldn't, and we bear that social reflection as parental guilt. We somehow failed to do our job of socializing our children to be responsible, civil, well-behaved adults. And we often wonder what we could or should have done differently to prevent this outcome. Although the answer to that self-questioning is "nothing," given what you learned in earlier chapters about the neurodevelopmental basis of ADHD, you may not have known that until now. So you have years of self-blame and guilt that you have had to bear for believing that in some important way you failed to raise this person properly and it has left them engaging in behaviors that show poor self-control. Hopefully this book will help you to expunge such feelings of guilt from your current life even if it cannot erase those past years of having felt this way. Your parenting, alone, cannot and did not cause your adult child to have ADHD and the related deficits in their self-regulation.

Estrangement

A not uncommon emotional outcome for those of us with loved ones who have adult ADHD can be periodic estrangement from, or abandonment of, them either by your choice or theirs. Because of the stress, disruption, repeated sacrifice, irritation, or anger you may have experienced for so long with your loved one, you may have decided that it is for your own best interests that you withdraw contact from him for a while. You want some peace and tranquility, a chance to renew your own life and sense of well-being or satisfaction. So you decide it is for the best if you don't contact your loved one for a time. This is especially likely if that loved one denied his disorder, resisted getting treatment, or ceased adhering to such treatment. For some years, this is exactly how I dealt with my brother: I withdrew from him and he from me.

Any and all assistance you provide to others is always by your choice. You may have reached a point where you feel it best for your own sake to become estranged from your loved one with ADHD for a while. This can be a brief cooling off period after some major confrontation with her over a problem in her life she is failing to address. This cooling-off spell might last a few weeks, or it may even extend to several years or more.

You shouldn't feel that something is morally wrong with this separation period. It is not an admission of failure when you elect to restrict or terminate contact with a loved one with ADHD for a time while you get your own life in order, get back your emotional balance, and attend to your own well-being and longer term welfare. No one is asking you to martyr yourself for the sake of a loved one with adult ADHD. In fact, doing so can backfire, leaving you less of a quality resource for them. That is because you are so emotionally, financially, medically, and otherwise compromised from your chronic martyrdom. In short, taking a break from each other can be good for both of you.

This estrangement, even if temporary, can also occur because the loved one with ADHD withdraws from you or because such an estrangement is mutually chosen. My own twin brother and I had very little to do with each other for some years in the middle of our lives. From my perspective, this was largely because I was now busy with a career, my marriage, and my children, as well as increasingly assisting our aging parents when needed. But I also felt he was making repeated mistakes, as well as seriously wrong life choices. He also held values I simply could not countenance: Such things as leaving his wife and children for a new girlfriend, continuing to forgo other employment to pursue small-time opportunities to play in rock bands while not supporting his children, continuing to engage in drug use, and denying that any of this and other problems were of his own doing. He seemed to see his problems as being due to overly critical or demanding wives; or to an unsympathetic or hostile father; or to hostile and selfish employers; or to "friends" who reneged on their apparent promises of money, housing, transportation, or other allegiances they owed to him as he saw it.

From his perspective, this estrangement arose because we had few shared values, I was living far away from him, he likely saw me as a workaholic in my career and as having a "materialistic" lifestyle, and I was obvious in showing my dislike of his own lifestyle choices. There was also my refusal to keep giving him money or bailing him out of legal difficulties whenever he called. We both needed some space from each other to pursue our own desires and choices. And I needed to be free of his periodic crises and need for financial help when these arose.

As you may know from your own experience, it is difficult to maintain a relationship with a loved one who has adult ADHD when the only time they contact you is when they are in trouble and need your help. Otherwise, they make no efforts to participate in the social glue that binds families together—the occasional visits, family reunions, joint holiday rituals, births of new children, assistance with the care of aging parents, periodic expressions of interest in the well-being or life course of each other, and the usual signs of interest in others that holds extended families together. This leaves one with a sense that the relationship is just one-sided self-interest rather than mutual care and reciprocity.

Emotional Devastation

There is another negative emotional impact that can arise on rare occasions from having a loved one with adult ADHD. I know it firsthand, and I pray you never experience it. Yet failing to acknowledge it here, infrequent as it may be, would be a major oversight for a book aimed at all those adults who have loved ones with adult ADHD. It is that rare but extreme emotional impact known as devastation. I felt it when I got that call from my brother-in-law telling me that my brother was killed in that car accident. And again when his adult son, who also had ADHD, committed suicide 7 years later. And I know from clinical practice that other family members of adults with ADHD have had the same experience. One family being seen by a close professional colleague of mine wrote to him a few years ago to tell their own story of tragedy and accompanying emotional devastation concerning their own adult son with ADHD. I share it with you in A Story of Emotional Devastation, with their permission but with all identifying information stripped away.

When severe consequences befall our loved ones with adult ADHD, for a moment the bottom seems to fall out of our world. We are so stunned that we feel we are suspended in time in our disbelief that this tragedy simply cannot have happened. We are so blind-sided by reality that for a brief time we cannot process the event itself, much less its far-flung and serious implications and consequences. Grieving surely follows this, as night follows day, but for

A Story of Emotional Devastation

Allan[1] was a young adult with severe ADHD who had left home but returned periodically to live with his parents because he simply had trouble functioning on his own. Yet upon his return, he would wreak havoc on his parents and their household. And so he was encouraged to leave yet again lest he destroy what family they had left by his misconduct and its serious consequences.

Allan had a history of drug use, including alcohol; risky driving; highly impulsive and poorly self-regulated behavior; and poor emotional regulation. All this came to a tragic event when one evening when he was driving with his girlfriend and her aunt in his car on the way to get his children from a babysitter. He was involved in a terrible car accident that left him and his girlfriend in the hospital with multiple broken bones. But the aunt stopped breathing from her injuries and had to be airlifted to a nearby trauma center because of her severe condition. She eventually succumbed to her injuries. Allan's blood alcohol level was multiple times the legal limit. He was sentenced to many years in prison for vehicular homicide. The only fortunate aspect of this story is that his children were not in the car at the time. This tragedy came after years of hard work by Allan's parents to try and launch their son into independent and responsible adulthood. Allan's mother described the emotional devastation she felt by saying it was as if "we [she and her husband] had been hit by the car."

[1]Not his real name.

that moment in time the term *devastation* applies—the landscape of our normal emotions and life has been wiped away. Our sense of some permanence in life has been annihilated by this unexpected tragedy. May this emotional impact of having a loved one with adult ADHD never enter your life. But you need to know that it can happen and has happened for others of us who have been trying to help such an adult loved one.

Satisfaction and Happiness

> We were so lucky to find a neuropsychologist who believes in ADHD and diagnosed our daughter, who was 20 at the time. She has all of the symptoms and they really interfere with her college work. She always had to work harder than the others in school just to keep up. She said she had to reread things two and three times because her mind wandered. She said no matter how hard she tried to stay focused on schoolwork or in class, her mind wandered. When she was younger and in elementary school, the school's answer was to put her in the slower classes. We knew our child was smart even though she didn't test well and struggled. Recently, after a full round of testing, our neuropsychologist identified it as ADHD. She felt ADHD medication would help her considerably.
>
> We brought the report and our neuropsychologist's findings to a psychiatrist, who prescribed the medication for our daughter. The response was immediate, and she found herself performing at an extremely high level in her college classes. It made a profound difference in her life. Not only now does she feel she is smart and belongs in the advanced honors level classes, it has increased her self confidence in all aspects of her life. She went from wondering if she could be college material at all to having a successful year at a very good college. She is a different person now.

Let me end this section with an antidote to this narrative on negative emotional consequences. It is the one I wish for you. It is to acknowledge that not all of the emotional impact of having a loved one with adult ADHD is negative. Apart from the thrill or excitement noted earlier that comes from first initially getting to know someone with ADHD, as in dating, other positive noteworthy reactions are the more noble and life-sustaining emotional reactions one experiences when a loved one with ADHD finds success, fulfillment, effectiveness, or happiness and even joy in their own life, often as a consequence of treatment and, with it, your constructive support of them. Because of your empathy, you may also experience this sense of happiness, joy, pride, and the shared celebration of their accomplishments one experiences when loved ones close to us overcome their ADHD-related problems and find success and happiness.

But the experience of satisfaction you feel for them is not just second hand—there is also a direct sense of accomplishment, pride, and success when you have played an active part in their improvement or otherwise helped them to overcome the obstacles that ADHD had placed in their life's path. After all, had it not been for your emotional, social, financial, and other assistance, their current success or positive adjustment might not have been possible or achieved to the degree it has.

When you are an active part of the successful treatment of a loved one with ADHD, you have every reason to share in a sense of accomplishment and satisfaction. Remember the success stories I discussed in the previous chapter? You saw there how a combination of the support of a loved one, helping them find a life's calling or other talent at which they excelled, getting treatment for their ADHD, and seeking out opportunities and resources in nontraditional careers can all result in not just a good, but even a great, outcome. The parents, siblings, and other loved ones in those cases actively assisted the children and young adults with ADHD in their endeavors to overcome the obstacles posed by their disorder. They helped their loved ones find the right niches in which they could not just succeed but excel. All of those who help the adult with ADHD to succeed deserve to take a bow. They also deserve to find a sense of satisfaction, of accomplishment, and of joy and pride in how well that young adult with ADHD has turned out. Bless them for doing all that they did to help.

DOES HELPING ADULTS WITH ADHD ENABLE THEIR BAD CHOICES?

You no doubt realize on some level that the disruption, dependency, and sacrifice that you may have experienced by being involved in the life of a loved one with adult ADHD seem different from the assistance people routinely provide to their loved ones with severe physical, mental, or developmental disabilities. Those people often feel far less put upon than you may have. That is because the need of their loved ones is obvious and serious—their loved one may not even survive without their help. But it is also mitigated by the fact that such disabilities are not just physically obvious to all but typically not of that loved one's doing. They are more like "acts of God" or accidents of nature visited upon the loved one by fate and so were unavoidable.

Yet when dealing with an adult loved one with ADHD whose executive disabilities are not physically apparent, it is far harder to feel that way. That is because an adult with ADHD does not manifest any signs of such disabilities that might make it obvious to all why he routinely needs our assistance. His disability is not in his physical status or appearance but in his behavior. It is also because the adversities he is experiencing seem far more likely to be of his own doing, stemming from his own impulsive, ill-considered choices or frank recklessness that do not have the character of mere random fate.

It can seem to you and to others that your loved one continues to bring repeated adversity onto herself by how she acts (her ADHD symptoms and executive deficits). Many of the delayed consequences she experienced are foreseen by others as being the likely consequences for acting that way. No wonder that people may begin to feel that the loved one with ADHD deserves what she gets. With choice comes responsibility—an ownership of the consequences of our decisions and actions. And so we get the haunting feeling that the loved one with adult ADHD is somehow responsible for all that is happening to her. That hardly brings out the understanding and even empathy of others toward our loved one who is disabled by adult ADHD.

This may lead you (and others) to wonder whether you are not actually enabling or contributing to a continuation of your loved one's problems by repeatedly heading off, reducing, or minimizing the adversities he may experience from the way he is behaving. This push and pull between conflicted feelings is common among people who have loved ones with ADHD. That loved one is in an immediate crisis or has a pressing problem with which he wants or needs your help. Yet it is often a crisis he brought upon himself by his ill-considered actions or omissions. You may wonder whether he is ever going to learn not to behave this way if you keep interceding between him and the consequences of his behavior.

You may even consider using the "tough love" approach to dealing with lazy or irresponsible young people. It essentially involves turning them out of your house and life, with no support. I do not advocate this approach; it is abandonment. It is recommended by some professionals in the erroneous belief that when the hard knocks of his lifestyle do happen, he will change for the better, learning from life's natural consequences. You may experience a nagging sense that by not using tough love you are enabling his life of self-destructiveness.

The answer here is, no, you are not. Unless you are actively encouraging him to stay home and play video games all day instead of seeking education or employment, you are not an enabler. Short of giving him money for drugs or otherwise directly encouraging his irresponsibility, avoidance of adult responsibility, or even outright misconduct, you are not helping to sustain his difficulties with his life by your periodic constructive assistance.

Yes, most of us learn from consequences—we learn that current actions often have immediate consequences. When you put your finger into a flame, it gets burned and you learn not to repeat the action. So do adults with ADHD. That is called Skinnerian, or operant, learning and all creatures with nervous systems possess that sort of learning by consequences. So does your loved one. Those are not the sorts of actions that are leading your loved one into trouble and for which you are being asked to assist them.

The learning that is not working so well with your loved one is a type of learning that takes place in the executive brain. It is related to how current actions have delayed and unintended consequences that are not immediate or obvious at the moment but could be foreseen as being the likely delayed consequences of those actions with just a moment's reflection before acting. The problem here involves your loved one's not recognizing the delayed, and hence the unseen, outcomes of one's actions. It is this special type of learning from delayed consequences that is involved in ADHD. It is learning across time and through the executive brain that we connect the now with the later, binding those events in our memory despite the time lag between them. It leads us to try to not make that mistake again and so avoid those future consequences again.

Notice here the time gap between behavior now and consequences later. This understanding that our actions have not just immediate but also delayed consequences is the basis of ethics and morality. It enables one to foresee delayed events and hence to be concerned about the long-term consequences of our actions for ourselves and for others. It enables us to act in opposition to the desires of the now in favor of our welfare later. The executive brain lets us defer immediate gratification and pursue larger but later consequences that will prove more rewarding to us than will giving in to immediate interests and gratifications.

Such human foresight is also the basis for social skills and cooperation, which are predicated on understanding that although we may have immediate conflicts with others concerning all of our self-interests, over the longer term our self-interests will converge if we act civilly toward each other. By subordinating our immediate self-interest, all of us can benefit in the longer term and live in a more peaceful and cooperative society. When we cooperate with others, we usually are sacrificing something of our own now (labor, resources) as do those others with whom we are cooperating so that all of us acting in unison gain a greater benefit later. People with ADHD have a more difficult time stopping to consider the later consequences of what they are doing. Their deficits in inhibition, self-reflection, and foresight prevent them from giving as much consideration as do others to the likely later consequences of what they are thinking or doing. It can leave the impression that they are not only impulsive and thus irrational (they don't stop and think as often as others) but also immoral (they fail to consider the consequences of their actions for others).

It is easy to see then how others who don't understand adult ADHD may come to see that adult's behavioral problems as a moral failing—a flaw in their personality and judgment for which they should be soundly condemned. The source of this moral failing is thought to reside in that person's willpower—they are choosing to behave this way. Thus, they are seen as selfish and greedy. Or they are judged as defective in their upbringing, in which case we blame not only them but also their parents. Either way, the adult with ADHD is judged to be immoral by those who do not understand the causes of ADHD. But those who make such judgments are dead wrong.

This type of learning across time requires the prefrontal lobes or the executive brain, the region from which ADHD arises. This is why adults with ADHD have serious deficits in their executive functioning. The important consequences in life are often those that are delayed, and the adult with ADHD is less able to consider them before acting. If the brain of an adult with ADHD cannot link the now with the later as well as others can, then they are prone to committing and even repeating those mistakes that often lead to such delayed adverse consequences.

Your loved one with ADHD has a neurological problem that reduces their capacity to link the now with the later—to easily and quickly foresee that current choices have later consequences, that immediate situations link up with distant outcomes. As I said before, they are time blind, or more precisely, nearsighted to the future. Consequently, they have more frequent problems than others who possess a typical brain. Typical people would have foreseen those outcomes and thus would not have engaged in that behavior. All of this means that adults with ADHD do not have a moral failing arising by choice or upbringing but a neurological condition over which they have no influence. Although they often receive it, adults with ADHD do not deserve the moral denigration that is usually heaped upon them when they act without regard for their own future welfare and that of others.

If a person survived a car accident in which most of his frontal lobes (executive brain) were destroyed and he subsequently acted in more irresponsible and immoral ways, we would not judge him so harshly. We would understand the neurological basis of his change in behavior, and instead, we would have sympathy and compassion. We would want to see that he was given the medical and psychiatric help he required to compensate for this injury. We would also strive to protect him from the consequences of his own actions. So, if someone with ADHD acts the same way for precisely the same reason (malfunctioning frontal lobes), shouldn't we take the same perspective about his conduct? I think so, but with the caveat I discuss next.

How a Wife Decided to Cut Ties—But Not All of Them

I work as a counselor for a small college in Oregon. My husband is from Brazil and has been in this country for 5 years. We have mutual friends, including some who share his cultural background, but for the 2 years I knew this man before marrying him, I learned virtually nothing about him that would have prepared me for actually living with him. A cultural feature of rural Brazil, where he's from, is that no one talks about anything that might be perceived as "crazy" or mentally deficient. What I've learned from being married to this man is that he has no ability to regulate his emotions. I wish our friends had clued me in to this somehow—even if they didn't know the right words for it.

I could see that my husband was beloved by his family. They chose to let me know after we married, however, that they were very grateful he had me because "he is special." That is, he had a very serious problem.

I had already begun to lose sleep because of his rants that seemed to blow up out of nowhere. I soon learned that his ex-wife was planning to sue for more child support because she misconstrued that I was rich. She bombarded him with text after text, after which he'd explode into a tantrum, eventually tiring himself out so he could not go to work.

After supporting us solely with my income for the better part of a year, I realized I was becoming consumed by my husband's behaviors. We weren't able to work through his ex-wife's demands in a meaningful way because his temper and lack of organization constantly undermined any plans or strategies we made.

When we went to a psychiatrist for help, the psychiatrist explained that people with ADHD sometimes miss their appointments because they forget or they don't really want treatment. The plan for keeping my husband in treatment was for the doctor to write 1-month prescriptions. My employer health care plan subsidizes only medications that are prescribed in 3-month blocks, so we had to pay $300 a month, cash, for the medicine. The doctor was fully aware of the financial burden his so-called tough love placed on us.

Though I was running out of money, I bought my husband an airline ticket to visit family and made an appointment for him to see an ADHD

How a Wife Decided to Cut Ties—But Not All of Them (*Continued*)

specialist in Rio de Janeiro. Without telling him, I then broke our home lease agreement and put our belongings in storage. Through a friend, I found a room to rent so I could have peaceful evenings, regular sleeping hours, normal talking and planning, and freedom from cleaning the endless messes. I devoted myself to supporting my husband in Brazil and paying off our bills.

He was upset when he realized that my plan involved him staying in Brazil for an indeterminate time, but he also understands that $100 here is worth $1,200 there. Because our life together was so chaotic, my friends and family told me to leave him. They said I should not continue supporting him. I haven't made up my mind yet to do that. I think if I'd left him abruptly he might have tried to commit "suicide by cop." I'm glad I decided to call on his support system in Brazil as a first step.

ADULT ADHD IS AN EXPLANATION—NOT AN EXCUSE

From the neurological perspective I have noted here, the adult with ADHD is similar to the adult with more obvious and more serious physical disabilities whose loved ones don't question the care and assistance she requires. Adults with ADHD also need the help of loved ones for dealing with their ADHD and its adverse consequences. As I have said, your assistance is not enabling a problem that would otherwise diminish or disappear if your loved one with ADHD would be permitted to experience all the hard knocks of life her conduct may be precipitating. Your help is no more enabling her misbehavior than the nursing care a parent provides to an adult child with severe cerebral palsy or mental retardation is enabling her physical incapacities or intellectual disability. Any help you provide is no more enabling than the help being provided to another adult who has a clear-cut injury to her frontal lobes. And so, to help an adult with ADHD, the solution here is not to withdraw your support to her. By your not stepping in and providing assistance, her disability will surely continue and her life circumstances may be considerably worse.

OK, so you accept that your assistance to your loved one with ADHD doesn't encourage his problems. But it doesn't necessarily help to improve them either. There is an important difference here between the assistance we provide to our loved ones with physical disabilities and brain damage and that which we provide to adults with ADHD. Notice that the problem the adult with ADHD is having is with the time lag to the later consequence. This deficit in time binding is not the disability in those who have physical handicaps, but it is in adult ADHD. The solution to the ADHD adult's disability is therefore not to excuse what he does wrong or minimize its consequences, delayed or otherwise. Instead, the solution is to tighten up accountability for their actions.

The key here is to understand that the time lag to those consequences is the problem and to try to reduce or eliminate it when you can. That means injecting more immediate accountability and more immediate consequences, even artificial ones, into the life of your loved one with ADHD, not giving up on accountability altogether. So, yes, provide assistance to her as we would to any loved one who is physically disabled. But then go further and couple that assistance with an insistence where possible or feasible that greater accountability be arranged in the future for her actions in that domain of life. Add that extra scaffolding, situational structure, supervision and accountability, and other artificial consequences that I discuss in more detail later in this book (Chapters 11–18). It is the concept that is important here, not (yet) the details of how to do it.

Accepting your assistance means she is agreeing to greater accountability to others, more frequent and immediate consequences, and more participation in ADHD treatment programs so as to reduce the chances that this adverse outcome will happen again. Your help should not be unconditional—it comes with a price. That price is the submission of your loved one to greater and more immediate accountability in that problem domain when and wherever it may be feasible to do so. It also means your loved one must participate in constructive solutions to her problems and not just attempt to minimize their consequences. Your offers of help should be not just reactive, as when a crisis occurs and you protect her from the harm her actions have caused. It must also be proactive, as when you encourage her to get extra vocational training or education, assist with its expense, or get her into a treatment program. You are also being proactive when you help financially with her transition to independence, you more closely monitor her adherence to such treatments, and you open other doors for her to improve upon her life.

HOW WE COPED WITH MY BROTHER

In my family's case, my brother, Ron, was eventually arrested for sleeping in his van on a public beach after his second wife kicked him out of their house for lack of sustained work and financial support, as well as his drug use. This, finally, got him to go into treatment, albeit court-ordered. It now became clear to my wife and me that the consequences of his years of drug use, crime, numerous but short-lived jobs, abandonment of his wives and children, homelessness, and social rejection by mainstream adults had left him penniless and in need of ongoing support and assistance. Such assistance spanned numerous needs—medical, dental, financial, and psychiatric. If they were not met, it seemed likely that he would become homeless or even die.

My wife and I then renewed a relationship with Ron. We arranged for him to live in an upstairs apartment in the same house as my mother, which we owned and maintained. We then assisted with his urgent medical and dental care. And we provided periodic financial assistance for his daily sustenance. We did all this with the same perspective one must have in helping to care for an aging physically disabled or seriously mentally ill sibling—one of forgiveness and compassion, not one of enabling bad choices. We simply could not live with what fate might otherwise have had in store for him or what tragedies might befall him if we didn't provide some help to him.

Periodic problems still arose because of his risky driving, alcohol use, poor management of his limited finances, and occasionally bad choices in friends. But these were of a lesser magnitude than the alternative as I saw it. That alternative was homelessness and likely malnutrition or even death if we did not become his safety net. I came to appreciate that we now had much more contact with each other by phone and in person, shared participation in family reunions, and other good times. There was also the satisfaction I felt from his jointly helping me look after our aging mother, each in our own way. Despite all the problems, I now had my twin brother back in my life, and that meant something important to me. All this ended in his death in that freak, one-car, low-speed accident when we were both 56 years old. Even though his life had a tragic ending, my wife and I like to think that he had a far better quality of life during his final years when we renewed our relationship with him than he might have otherwise have had if we had continued our estrangement from him. And we got to know and even assist his children (now young adults), whom we had not seen since they were babies and who had become estranged from him as well.

KEY POINTS TO REMEMBER

As someone who has a loved one with adult ADHD, to the extent that you are involved in their life, you are likely to also experience the emotional impact of their ADHD in various ways. Many people with such loved ones have told my colleagues and me of the various effects their loved one's ADHD and poor self-regulation have had on their own life. This includes the disruptions to their own lives caused by the problems, issues, and crises that can frequently happen to an adult with ADHD in which loved ones like you can be swept up in their wake. These disruptions can be felt in your own family life, your work, your sleep, and even your own social life. Helping the adult with ADHD to cope with their problems and crises can also lead you to make various sacrifices beyond the disruptions noted, including financial ones to help lessen or mitigate the adverse consequences of those crises.

Moreover, there are the numerous emotional impacts that a loved one's adult ADHD can have on others, such as her parents, spouses, partners, siblings, and even close friends. Among these are added stress, irritation, anger, embarrassment, humiliation, shame, discouragement, demoralization, depression, guilt, learned helplessness, and on rare occasions sheer devastation as a consequence of the tragedies that may befall your loved one. On the upside, there is also the spontaneity, excitement, thrill, fun, humor, and adventure that comes from loving someone with adult ADHD, at least when you are initially introduced to their talkative, engaging, sensation-seeking, devil-may-care, and impulsive lifestyle. Of course, this is great fun for short periods, as if on vacation, but it can be a poor way to deal with life's mundane but important responsibilities. It also may eventually lead you to have the negative emotional consequences noted. Doing it "your way," like an adult with ADHD, is a great lyric for a Frank Sinatra song but no way to lead a mature life. A good life means that you fulfill your promises, commitments and other responsibilities while seeing to your (and others') long-term welfare. Yet when your loved one with ADHD profits from your assistance, gets effective treatment, finds a life-calling in which they can excel, and overcomes the early obstacles created by their adult ADHD, you can also experience joy, happiness, pride, and a sense of accomplishment for your loved one with ADHD and for yourself.

II

WHAT YOU CAN DO TO HELP

CHAPTER 9

HOW TO TALK WITH A LOVED ONE ABOUT GETTING PROFESSIONAL HELP

If you have read this far, you probably have a good idea about whether your loved one has adult attention-deficit/hyperactivity disorder (ADHD). If so, and she has already received a professional evaluation, been diagnosed with ADHD, is receiving treatment for it, and is cooperating with such treatment, then you may wish to skip this chapter. You are way ahead of the game. But if you think a loved one has adult ADHD and has not already been diagnosed and receiving professional assistance for its management, then take time to read this chapter. Before you launch into helping him find a professional to get an evaluation of his possible ADHD, it may be necessary for you to review your concerns with him. In that case, the next step is discussing ADHD with him so as to encourage him to seek such professional help. How should you broach the subject? Carefully, sensitively, and diplomatically, of course.

This brings us to the topic of a very important concept in clinical psychology: a person's *readiness to change*.[1] This concept comes out of the recognition that not all people are at the same stage of being willing to acknowledge their problems, learn about them,

[1]This idea was first developed by psychologists James Prochaska, PhD, and Carlo DiClemente, PhD.

get help for them, and hence change how they are functioning. The theory sees a person's readiness to change as falling along a spectrum or dimension. That dimension reflects the person's degree of openness to information about a problem she has and her willingness or motivation to do something about it—that is, how ready and willing she is to change. At one end of the spectrum, the *precontemplative stage*, the person does not even realize she has any problem (and so would not be ready to change); at the other end, the *maintenance stage*, the person is changing or has changed and is striving to maintain the change in her behavior. At this latter stage, she has already acknowledged the problem, gotten professional help for it, and is doing what she can to remain in treatment if that is needed to continue dealing with her problems.

Between these two stages are three others. You will be more likely to succeed in encouraging him to get help if you already have some sense of where he is along this spectrum of readiness to change. You should only try to help him move from one phase to the next, as needed, to make it more likely that he eventually gets professional help for his problems. You may be ready for him to change, but he may be at a very different stage where he is not yet prepared to take action for his problems (get professional help) or even acknowledge that he has a problem. Think for a moment about your loved one, and then consider which of the following stages he may be in. In each phase, I also present some suggestions for how you can approach him about his problems so as to, hopefully, get him to the next stage.

DENYING OR NOT ACKNOWLEDGING THE PROBLEM: THE PRECONTEMPLATION STAGE

Some adults who have ADHD not only do not know they have it but also are completely oblivious to the fact that they are having problems due to it. Thus, they are hardly prepared to act on their problems or get professional help. They are not even thinking about their problems as such or about doing anything to change them. If this is the case with your loved one, then you are going to need to be thoughtful, careful, and diplomatic in even bringing the problems to their attention. In that case, see if you can find a time to talk with them privately about your concerns when both of you are reasonably calm.

Where to Start

Before having this talk, make up three lists.

1. *Family history.* The first list should be of any relatives of your loved one you can recall who may have had problems with or diagnosed as having ADHD (or related disorders, e.g., learning disabilities, bipolar disorder, substance abuse). This assumes you are genetically related to this loved one and share a common family lineage in some way. If not, as a spouse or partner, you may know something about the extended family of your loved one that can be useful here. You are going to use this list to show your loved one that (a) he is not alone in experiencing difficulties in dealing with life and that other family members had similar struggles and (b) his problems may well have some genetic basis to them, which is another way of saying he is not entirely at fault.
2. *Adverse consequences.* The second list should be of what you perceive to be the adverse consequences your loved one seems to be experiencing as a result of her ADHD—her impairments. Go back through the earlier chapters here on the adverse effects of adult ADHD on major life activities. List those domains in which you feel your loved one is having problems. Under each domain, note what the specific

problems or consequences in these areas have been for her. List those she may already have mentioned previously but also others you think may be problems but that she has not commented on with you. The domains to consider include intimate, marital, or cohabiting relationships; educational problems; occupational difficulties; trouble with friends or socially with others; money management, bills, and credit problems; difficulties raising her children; driving problems; legal difficulties; substance abuse; health or other medical issues; and other psychiatric disorders besides ADHD.

3. *ADHD symptoms.* The third list can be your loved one's symptoms of ADHD that you have observed. You can even make a photocopy of the symptom chart in Chapter 1 and circle the symptoms of ADHD you believe your loved one is experiencing often. But don't forget to also make note of all of those executive deficits mentioned in Chapter 2 that might apply to your loved one: other examples of inattention, impulsiveness, and restlessness, besides what were shown in the symptom chart; poor working memory and organization; difficulties with time management; problems with self-motivation; poor emotion regulation; and any other problems you noted.

How to Begin

When the opportunity arises to speak with your loved one candidly, it helps to start with a statement of how long you have known her, how fortunate you feel to have her in your life, and how much you care about her. This may help her to be more open to listening to what you have to say. It should also disarm any defensiveness she may have if you were to simply launch into a list of her problems. It's hard to be defensive or angry with someone who just told you how much they care about you. If you open this discussion with accusations or criticism instead, it is likely to close her off completely to hearing what else you may have to say.

Next, start this discussion of your concerns by repeating back to her any concerns you have heard her express to you about herself, such as "I know you mentioned the other day that you think you are not doing well at school" (or work or socially, etc.) or "Last week you told me that you were worried about your bills and money" (or any other issue she raised). In other words, start with problems she has already acknowledged, even just in passing. This way you don't blindside her with concerns she may not have heard about or recognized in her life.

It also may be helpful to start discussing the list of impairments (problems areas in major life domains) you made before discussing her behavior or symptoms that you think may have led to her problem areas (which can be more personal and so harder to acknowledge). In short, start with reviewing "here are the problems that are happening" before you discuss "here is what you are doing to create these problem areas." For instance, you can say, "I remember you telling me you are worried about making your car payments while you start your new job" instead of "You're going to miss a car payment again because you didn't set aside enough money before your impulsively quit that last job. Now what do you intend to do about it?" Note that the second example is very accusatory and critical, whereas the first is not.

Sometime in this initial discussion, when it seems best to do so, you can bring up your list of your loved one's relatives who have been diagnosed with a psychological difficulty. Do this in such a way as to say that you recognize that your loved one may have come by some of their current problems "honestly," that is to say they are predisposed to those problems genetically; the problems may have been inherited. It can sometimes be easier to accept that one may have a disorder if a person knows that other relatives have had the same or similar disorder. In doing this, emphasize that this pattern among relatives means that your loved one is not entirely at fault for the problems they are experiencing. Acknowledge your understanding that they are trying to cope with or fight against a genetic predisposition toward those ADHD symptoms. This can be even more helpful if some of the relatives you mention can serve as role models in that they not only got diagnosed but also have been successfully treated or at least became successful despite their disorder. It is easier to accept a disorder that one knows is "running in the family" than to believe that you are the only one of your relatives who is having these problems. Given how highly genetically determined ADHD is, as I explained earlier, there are bound to be a number of relatives who had this or a related disorder that you can use to make your point with your loved one.

Keep It Short and Simple

Remember that you don't have to cover all of your lists in one sitting. In fact, you probably shouldn't if they contain more than just a few problem areas or symptoms. Especially if you begin to sense some defensiveness or denial arising in the discussion, then back off. Don't raise any further issues, and just wait to discuss them until another time. In this first discussion, raise just one or two problem areas and even one or two ADHD symptoms that contributed to them. But keep this first talk fairly short. The purpose of this discussion is to get your loved one to open up and begin contemplating his problems (the next stage), not to unleash the entire list of his issues and faults. This first conversation is really intended to be an expression of concern, not a courtroom trial.

Moving someone from the "not aware of the disorder" (precontemplation) to the next stage, "aware of the disorder" (contemplation), isn't going to happen immediately, much less getting her to arrange for an appointment with a professional. Although the ultimate goal is to get her to seek professional help, the initial goal here is simply to get her thinking about her problems as problems. Keep the first discussion fairly brief, and you may find that the next time you want to discuss these issues it can last longer, if necessary. You may also find it very helpful to close this discussion with a reiteration of your care or affection for her. This can be helpful in gaining her willingness to speak to you again about her problems.

Other Useful Suggestions

Some other suggestions are listed here.

- Avoid blaming or making your loved one feel guilty.
- Express your concerns in a brief, direct, yet compassionate manner.
- Don't make threats or use ultimatums.
- Keep some literature or a brief video available that your loved one can read or watch to learn more about ADHD, its symptoms, causes, and impairments, if they seem at all open to learning more about it. Although a trade book on adult ADHD may seem useful, it is probably too much information for this stage of getting ready to change. Instead, a brief fact sheet copied from the Internet might come in handy, such as those on my website (http://www.russellbarkley.org), at Children and Adults With ADHD (http://www.chadd.org), or at Attention Deficit Disorders Association (http://www.add.org). Or you can go to YouTube, find my short videos about ADHD, and bookmark them in your browser so you can get to them right away if your loved one expresses any curiosity about ADHD or just learning more about their problems.

- Periodically ask your loved one if she is concerned about the problem being discussed, especially if it is not one she has raised with you previously.
- Then give time a chance. Before you ask for another discussion time with her, let her have some opportunity to think about the few issues or problems you have raised. Don't raise her problems every day, as you will be seen as nagging or nitpicking, or just unkind, all of which can lead her to justify ignoring you.
- Watch for that window of opportunity to have another discussion. You will know when that window is open if you hear her mention her own concerns or problems without prompting. It is also open when she says things like she has been thinking about what you said to her in that first conversation. Or you can think of the window as being open when she asks out loud, "Why do I always do that?" or "Why am I having such trouble with ____________?" If she does, then use this situation to discuss one or a few more of your concerns about her, again following the advice for doing so suggested earlier.

> My partner found some videos on YouTube where ADHD was explained so well and shared them with me. They even got me crying at some point. ALL the things it said, all the symptoms it mention is how I feel and how I deal with my everyday life. I have always blamed myself for having this weird tendency of being "lazy." I call it "weird" because I also know that at the same time I have a strong drive, I have a strong passion, and big dreams. That's why I call it a "weird laziness" because I wasn't able to explain why I was working at my goals like this but having little success. I feel like the goals that I was able to achieve, such as in my acting life/career, took me too long and that if I only had a stronger focus, concentration, and motivation, I would be able to achieve them much faster, which would result in me doing many things in a shorter time. Now I understand much better where this is coming from and why

> I'm like this. There is not something wrong with me, but it's a disorder that I am suffering from. I would like to get in touch with someone who can help me through counseling therapy.

Dealing With Denial

As I mentioned in earlier chapters, it is very common for adults with ADHD to not monitor their own behavior as well as others. That means they are not as aware as others of their own problem behavior and functioning in a major life activity. This can come across as denial when it is really just lack of self-awareness. If that is the case with your loved one, the advice given earlier in this chapter should help you open a dialogue with them about their difficulties. Lack of awareness is not really denial.

However, as Cynthia Last, PhD, nicely explained in her own book for adults who have loved ones with bipolar disorder, real denial can also occur, and it has many faces. When you try to discuss personal problems with another adult, you can expect some adults to try to minimize or normalize the abnormal, blame others for their difficulties (including you, perhaps), blame their current location or living circumstances, or in other ways deny that they have a problem.

All this can be understandable if the person views the suggestion that he may have a mental disorder as stigmatizing, such as being "crazy." You might feel the same way if someone said that to you just out of the blue. So keep that thought in mind as you try to deal with his initial denial of his problems.

Normalizing Problems

As you deal with your loved one's efforts to make his problems seem like normal ones, be sure that you talk with him when he is calm and seems open to your discussion. Also, when you start by reminding him of his own expressions of concern about his own functioning, it is harder for him to claim that things are normal. If he asserts that "everyone has problems," then remind him that you are not concerned with everyone but with him. And keep coming back to his own statements that he is having trouble with some area of life. Tell him that it is his troubles, not those others may be having, that are important to try to address. Just because many people have been burned from a fire may make getting burned occasionally a "normal" event, but it doesn't mean we shouldn't avoid getting burned again. Also, steer clear of words that are sensational, stigmatizing, or humiliating, such as his being crazy, mentally ill, sick, stupid, or other such characterizations of his personality. During day-to-day interactions look for chances to "plant seeds" as Dr. Last calls them—these are opportunities to briefly acknowledge a concern that he has raised previously (you can say you are concerned about it, too). Or you can use these opportunities to briefly note a concern you have, such as on the day after some problem has occurred again. Through planting seeds, you can then use them to open your longer discussion of their problems. You can also "water the seeds" by just periodically and uncritically repeating them back to your loved one at opportune times.

Blaming Others or "The Situation"

Some adults with ADHD will blame others for their own difficulties, such as partners, spouses, friends, supervisors, or strangers. My brother certainly did this in his teen and young adult years. The culprits for his problems were always others in the current situation. For instance, sometimes he blamed our parents (especially our unsympathetic and strict father), other times the fault was with his partner, sometimes the other guys in the band, occasionally his bosses at work, and even "society" at large (e.g., that legal sanctions against drugs were simply stupid when he was using those drugs). The bottom line was that if these people would just let him do whatever he wanted, and then give him the help he wanted whenever he asked for it, his life would be going along just fine.

Whenever someone with adult ADHD has a problem dealing with another person, she may initially see this as being that other person's fault. You can try and help her overcome this form of denial by pointing out how often such problems have been occurring, how many others this same issue has arisen with (bosses, coworkers, neighbors, the grocer, and so on), and especially by reminding her that she is the common thread across these difficulties with other people.

You can also help your loved one by building your argument on top of their own thinking. If they try to externalize blame for the problems by shifting it to others or to situational factors, then start by just acknowledging that they seem to be under stress or may be angry or upset about something. That is why you want them to see a professional—because of their stress, upset, and anger. Don't agree with them that all this is someone else's fault, but do use their own statements about their distress to open the door to the possibility of seeing a professional about those feelings. You can acknowledge their distress without agreeing with them on the source they are blaming for it (often wrongly).

Likewise, your loved one may try to blame her problems on where she currently lives (location) or her living arrangements (back in her parents' home, the college dorm, the apartment she shares with others, etc.). If only she could go back to a place or arrangement she lived in earlier before her problems arose, things would be just fine, she claims. Or she may pine to live in a new place where she has heard things or opportunities are so much better. She tells you that she wishes to quit her job, move out of her current home, or even relocate to a new city. The change, she says, will solve the problems. In short, what she is saying is: "It's the situation, not me." To address this form of denial, you can follow the same tactics I discussed. Point out that she has had similar difficulties in the past when she lived in other places or under different arrangements. Again, the common thread you are trying to point out across all these different places is that *she*, not the place, might be the problem.

Minimizing the Problems

It is not uncommon for adults with ADHD to minimize the level of their difficulties. This is different from outright denial of their problems. Denial involves your loved one believing that there is nothing wrong with him at all. In contrast, minimizing problems involves the person accepting that he may be having some problems but not feeling they are so serious as to require any professional help. Just as with denial, this can certainly lead to your loved one not pursuing any professional attention for his difficulties. Typically, this attitude of minimizing the seriousness of his ADHD-related difficulties is often coupled with the attitude that he can handle the problems, often by proclaiming that he simply needs to try harder to do so. My colleagues and I see this attitude frequently in young adults with ADHD who are confronted for the first time with convincing information about their ADHD, even when it is given by a professional at the end of a diagnostic evaluation. At one level, the person accepts that they are having some difficulties right now in some area of their life, like college or work. OK, he gets that. Yet at a deeper level he has not acknowledged that it is a serious problem or that the ADHD requires professional intervention.

Your loved one might downplay the seriousness of the problems if she has already received a diagnosis. If the professional did not provide an adequate explanation of the disorder, this could make it easy for her to minimize the problem—"Hey, it's just a problem with concentrating," she says. "I can just deal with it by getting more sleep, drinking more coffee, or just motivating myself to pay attention when I need to. What's the big deal?" If this is the case, you may need to get more information on ADHD for your loved one to review (see the Resources section at the back of this book). Sometimes, hearing the information from a professional, and not you (just a loved one), can make it easier for her to accept the information.

This problem with minimizing the disorder can also occur if other members of your loved one's family or your loved one's close friends have also been minimizing the disorder and even saying so directly to your loved one. This sometimes occurs because these other adults simply want to help your loved one not feel so bad about his problems. Perhaps those friends are just trying to cheer him up a bit when he expresses demoralization over his problems. Despite their best intentions, these people can foster or even create a counterproductive attitude in your loved one. Their opinions reinforce the notion that your loved one doesn't need any professional help.

This difficulty with downgrading the seriousness of his ADHD also may occur because your loved one fears the stigma of getting a diagnosis. He doesn't want to be viewed as crazy or mentally ill even though he knows he is struggling with some difficulties in his life right now. You can certainly understand his fears (and acknowledge them) because some others in society still hold derogatory views of mental illness.

To deal with this attitude of minimization, you will likely need to follow the suggestions I gave earlier for dealing with denial. If the problem with minimization is because other friends or family members have also been downplaying your loved one's problems, then consider speaking privately with these other individuals about their comments. Explain to them why you believe that there is a more serious problem here than they are conveying. Let these others know that such opinions may actually not be helpful, even though they were intended to be. Instead, explain that those comments may be harmful in forestalling your loved one from getting professional help. Doing so may bring them around to your own point of view. You can tell them that it is one thing to want to perk someone up because he is having a temporary setback and feels down about it, yet it is entirely another thing to help someone engage in routine denial or minimization over chronic and serious problems he is having and thus dissuade or obstruct him from seeking treatment. You may need to do some educating of these others about adult ADHD. You can do that yourself or recommend some books, YouTube videos on ADHD, or other sources of information, such as the Internet sites I mentioned earlier in this chapter (CHADD, ADDA, etc.). If you think it is appropriate, share with these other people your list of the various impairments your loved one is currently experiencing. You can do this to try to help bring them around to not only supporting your view that help is needed but also to assisting you in encouraging your loved one to seek assistance.

If the problem is one of fear of being stigmatized with a diagnosis, talk with your loved one about how openly ADHD is discussed these days in the mainstream media, on the Internet, by celebrities, and in other social media. Show them the websites I discussed in the chapter on ADHD success stories (Chapter 7) and how open these prominent people are about their ADHD diagnosis. Even just entering *ADHD* into an Internet browser can bring up millions of search results showing how often it is discussed. Having a diagnosis of ADHD these days is nowhere near as stigmatizing as it was 20 or 30 years ago. Its widespread discussion in the media guarantees that your loved one has likely already heard about the disorder. They may also have some acquaintances that have the disorder and have been open about it. You can talk with your loved one about those possibilities as a means of destigmatizing the diagnosis.

THINKING ABOUT AND ACCEPTING THE PROBLEM: THE CONTEMPLATION STAGE

This next stage along the spectrum of readiness to change can be a little easier to address in your loved one because you are now past most or all of the difficulties that can arise from the earlier stages of denial, lack of awareness, or minimization of the problems. At least now your loved one with ADHD has acknowledged that she has some problems. That can mean she is not just thinking about her problems but may even be contemplating doing something about them. At this stage, as Kim Muesser, PhD, and Susan Gingerich, MSW, recommend in dealing with a loved one with a serious mental disorder, you can move her to the next stage. That stage is acceptance of a problem and contemplating doing something about it, called the *contemplation stage.* It is one in which your loved one may be preparing to act to change her problems. You can help move her toward that next stage, *action*, using several means.

- First, encourage her to talk about her concerns, problems, or symptoms and about what can be done about them. Here you want to encourage change, but without pressuring her too much.
- Next, talk with your loved one about how her life could be so much better if she could get effective treatment for her ADHD.
- You can also help her through this stage by asking questions in a nonjudgmental way about how difficult it must be to have to face the problems she is having. Use this to offer hope that getting treatment might make these problem areas better. For example, you might say,

> I understand how difficult it must be for you to deal with a supervisor at your job who is constantly on your case about getting your work done on time, and that your feeling so distractible is

> contributing to this. No one likes that kind of pressure or nagging. You know, there are some good professionals I found who specialize in ADHD that can help you with that issue.

And as discussed earlier, you can keep some literature on ADHD around to share with your loved one when she seems open to getting such information (see Resources).

GETTING READY TO CHANGE: THE PREPARATION STAGE

This stage of being ready to change can be even less difficult to address because it means that your loved one agrees that there are problems, has accepted them, and acknowledges a need for help. That means he is preparing to engage in treatment or in other ways to try to change these problems. You will know that your loved one is at this stage because he doesn't just acknowledge that he has symptoms of ADHD or problems functioning in life areas related to it but he is also asking questions about what sorts of treatments are best to use. He is gathering information about possible therapies. Perhaps you see him leafing through the books on adult ADHD you have kept nearby for him to use. Or maybe you have observed him surfing the Internet for websites about adult ADHD and its management. Regardless of where he is seeking such information, the good news here is that he is considering treatments for the disorder. You can help your loved one along with progress at this stage by doing such things as

- discussing the types of effective treatments available (see the next chapter);
- helping her to make plans to see a professional by getting information about experts in your area (see the next section of this chapter);

- getting your loved one trade books about adult ADHD to peruse and longer videos on the Internet to watch that were created by those who have ADHD (e.g., by Ty Pennington, Glenn Beck, or as seen in the CBC/PBS documentary *ADHD and Loving It*);
- searching for websites about famous people with ADHD that contain short biographies about them (you can find these Internet addresses in the footnotes in Chapter 7 on ADHD success stories; bookmark those websites so you can get to them easily when your loved one seems open to reading them); and
- sharing with your loved one good websites that post current ADHD research findings, new developments, and practical suggestions, such as those operated by Dr. Jeff Copper at http://www.attentiontalkradio.com, http://www.attentiontalkvideo.com, and http://www.attentiontalknews.com, or those by CHADD (http://www.chadd.org) or ADDA (http://www.add.org).

Sharing such websites with your loved one may help him to further his preparations to seek treatment for his disorder.

GETTING HELP: THE ACTION STAGE

Some adults who may have ADHD are already open to hearing this sort of information from a loved one. They not only realize they are having problems with the various symptoms of ADHD but also have already even mentioned to you that they think they need professional help dealing with their problems. They are not in denial but clearly recognize that they have a disorder and need some help with its treatment. If so, that is great because all they may require here from you is some encouragement and support to take that next step of making the initial appointment with a professional. When that is the case, you can easily sit down with your loved one privately and discuss ADHD. You can even share the results of any research you have done about area professionals who specialize in the disorder along with phone numbers she can call to make an appointment. Your loved one is now ready to take action to get the help she needs to not only get an appropriate diagnosis but also effectively treat her disorder. She may even beat you to it by telling you of the appointment she has made to see such a professional.

At this stage, you can help your loved one along in their readiness to change by using these helpful tips I adapted from a book by Kim Muesser, PhD, and Susan Gingerich, MSW, on helping a loved one with a mental disorder:

- Provide lots of encouragement and support, even financial support, to help defray the costs or copays of the appointment if you can afford to do so.
- Help her with overcoming obstacles that might occur in making or especially keeping her appointments (with transportation, parking, parking fees, etc.).
- Assist him with problem solving—when he mentions a particular problem he is having in some domain of life, you can talk him through various options for dealing with that problem situation (see the later chapters here on how you can help with problem solving).
- Don't get discouraged or show any discouragement if your loved one slips up, misses an appointment, occasionally forgets to take her medication, and so on. Understand that we all make occasional mistakes, are sometimes forgetful, or just slip up in getting and staying with our treatments.
- Remind him occasionally of the reasons he elected to get treatment. Typically, these will be those areas of impairment you had on your list of problem domains. Explain why he does not want to go back to having those problems again.

- Talk with your loved one about the benefits of, and even locating, a group therapy program at a mental health center or self-help groups for adults with ADHD that may be in your area. You can also find such support on the Internet, such as at http://www.add.org or http://www.adhdrollercoaster.org, WebMD (http://www.exchanges.webmd.com/add-and-adhd-exchange/groupstory/17376426), or similar websites.
- Consider finding an ADHD coach for your loved one (e.g., at the websites http://www.paaccoaches.org or http://www.totallyadd.com/coaching-directory-search/). Help to defray the cost if you can afford to do so. Well-trained ADHD coaches can provide periodic contacts throughout the week with your loved one using various media and technology (video chat, collecting data with a health app, setting up a calendar or system of alerts on a smartphone or other device, phone calls, e-mail) to keep her accountable to someone and focused on her goals, plans, treatments, and advise her on coping with particular problem areas.

Where Can Your Loved One Find a Professional?

Once a loved one reaches the action stage, there are things he (or you) can do to find a professional experienced with ADHD in his geographic region. You can help by encouraging him to do the following things, or consider assisting him in doing so, or even do these things yourself and share your findings with your loved one.

- Call your primary care provider (internist, family practitioner, general practitioner) and ask if she knows specialists in your geographic area working in adult ADHD. You can't speak with your loved one's primary care provider without her permission, so if you are the one doing the legwork here to find a professional, you are better off starting with your own primary doctor to get that information.

- Call or visit the website for the state psychiatric or state psychological association. These associations usually keep lists of their clinical professionals organized by specialty. See if they have any who are listed as experts focusing on ADHD in adults.
- Check the CHADD or ADDA websites to see if there is a support group in your region. CHADD is a large national nonprofit organization that promotes awareness of ADHD in the United States. ADDA is another one, albeit smaller, but focused chiefly on adults with ADHD. Call that local chapter and ask if that person knows of any ADHD clinical experts in your area.
- Call the local university medical school psychiatry department. Even if it is not nearby, they can usually direct you to who they know in your area that does adult ADHD evaluations.
- Call the local hospital psychiatry department for the same information.
- Call the local university psychology department and see whether they operate a clinic; if so, again ask for the same information.
- Call the local mental health center.
- Check the Yellow Pages for psychiatrists and psychologists specializing in adult ADHD.
- Search the Internet for ADHD professionals in your city or state. Then check the information on each to be sure they are licensed psychologists, psychiatrists, social workers, or physicians. Call the one that seems to have the most experience with adults with ADHD rather than being a general practitioner. You can also check the state licensing board for this profession to see if they have received any complaints about this professional.

KEEPING THE IMPROVEMENT GOING: THE MAINTENANCE STAGE

Once a loved one gets diagnosed and treated, helping him to stay in treatment to keep his improvement going can be an important goal. Research shows that many adults with ADHD do not stay on their medication after the first year or two, or remain in therapy programs for more than a few weeks or months before dropping out. You can help your loved one by (a) praising his continued accomplishments and involvement in treatment; (b) focusing your attention on the improvements or successes he has achieved in major areas of his life, such as education, work, friendships, finances, and so on; (c) continuing to support his involvement in therapy groups or with an ADHD coach; (d) getting him involved in such programs (discussed earlier in this chapter) if he is not already in them; and (e) helping him handle difficult situations using the problem-solving approach recommended in Chapter 16.

TAKING ACTION TO HELP YOUR LOVED ONE WITH ADULT ADHD

Stop here and think about where your loved one is along this dimension of readiness to change. How far along are they in the following stages? The way you approach helping them will depend on how open to and ready they are to change. Circle the one you think best applies to your loved one's awareness of the disorder and willingness to engage in treatment for it:

- *precontemplation*—not aware of or not acknowledging their disorder;
- *contemplation*—thinking about their disorder but not yet considering treatment;

- *preparation*—thinking about their disorder and preparing to get treatment;
- *action*—know they have a disorder and engaging in treatment; or
- *maintenance*—engaged in or completed treatment for their disorder and now trying to maintain the improvements.

Then go back to the section of this chapter that pertains to that stage and look again at what you can do within that stage to help them progress to the next one. If your loved one is at one of the early stages, don't try to undertake the recommendations I have made for people in later stages of readiness because your loved one won't benefit much if at all from them. Target your current assistance to their particular stage of readiness. Once your loved one has then moved on to the next stage, try those recommendations I have made in this chapter for that new stage to get them through it and on to the next one. As you can see, there is a sequence here to the types of assistance you can provide to your loved one and it is based on where that person is in the sequence of being ready to commit to self-change. Adjusting your approach to helping your loved one based on your sense of how far along they are in their willingness to change can go a long way toward moving them eventually to the point of taking action to get professional help.

CHAPTER 10

HELPING YOUR LOVED ONE UNDERSTAND AND ACCEPT ADULT ADHD

Following an evaluation and diagnosis of adult attention-deficit/hyperactivity disorder (ADHD), it may surprise you to learn that the next issue does not concern what treatments may be best to use. Instead, it is how well your loved one has understood and accepted their ADHD. Over the years of working with adults with ADHD my colleagues and I have learned that the next step is a crucial one: It is all about the attitude your loved one adopts toward this diagnosis. Unless they develop an attitude of owning their disorder, accepting the diagnosis for what it means, and then getting educated about the condition, they are not likely to get treatment for it. Even if they are offered treatments, they are certainly not likely to cooperate fully with the treatment plan without this sense of ownership.

In the next few chapters, I discuss the most effective therapies for the management of ADHD in adults. But here I discuss this critical first step in engaging treatment. That step is *acceptance.* It is important for both you and your loved one to understand what it means to have ADHD and that no treatment cures it. In that sense, ADHD is like diabetes. It is a condition whose symptoms can be managed quite effectively on a day-to-day basis. Yet, the underlying cause of those symptoms cannot be cured or easily corrected. The goal of treatment then is essentially the reduction of any possible harm that might come to adults with ADHD if their disorder were not managed well. Harm can include all the secondary consequences arising from the areas of impairment I discussed in earlier chapters (work, education, family life, driving, etc.).

From this point of view, ADHD must be managed on a daily basis if those secondary consequences are to be prevented or at least reduced. And that means treatment can go on for years, just as it does for diabetics. Yet, similar to people with diabetes, adults with ADHD can lead a relatively normal and fulfilling life when their disorder is well managed. Fully engaging in this sort of ongoing or continuous treatment, at least as needed, requires that a person first accept that they have a chronic disabling condition. They must first adjust their attitude toward themselves and their disorder. They must incorporate the diagnosis into how they personally view themselves and what that means for getting help for it.

> My 22-year-old son was just diagnosed with ADHD; generalized anxiety disorder; and major depressive disorder, mild. He has always had above average intelligence (proven on IQ tests). He eventually dropped out of high school, however. He is now addicted to video games and has angry outbursts. I am looking for a good doctor for him because we need help ASAP—he is going downhill quick. I really don't think he fully understands that his troubles are due to his ADHD—to him it's just some label a doctor gave to him, and I just don't want to spend years searching for a doctor who "gets it"—as I had to do for my own medical condition. Both my son and I are working with our family physician, who is prescribing our ADHD medications. I just wonder if we should both (mostly my son) be seeing some type of specialist—but I am not sure what type of doctor to turn to. My son is very stubborn and often refuses to keep his appointments because he sometimes doesn't think he has a serious problem. So I almost have to get it right the first time. Though he is 22 now, he acts more like a 14-year-old.

The first thing both you and your loved one with ADHD need to do following a diagnosis is to accept that he has a chronic psychological condition. Clearly, this son has not. If you are like the mother in this story—frantically searching for a doctor or therapist who understands the condition—you may indeed find the perfect match, only to have your efforts fail if your loved one does not first accept his ADHD for what it is. In a situation like this mom's, I might advise her to quit focusing on finding the "perfect doctor or else" and instead focus on further educating her son about his ADHD and that it is like diabetes, in need of a package of treatments that are done frequently. Her son does not yet clearly own his disorder but sees it as something his mother is to take care of in his life.

Your own loved one will need to *own it, learn about it, and then deal with it.* You and your loved one must first accept the diagnosis as part of who she is and not disown it. Absent such acceptance, it is likely that nothing further can be done to help her manage her disorder. Both of you must then learn as much as you can about this condition. And, hopefully, having that knowledge will enable her, and you, to manage her disorder as best as one can.

ADHD may be running and even ruining your loved one's life right now. But it doesn't have to do so. Your loved one is really only at the mercy of this disorder to the extent that he chooses to be put in such a subordinate position. Yes, it is a disorder, not a gift. Yes, it is a chronic handicapping condition for most people, not some episodic state that overcomes your loved one just once in a while. However, the extent to which it disables your loved one is directly related to the environments he places himself into and what he makes of those surroundings. It is also related to the kind of people he chooses to be surrounded by and with how well (or poorly) those people contribute to your loved one's impairments, either worsening or improving them. The degree of the impairment your loved one experiences is also related to the resources he may have available and how well he uses them. Understand that whereas disorders belong to people, handicaps belong to situations. Change the situation well enough, and a person can reduce or eliminate the degree to which the disorder results in how handicapped or disabled he will be within it. But you can't expect someone with ADHD to change the situation to help their ADHD if they have yet to accept it, own it, and understand that they can do something about it.

For instance, people who are so physically disabled that they must use a wheelchair can still enter and exit buildings, use cars, and otherwise participate in most daily life activities because their environments can be modified to help them do so. Putting a ramp for them on a building entryway does not eliminate their disorder. However, it does reduce or eliminate the impairment they may have had in that setting had no ramp been available. Or consider an opposite situation—that young adults with ADHD may choose to surround themselves with other impulsive, antisocial, drug-using, and otherwise criminally inclined people (as did my brother sometimes). In that case, those young adults with ADHD are highly likely to find themselves getting into serious trouble with the law, even winding up in prison as a result (as my brother did). Such an outcome is not automatically going to occur to your loved one simply because she has ADHD. It is much more the result of the environments she chooses to place herself within and the people with whom she elects to socialize with, not to mention the treatments she agreed to use or refused to accept. However, that willingness to modify settings so that one is less handicapped by their disorder first requires that the disabled person and their loved ones accept that she has a disorder. The adult with ADHD has to own it!

OWNING ADULT ADHD

After getting the diagnosis, and after improving their knowledge of ADHD, comes a step that can be difficult for some adults with ADHD to take. They have got to own the diagnosis of adult ADHD. That means that they don't just passively accept a diagnosis given to them by a professional, like the son in the previous example. It means that they buy into it. They incorporate it into their basic perception of themselves and who they are. Like the rest of your loved one's core personality traits, which are not likely to be completely overturned or revised no matter how hard your loved one may wish them to change, ADHD is a part of your loved one's psychological makeup. Just as with his physical appearance and his need to develop a realistic self-appraisal and self-image, he has to take that next step of understanding his problems and his diagnosis. He has to accept that ADHD is a part of who he is and is likely to be from now on. That is what I mean by "owning" adult ADHD.

Some adults with ADHD who have come through our clinic could acknowledge the disorder at some detached intellectual level. They could even sit through counseling sessions nodding their head in recognition of what we were saying, like the son in the present example. But we could tell that in their head, in their personal life, in that inner sanctum of their mind where we hold our self-image, they didn't "get it." These adults had not really owned the disorder at all. They paid public lip service to the diagnosis, but privately they denied that this disorder was really a part of their self-image. So your loved one might adopt some intellectual understanding of the information about ADHD but not take on the entire package of the disorder or even accept that it is a disorder.

Sure, your loved one might admit that she cannot concentrate as well as others or makes impulsive decisions more than others—that part she acknowledges. But then she goes on to say that it doesn't mean she has a "disorder" or that she is all that different from the majority of other people, who may also have these troubles from time to time. Yes, she may confide, her spouse, partner, family, friends, coworkers, or employers have told her she has problems that sound very much like the traits or symptoms of ADHD. But then she says, "What do they know?" or "They're not experts" or goes on to make these others out to be the actual source of the problem: "If they would just get off my back, I'd do just fine." I hope you can appreciate this difference between your loved one knowing about ADHD and owning her ADHD. Your loved one needs to admit that she has it, accept the diagnosis, own it as she owns other features of her self-image, and then she can really begin to deal with and master it.

> I am a 42-year-old woman, TV reporter for our local station, and mother of two teenagers. My whole life I have searched for a solution to my problems. Last autumn I found it—finally. I have ADHD. Now all the things I know about myself get light. I have known that I am not stupid, but all my life floated past me as I was not able to accomplish what I know I have the ability to do. Now that I know what I have, maybe I can get help and do the things I want to accomplish.

When adults with ADHD accept their disorder and truly come to own the diagnosis, it is not demoralizing—in fact, it can be liberating. They come to understand that they are not dumb or stupid as many had come to believe. The cloak of demoralization and moral self-criticism is lifted, freeing them to better understand the struggles of the past. They also no longer have to play mind games with themselves or others in which they deny, excuse, defend, distort, massage, or in other ways avoid accepting the disorder, what it is, and what it means for their life. It takes a lot of time and emotional energy to engage in those sorts of mental avoidance. Your loved one's happiness can only come from acceptance of who he is—ADHD and all. He must realize not only that no one is perfect, including him, but also that owning his ADHD doesn't make life a catastrophe.

So, owning one's adult ADHD, as Dr. Kevin Murphy writes,[1] doesn't have to demoralize your loved one, because when your loved one really owns it, she can then conclude, "So what if I do?!" (2015, p. 744). Just as everyone else has a long list of frailties, weaknesses, faults, imperfections, or other inadequacies, your loved one just so happens to have ADHD as one of her imperfections. Big deal! I could just as easily list hundreds of worse conditions that your loved one likely doesn't have if that would make you or her feel any better about her having ADHD. But you get the point. If she (and you) have not accepted that she has the disorder, your loved one cannot seek help for ADHD; discuss it rationally with others; evaluate what types of accommodations, if any, she may need for it in work, school, or home life; adapt to it; and cope with it as may be necessary. Again, think about diabetes: You can't manage it well if you don't really believe you are a diabetic. But once you acknowledge it and really own it, you shift to becoming proactive in learning the best things to do about it so you can lead a better life. It's the same for adult ADHD.

Please do not misunderstand what I am saying here. The attitude of "so what" I am encouraging your loved one (and you) to adopt is not one of denial of reality or of ADHD specifically. It is not an attitude of minimizing the seriousness of the disorder or its consequences when it goes for years without being diagnosed or managed. I discussed that issue in the last chapter. No, the "so what" I am describing here is one of complete change in perspective and hence acceptance of the facts. The fact is that your loved one

[1]Murphy, K. R. (2015). Psychological counseling of adults with ADHD. In R. A. Barkley (Ed.), *Attention-deficit hyperactivity disorder: A handbook for diagnosis and treatment* (4th ed., pp. 741–756). New York, NY: Guilford Press.

has ADHD. Another fact is that he is going to need to deal with it. But those facts don't have to come with a lot of drama. Acknowledging these facts can actually be liberating and contribute to an inner peace of mind that arises from your loved one (and you) truly admitting that he has ADHD. In doing so, your loved one adopts it as part of his persona and self-image, just as if he were accepting that he is visually impaired and needs to use glasses. One accepts the facts and treats the disability as best as one can, and then gets on with life—with seeing to their happiness and long-term welfare.

Also, you and your loved one both need to appreciate that getting to the point where one can accept the disorder as part of one's self and life is neither instantaneous nor easy. Many adults with ADHD, when diagnosed and counseled about it, have one or more of the various reactions associated with grieving. By recognizing these reactions and understanding their origin (grieving their diagnosis), you can help your loved one negotiate these initial reactions and hopefully come to a state of calm acceptance of their disorder. Some of these reactions I discussed in the previous chapter, such as denial. Other emotional reactions you and your loved one may need to work through are described next.

Relief

> My daughter, who is 23, has been recently diagnosed with ADHD. For years we have been trying to figure out why she could not accomplish goals or complete tasks, despite being very bright. I thought it was her just being lazy. She actually said no one realizes what it is like to not have the ability to live up to your expectations. Then we saw a YouTube lecture on ADHD that was an eye opener for her and us. She actually started crying and said it could be just the answer for her. So she went and got a professional evaluation and was finally diagnosed with ADHD. Now she not only better understands her difficulties but also knows the treatments she needs to use

> to improve them, and she actively participates in her treatments, appointments, and other things we have helped her arrange to deal with areas of her life with which she struggles.

Fortunately, most people clinicians see are open to accepting their diagnosis and moving on to learning about ADHD. This is largely because they initiated the request for the evaluation to begin with and so were open to hearing about the nature of their problems, symptoms, and impairments. These adults may experience a sense of profound relief at finally knowing what they have and how it accounts for their life-long struggles. They can reframe their past from being one in which the problems were due to being stupid, lazy, or unwilling to improve. Rather, they now know that ADHD is a neurological disorder of the brain's executive system. They also experience relief in knowing that the likely reason for many of the problems these adults with ADHD experienced in school, work, and/or social relationships was a subtle neurobiological deficit in the brain over which they had little control. As my good friend Dr. Kevin Murphy explains it,

> Their problems were not the result of deliberate misbehavior, low intelligence, or lack of effort. These misguided and damaging perceptions should be recast in a more positive and hopeful light, so patients can begin to rebuild their self-confidence and believe that successful treatment is possible. As a consequence, patients will ideally be in a better position to break out of the shackles of feeling stuck, demoralized, and chronically frustrated (see Footnote 1, pp. 748–749).

Demoralization

Upon receiving the diagnosis, some adults with ADHD experience temporary demoralization or depression. That is because, after all, it is a chronic disorder that has no quick cure, such as some antibiotic that may treat a transient infection. No advice, therapy, or drug to date gets rid of ADHD. You can therefore understand why the diagnosis might be at first disheartening to your loved one. As Dr. Murphy (2015) has written:

> Most adults with ADHD have suffered years of feeling demoralized, discouraged, and ineffective because of a long-standing history of frustrations and failures in school, work, family, social, and daily adaptive domains. Many report a chronic and deep-seated sense of underachievement and intense frustration over squandered opportunities, and are at a loss to explain why they cannot seem to translate their obvious assets into more positive outcomes. . . . The cumulative effect of such a history can sometimes lead to . . . a sense of anticipating failure as the predictable outcome of their efforts. Sadly, some appear so wedded to this belief system that they eventually give up believing life could be different for them. Many are completely unaware that their condition is a highly treatable one. (see Footnote 1, p. 746)

What other reactions might you see in your loved one immediately following a professional diagnosis of ADHD? Some possibilities are listed here.

- *Anger.* Many adults we have seen, upon learning of the diagnosis, react with anger and frustration for various reasons. Not the least of these reasons is the long delay to finally receiving the appropriate diagnosis for their problems, especially if they have sought help previously, only to be told they had a different disorder or no disorder at all.
- *Sadness or loss.* Other patients, upon their diagnosis, show a mixture of both sadness and anger because of previous adverse events they have experienced that likely stemmed from their disorder. The sadness comes from recognizing that some of these adversities cannot be repaired. These irreparable harms

might include lost relationships or marriages; visitations with or custody of their children after an acrimonious separation or divorce; lost education and related opportunities; lost jobs and other employment opportunities; previous drug abuse and its consequences; and even previous arrests, jail time, or related harms caused to victims of their impulsive and even antisocial activities. And then there are the many social relationships that fell victim to the individual's inappropriate ADHD behavior. Those relationships may be difficult or impossible to reestablish or reclaim. The list here could be nearly endless, but the point is that many adults come to realize that even now that they have the proper diagnosis and a treatment plan, little can be done about some of the past irreparable harms that have befallen them because of their previously undiagnosed ADHD.

- *Grief.* All of the reactions in this list are actually part of human grieving. So it is understandable that your loved one with ADHD may feel grief when she receives a diagnosis of ADHD. She is grieving what has been lost and may not be recovered. Yes, some relief comes in knowing what the core problem is and what can be done about it. But there is also a profound sense of loss about the harm that might not have occurred had her condition been diagnosed and treated earlier. This sense of loss might necessitate counseling sessions with a professional to assist her in understanding, venting, and resolving these reactions. Also, your loved one may start to think and act from this grief reaction, which may cause her, out of desperation, to try any quack remedy for adult ADHD she may have heard about on the Internet or from other sources. She may start to think with her grief and not with her brain. That means that she may look for the promises of quick cures rather than the evidence-based treatments that do not make such promises but are more likely to be effective in the longer term.

You can help your loved one negotiate and resolve many of these reactions by being a sensitive listener. Acknowledge that you understand how they can feel that way. Sympathize with the unfairness of it all—that it had to take this long to get the right diagnosis and treatment. Then encourage them to move past such grief responses to a healthy acceptance of the disorder. Hopefully, after the catharsis and exorcising of past regrets comes an acceptance of their condition. With that acceptance or ownership of the disorder, they can adopt a more forward-looking perspective of hopefulness based on the knowledge that ADHD is highly treatment responsive and that one's future does not have to look like one's past.

Acceptance Does Not Mean Making Excuses

Important to recognize here is that *owning the disorder* does not mean using it to make excuses for one's inappropriate behavior. Rather, the diagnosis is a means to motivate one to understand ADHD and accept what it represents in their life. Owning the disorder does not mean one is allowed to violate social etiquette or even laws and claim not to be responsible—It was my ADHD that did it! Nor does it mean committing criminal acts or becoming drug dependent or a drug abuser and then claiming it could not be helped—It was my ADHD that did it. No way! The diagnosis of ADHD provides an explanation but not an excuse. It can help you and your loved one understand why he may be having difficulties behaving in a less-than-optimal or inappropriate way. But it does not excuse such behavior, and one remains accountable for its consequences.

LEARNING ABOUT ADULT ADHD

Your loved one cannot deal effectively with something they do not fully understand (nor can you). That means that the second step in helping your loved one build a treatment program after they have owned their disorder is for them, and you, to learn as much as possible about ADHD. Reading these pages is a great start, and you can suggest books and videos on adult ADHD to your loved one (see the Resources at the end of this book). In all this, remember: Truth is an assembled thing! It comes from no one book, source, expert, guru, video, or website. The more widely you pursue information, the more likely you and your loved one are to differentiate the knowledge that is reliable and trustworthy from that which is fashionable, flimsy, baseless, or outright false. Much of the knowledge about adult ADHD out there in the informational world is reliable and science based. Yet there is also much hoopla, misinformation, and blatant propaganda that one needs to filter out as unreliable, unrepresentative, and even intentionally misleading.

While you and your loved one are becoming informed on ADHD, please try to be skeptical. Don't let this be you:

> After our college-aged son was diagnosed with ADHD, we turned to the Internet and immediately were awash in a flood of frightening misinformation about ADHD. We read so many scary articles about the "horrible side effects" and "lack of long-term studies" on ADHD medicines that I quickly decided that I would never medicate my son.

Beware of the Internet. It can be both blessing and curse in finding information about any disorder. If you enter "ADHD" into your search engine, you will get millions of search results. Yet, only about 10 to 20 websites offer truly accurate, science-based information. These are listed in the Resources section of this book. Check to see whether the website you are reading is a charitable foundation dedicated to ADHD, such as CHADD, or a professional association, such as the psychiatric and psychological associations that have fact sheets on various mental disorders. Beware of websites that are trying to sell you something, like a "natural remedy."

Question what you read. Look for the evidence behind the assertions. Challenge the claims about treatments that seem too good to be true (they usually are). By seeking the evidence behind the claim, you can not only evaluate its truth but also broaden your knowledge of ADHD and related topics. Sort out for yourself what makes sense, and help your loved one do the same. Look for what seems to be the consensus of the clinical and scientific experts who specialize in the disorder. If you really want to read the science behind any topic related to ADHD, then do not use a general browser like Google, Firefox, or Safari. Use Google Scholar—a browser that searches just the scientific journals and textbooks for what is known on that topic.

If you know other adults with ADHD, ask them what they found to be of value to them. Remember, of course, that all cases of ADHD are not the same, because all people are not the same. Your loved one may have many of the features of ADHD and its impairments discussed so far in this book. But he surely doesn't have all of them. Your loved one will have his own mix of symptoms and impairments. These symptoms link up with the rest of his personality, other psychological abilities, physical attributes, personal strengths, and weaknesses, not to mention specific living and working environments. All of these combine to make your loved one's case decidedly unique from all the others. You must therefore take all the general information on ADHD you are going to learn and conform it (like shrink-wrap) to your loved one's unique life circumstances.

Whatever approach makes the most sense for you or your loved one with adult ADHD, both of you can start learning more about adult ADHD. Your loved one cannot make the most informed decisions about her ADHD and how best to help her take charge of and master it unless you (and she) know what it is and what the most effective methods are for treating it.

KEY POINTS TO REMEMBER

For treatment for adult ADHD to be effective, it is first necessary for the adults who have it to own their ADHD—to accept it as part of who they are. Without this acceptance, your loved one is not likely to engage or fully engage in treatment. This also applies to people such as yourself who wish to help. You, too, must accept the fact that someone you care deeply about has this chronic psychological disorder. Your loved one (and you) must also learn more about adult ADHD, what it is, and how it needs to be managed. What will you need to do to help your loved one with owning, understanding, and dealing with their adult ADHD? To accept it and understand it yourself. Then you will need patience, tolerance, a sense of humor, realistic expectations, an ability and willingness to help them through crises, and a willingness to hang in there with them no matter what may be around the next corner. Next, I take a look at the specific types of treatments that are most likely to help your loved one in managing ADHD.

CHAPTER 11

WHAT ARE THE BEST NONMEDICAL TREATMENTS FOR ADHD?

The effective management of attention-deficit/hyperactivity disorder (ADHD) in adults is typically achieved through a combination of therapies, both psychological and medical (i.e., medications). Here, I discuss those treatments that are psychological in nature, leaving the discussion of medications for the next chapter. However, I start out with some commonsense suggestions that can help manage the symptoms and impairments from the disorder given what we know about it. They come from taking the big-picture view of ADHD as a disorder of executive functioning (EF) and self-regulation, not just one of inattention (see Chapter 2). The following suggestions can be implemented with or without any of the professional types of therapies that I discuss later in this chapter.

DEALING WITH ADHD: THE BIG PICTURE

Adult ADHD is a disorder of self-regulation and EF. As a result, people with ADHD are "time blind." Any situation, task, or activity that involves long lags in time or events that are delayed into the future is the enemy of adults with ADHD. Let's revisit some other essential ideas from Chapter 2.

ADHD Is a Disorder of Performance, Not One of Knowledge

The problems those with ADHD experience in major life activities have more to do with not using what they know when and where it would be wise to do so and less to do with not knowing what to do. Adults with ADHD are as smart and knowledgeable as anyone else of their background and educational level. But they don't put that knowledge into play as often as others for more effective functioning in day-to-day major life activities. Think of it this way: The back part of your brain is where you learn things (knowledge), and the front part of your brain is where you apply that to everyday functioning in life to get to your goals and improve your welfare (performance). ADHD partially disconnects these two regions. What they know does not guide what they do as often as it does in others: Adult ADHD is therefore a disorder of performance—a problem of doing what one knows. Thus, the individual with ADHD may know how to act, but she may not act that way when placed in social settings where such action would be beneficial for her in the long term. ADHD disrupts the timing and timeliness of applied knowledge, not basic knowledge or skills.

From this vantage point, treatments for ADHD will be most helpful when they help the adult do what he or she knows is best to do where and when it would be best to do it. I call this the "point of performance." That point is the place in the natural environment where they are having problems. Addressing ADHD requires helping that person to show what they know at those crucial places—at those points of performance. A related idea is that the further away in space and time a treatment is from this point, the less effective it is likely to be in assisting with the management of ADHD at that point in the natural environment. For example, I can meet with an adult with ADHD in my office and give them lots of suggestions about time management. These might include using computer-based calendars, reminders within timers on a smartphone, simple low-tech "to do lists," and sticky notes kept in front of them at their desk to guide behavior while working, and using software like SelfControl[1] to block distracting websites from being used while working. This rarely works. Why? Because we are in my office and the knowledge I just gave them won't get carried over and used at the point of performance, which is their workspace. The office is not where the problem arises. What needs to be done is to help the adult with ADHD to actually rearrange and implement these changes in their actual workspace (the place where and when the knowledge I taught must be implemented).

This will not be achieved simply by training a person with ADHD in what to do; the particular problem setting needs to be arranged in such a way as to assist her in actually doing it. Nor will that kind of assistance lead to any lasting value or maintenance of treatment benefit if it is removed within a short period of time. The value of such treatments at the point of performance rests not only in helping the adult with ADHD show what she knows but also in maintaining the changes at that point of performance so that the improved behavior can be sustained over time in that natural setting.

Information Alone Does Not Guide Behavior Very Well

Adults normally self-regulate much of their behavior by using mental information (held in mind—their working memory) to guide what they are doing—in other words, what we think about can guide what we do. This process is far less effective in those with ADHD.

[1]This application is available at http://www.selfcontrolapp.com/

HOW CAN YOU HELP?

- *Don't rely so heavily on mental information. Instead, make that information physical in some way in that problem situation—"externalize" it.* You and your loved one can do that by putting it in a physical form to remind them of what needs to be done. For instance, if your loved one's boss or someone else has given her a set of instructions to get something done over the next few days, have her stop trying to carry this around in her head so she can remember it over that period of time. That doesn't work well if you have ADHD. Instead, have her always carry a small journal and pen and instantly write down the task, any steps given to her to get it done, and the deadline for when it's due. Then make sure she keeps this journal in front of her where the work is to be done over the next few days. The journal can serve as an external type of working memory. You can help your loved one translate this written plan into smaller steps and insert them into her day planner as goals for each hour of that day and even over the next few days before the work is due. After a task is done, it can be helpful to record in the journal how much time the task actually took. The technique here is not what is important—the principle behind it is! Make important information, plans, goals, and deadlines external (in a physical form) around your loved one in problem situations if you hope to improve her chances of getting things done. In "techspeak," download the information that must be held in mind to some other, more physical medium that exists in that situation or workspace.

ADHD Means Being Blind to Time

This is one of the most important ideas about adult ADHD. It gives you not only a deeper understanding of its nature but a richer understanding of how to help. Difficulty with organizing behavior across time, known as "time management," is one of the most significant disabilities created by ADHD. You could say that ADHD is to time what nearsightedness is to vision—ADHD has created nearsightedness toward the future. The individual's behavior is governed by events close at hand—the immediate situation—and not enough by thoughts of events in the future. He simply doesn't stop to think of future consequences before he acts. Instead, he acts on impulse and often pays a heavy price for doing so. Knowing this helps you to understand why adults with ADHD make the decisions they do, shortsighted as those decisions seem. If one is not able to consider future consequences, then much of that person's behavior will be aimed at maximizing immediate rewards or escaping from immediate hardships without concern for the later negative consequences of those actions.

HOW CAN YOU HELP?

- *Make time physical.* That is, make time more visible in situations where time matters. You can do this with kitchen timers, clocks, computers that give periodic reminders about deadlines, day planners or week-at-a-glance desk calendars that show the days broken down into hourly units, cell-phone timing devices, smartphones with deadline reminders, and so on. The ways to do this are countless, but it's the principle that is important here: The more external or physical you and he are able to make the passage of time in front of him, for example, by structuring time with periodic physical reminders, the more likely your loved one with ADHD is to better manage his time.
- *Reduce or eliminate the problematic timing elements* of a task when feasible. Rather than have your loved one take on a task that has large time gaps in it, such as one that extends over days or weeks, reduce or eliminate those gaps whenever possible. When she must take on a project that must be done over the next

month, encourage her to break it down into much smaller steps and try to do a step a day toward the eventual goal. That way, each step does not seem so overwhelming, as the entire project might when viewed as a whole. Breaking big projects into very small steps makes it much easier to get motivated to do these smaller chunks. When those small tasks are done every day, the work will likely have been done when the deadline arrives.

ADHD Impairs Internal or Self-Motivation

Viewing adult ADHD as an EF disorder implies that it greatly reduces a person's ability to create internal motivation; what we generally call self-motivation, drive, persistence, or stick-to-it-iveness. Your loved one can't self-motivate like other adults can. When a task holds little reward or excitement, she cannot do as well as others at getting herself pumped up or activated to start it or sustain her activities over time toward deadlines and goals.

How Can You Help?

- Encourage your loved one to *arrange for frequent external types of motivation to help him get through the job.* For instance, break a project into smaller pieces so that each piece takes just a short time to do. Then have him give himself small rewards when he completes each piece, such as at the end of each hour, or even half hour, of sustained work. Then he can stretch; get a soda or coffee; check his smartphone for new e-mail, text messages, or Facebook posts; and so on—but only briefly!
- Tell her to *arrange small rewards for completing smaller work quotas* instead of waiting until the work is all done. Such artificial reward programs become for the adult with ADHD what a prosthesis is for the physically disabled: The rewards are like the wheelchairs, mechanical limbs, or crutches that some-

one with a physical disability needs to function more typically in a situation. The motivational disability created by ADHD makes using such artificial motivational devices nearly essential if longer term projects, assignments, personal plans, or social promises are to be successfully fulfilled.

- Encourage him to *make arrangements to be more accountable to others*, such as finding a coworker or supportive supervisor for him to check in with frequently to review his progress toward completing an assigned project. Doing so can boost a person's motivation to get work done, compared with situations in which he has no accountability to others and must work independently.

Reject Treatments That Don't Address the Point of Performance

Your loved one should likely reject most treatment recommendations that do not involve helping her with these sorts of active interventions at the points of performance in her daily life where she is having major problems due to ADHD. These are treatments like talk or insight-oriented therapy, psychoanalysis, weekly group therapy focusing on complaining, and so on. Those treatments are just not going to do it for the executive deficits ADHD creates because they don't take place at the point of performance.

Manage the External Environment to Manage the Symptoms

As I noted earlier, ADHD prevents your loved one from thinking as well as others both before and while she is behaving—she is less capable of using mental information to contemplate what she needs to be doing and to guide her along so she does it. The solution to this problem is not to nag those with ADHD to simply try harder or to remember what they are supposed to be working on; instead, she should take charge of that immediate context and fill it with physical cues to help them remember what to do and to stay on task. The external environment, which is often filled with irrelevant and distracting events, has a stronger pull on or influence over the behavior of someone with adult ADHD. This means that the more you can control and arrange the environment around them when something has to get done, the more likely those changes are to help them get things done.

How Can You Help?

- Encourage your loved one to *get rid of those distractions in the places where they typically do work.*
- Help your loved one *replace the distractions with cues, reminders, cards, lists, signs, sticky notes, day planners, or whatever else that will keep his mind focused on the task and goals at hand.*

Rules Alone Don't Guide Behavior Very Well

Adults normally possess sets of internal rules for what to do or how to act in particular situations, such as at work, in school, while driving, or at social gatherings. Adults activate these mental rules as they enter those settings to guide them more effectively through the situation. Adults with ADHD are far less likely to recall these rules and hold them in mind as they move into a new situation. Even if they do, the rules or instructions they recall don't control their behavior very well. Remember, ADHD makes mental forms of information very weak as a means of controlling one's own behavior.

How Can You Help?

- Encourage or even help your loved one to *make the rules into physical lists*, like on 3 × 5 file cards or "to do" lists. Externalize the important rules! The rules or instructions for a particular task can be externalized by posting them on, for example, small signs, lists, charts, sticky notes, and so on, in the appropriate place at school, at work, or in a social environment. Encourage her to *refer frequently to these lists* or other cues while she is in those situations.

- Recommend that your loved one *talk out loud in a low voice or whisper to himself and state these rules aloud* before and during these situations as another way to stay on task. Instructing ourselves out loud, quietly, is a great way to help keep our mind and behavior focused on our work.
- Suggest that he *digitally record these reminders on a digital recorder and then play them back again* in that situation, perhaps listening to them through earphones so as not to disturb others while he is working.

View ADHD as a Chronic Disability

As I have said before, the approach taken to the management of ADHD must be the same as that taken to other chronic medical disorders or to other chronic developmental disabilities. Take diabetes as an example. At the time of diagnosis, all involved realize that no cure exists for diabetes. Still, multiple means of treatment do exist that can provide symptomatic relief from the deleterious effects of the condition. These include taking daily doses of medication and changing settings, tasks, and lifestyles. Immediately following diagnosis, the clinician educates the patient and family on the nature of the chronic disorder, and then designs and implements a daily treatment package for the condition. This package must be maintained over long periods so as to maintain the symptomatic relief that the treatments initially achieve. Ideally, the treatment package, so maintained, will reduce or eliminate the secondary harmful consequences of leaving the condition unmanaged. However, each patient is different, and so is each instance of the chronic condition being treated. As a result, symptom breakthroughs and crises are likely to occur periodically over the course of treatment. These may demand reintervention or the implementation of modified or entirely new treatment packages. Don't get discouraged if this happens with your loved one's course of treatment for ADHD. It is typical, and it just means that treatments must be periodically adapted to the changes taking place in your loved one's life. Don't assume that changes to the environment that may assist those with ADHD are somehow correcting earlier faulty learning or leading to permanent improvements that can permit the treatments to be withdrawn. Instead, the more appropriate view of psychological treatment is one of designing an artificial social environment that serves to help your loved one better cope with and compensate for her disorder. Throughout all this, the goal of the adult with ADHD, their family members, and their treating professionals is to try to achieve an improvement in the quality of life and success for the individual, although life with ADHD may never be totally typical.

This is why adults with ADHD can be greatly assisted by having loved ones such as yourself available to help them accept their disorder, learn more about it, and deal with it following the general principles I have outlined. With proper treatment, adults with ADHD can make significant, and sometimes dramatic, improvements in their lives. Such treatment includes education about ADHD, counseling, medication, behavioral strategies, hard work, advocacy, and the support of family and friends, such as loved ones like yourself.

Treatment Works Better When You Instill Hope

You can make a great difference in how your loved one copes with ADHD by encouraging him to approach his treatment with a hopeful attitude. Absent such hope, your loved one is not likely to undertake the various treatment programs and coping strategies that are necessary to successfully manage this disorder and its associated impairments. He must come to feel that getting treatment has a high likelihood of improving the quality of his life, which it does. He also needs to know that not just his clinician but people close to him, such as yourself, sincerely believe that he can benefit from treatment. He also needs to know that loved ones may even opt to be partners in that treatment process, if possible, to help him engage. Now let's look at some different types of psychological therapies for adults with ADHD.

GENERAL COUNSELING

The first step in treating an adult with ADHD after she has been evaluated and diagnosed is to make sure she is well educated about the disorder, its true nature, causes, risks, and treatments. Adults with ADHD can't fully benefit from or participate in treatment if they are not fully aware of the broad knowledge that exists about the disorder. Counseling them about ADHD serves that important purpose. Self-education through trade books, the Internet, and other sources is fine. But many adults with ADHD often choose to also receive one or a few sessions of general counseling with a mental health professional who is knowledgeable about the disorder. This can also help them to get their specific questions about their own unique case answered. Consulting a knowledgeable and trusted professional is a better way of getting reliable information than is attempting to sort through the ocean of information, the multiple points of view, and even the propaganda about the disorder that one encounters through other sources, such as the Internet.

Short-term counseling with a professional can often help to address some of the phases of grieving or adjustment to the diagnosis I discussed. Some of those reactions can be serious enough to warrant working through them with a competent professional. That can be far better than struggling with them on one's own. Like you, professionals can also help instill hope in your loved one with adult ADHD. But they can also give them specific advice on how the other treatments discussed here may need to be tailored to their unique circumstances. All knowledge about ADHD and its management is general in form and needs to be adjusted to fit the individual circumstances of anyone diagnosed with the disorder. Counseling does that, tailoring general information to your loved one's specific case.

Although short term, such counseling sessions may be needed periodically as new problems or impairments arise, new issues come to the fore, or symptoms break through from being effectively managed. All this can require readjustment of the treatment components, such as medications, to deal with them. Such counseling may also serve as a central hub for the other components of the treatment package needed to manage an adult's ADHD. For instance, the therapist can help in

- arranging for a vocational assessment and consultation on occupational problems, where appropriate;
- referring your loved one to an expert psychiatrist or other medical specialist for consideration and management of their ADHD medication;
- consulting with college student disability services on ADHD accommodations in that setting;
- getting appropriate couples counseling with a knowledgeable marriage counselor as may be needed; and
- locating appropriate individual, group, and medical therapies for substance use disorders or for other coexisting disorders such as those I described in Chapter 6.

As someone who might be living with an adult with ADHD, you may also need some counseling with this general therapist. You also might need more specialized assistance to help you with your relationship with an adult with ADHD. A therapist can also help you to better understand the disorder and the types of treatment that may be needed for your loved one.

Expert counselors can also assist the adult with ADHD (and you) in transferring the general strategies for coping with this disorder from the big-picture perspective to your loved one's particular circumstances. Further advice on how best to cope with working memory problems and forgetfulness, poor impulse control, challenges with organization and problem solving, emotional self-control, and time management may all be provided by this counselor. Or the counselor can arrange for a consultation with someone more expert in cognitive behavior therapy that focuses on the executive deficits associated with adult ADHD (see the next section, Cognitive Behavior Therapy).

Helping the adult with ADHD includes not just identifying problematic behavior and impairments and what to do about them but also identifying positive qualities and assets they may have. Those assets can be brought to bear to help deal with problems or help offset the adverse consequences or demoralization one may experience from them. Skilled therapists can help offset or counterbalance negative self-perceptions; promote greater self-acceptance; and reinforce strengths, talents, and other qualities as needed for adults with ADHD.

COGNITIVE BEHAVIOR THERAPY

One of the best scientifically investigated nonmedical treatments for adults with ADHD identified to date is known as cognitive behavior therapy (CBT). CBT is widely used in psychology to treat various disorders, including anxiety, depression, posttraumatic stress disorder, substance use disorders, and personality disorders, to name a few. This method of therapy has now been specifically adapted for adult ADHD and targets the adult's deficits in EF, among other ADHD-related symptoms. Traditional CBT helps a patient identify inappropriate or maladaptive thoughts and associated negative emotional reactions, environmental triggers for such unreasonable or irrational thoughts and emotions, and ineffective behavior that may flow from or exist in conjunction with them and suggest various ways to correct them. These suggestions typically focus on helping patients modify or avoid problematic settings. They also help them learn to refocus their attention to less emotionally provocative aspects of the setting, and they especially teach them to rephrase and reframe inappropriate thoughts and conclusions to more rational and constructive ones. Some CBT methods also teach adults to self-soothe and otherwise deal with negative emotions, construct more appropriate coping strategies, and reduce or prevent inappropriate actions. Therapy can also teach an adult how to substitute more constructive behaviors that may all flow from the problem situation and the patient's thoughts about it and reactions to it.

CBT for adult ADHD goes beyond this traditional paradigm. It strives to identify problematic behavior and thoughts and substitute more specific coping strategies for the specific EF problems these adults have with self-restraint, time management, planning, self-organization, problem-solving, emotional self-control, and self-motivation, among others. It is referred to as "EF-focused CBT."

Professional manuals on these methods for therapists are now available, such as those written by Mary Solanto, PhD, now at New York University Medical School; Steve Safren, PhD, and colleagues at the University of Miami; and J. Russell Ramsay, PhD, at the University of Pennsylvania Medical School. Trade books for adults with ADHD also provide advice on these strategies, such as those by Ari Tuckman, PhD; Craig Surman, MD; Tom Brown, PhD; Lenard Adler, MD; Edward Hallowell, MD; and myself (see Resources).

Important to appreciate is that these therapies are not an alternative to or replacement for the ADHD medications discussed in the next chapter. Most adults with ADHD benefit the most from these therapies if they are also taking their ADHD medications when they participate in EF-focused CBT. The medications are usually more effective than just CBT alone, but using CBT with medication can further improve the treatment response of the typical adult with ADHD.

COACHING

> I was diagnosed with ADHD 8 years ago at the age of 22. I medicate daily and I see a psychologist twice a month for CBT. But recently I watched a video of a lecture, and it helped me understand why there are still many aspects of my daily life functioning that aren't improving. I have grown concerned that there are critical parts of my developmental deficit that are going completely untreated. My question is this: Aside from medication and counseling, are there any treatments available to help me? I remember from that YouTube lecture how it compared behavior modification for schoolchildren to a prosthesis, arguing that no amount of just skill development will help overcome ADHD symptoms. Rather, it said that motivational and other executive deficits also need to be treated by increasing the frequency and accountability of consequences at the point of performance. The argument makes perfect sense to me, but at 30 years old, I don't think I will be affected much by Smurf stickers or charts with gold stars. What options does an adult with ADHD have to get such accountability if medication and counseling don't appear to be enough?

Another approach to helping adults with ADHD is coaching—the adaptation of the life-coaching therapy modality to specifically help adults with ADHD. A small amount of research has been done to date on this therapy. It suggests some promise when used in combination with the ADHD medications discussed in the next chapter. Professional associations now exist to provide training and guidance to professionals who wish to practice coaching with adults with ADHD.

Coaching involves providing an ongoing professional relationship that focuses on the client taking action toward the realization of their vision, goals, or desires. It uses a process of inquiry and personal discovery to build the client's level of awareness and responsibility and to develop new skills. Coaching provides the client with structure, support, and feedback. Like general counseling or CBT, coaching is a supportive, pragmatic, educational, and collaborative process. But coaching for ADHD differs from traditional general counseling in that a coach is in much more frequent contact with an adult with ADHD, often several times each week. This is typically done using other means of communication than just face-to-face sessions, such as telephone calls, e-mail, texting, and other social media. Contact is usually made using daily or less frequent 10- to 15-minute telephone conversations. These serve to identify goals and strategies to meet those goals as well as to provide compassionate, constructive, and otherwise supportive advice to the ADHD client. Coaches can also provide the structure, accountability, and at times gentle confrontation that may be needed to address EF deficits, typically by giving many of the same suggestions as I gave earlier and that you will find in the final chapters of this book.

Pete Quily has identified 26 targets or benefits from using adult ADHD coaching on his website.[2] That list clearly shows the types of things an ADHD coach can assist your loved one with doing. More information on this treatment approach can be found on the Internet.[3] ADHD coaches can be located through several websites, including

---

[2]Quily, P. (n.d.). *26 benefits of adult ADHD coaching.* Retrieved from http://www.addcoach4u.com/adhd-coaching/benefitsofbeing.html

[3]See information at http://www. chadd.org, http://www.additudemag.com/adhd/article/4002.html, http://www.nancyratey.com/adhdcoaching, http://www.adhdcoaches.org/, and http://www.psychologytoday.com/blog/pills-dont-teach-skills/201101/26-benefits-adult-adhd-coaching.

http://www.totallyadd.com/coaching-directory-search/. Be aware that, as of the time of this writing, there is no licensing at the state or national level, nor is there any credentialing or certification for adult ADHD coaching that has been widely adopted by the field. But that is now changing for the better as professionals in the coaching community develop a consensus on what training is essential to be an ADHD coach. For now, understand that coaches can vary markedly in their educational background and depth of training about ADHD and mental health services. I caution you to investigate the quality and education of any coaches your loved one may be considering employing, just as you would do with any other unlicensed services.

MARITAL/COUPLES COUNSELING

No research yet focuses on the effectiveness of couples counseling for those couples in which one has ADHD. But couples counseling is often a necessary therapy for adults with ADHD and their cohabiting partners, given the findings I discussed earlier about the social impairments often seen in ADHD. Among the many problems couples may face when one member has adult ADHD are low marital satisfaction; impulsive emotional reactions; difficulties managing home responsibilities and finances; driving problems; excess tobacco, alcohol, and drug use; greater health problems; risky sexual practices and a propensity for casual sex (one-night stands); and even a propensity for reactive aggression in intimate relationships. Helping couples address these problems through marital/couples counseling will be essential for a substantial number of adults with ADHD. Fortunately, a few trade books exist to provide some preliminary guidance to such couples about these problems and possible ways to address them. One excellent book is by Gina Pera, *Is It You, Me, or Adult A.D.D.?* Another book is *The ADHD Effect on Marriage* by Melissa Orlov. And a new manual for clinicians to use in couples counseling specifically for adults with ADHD has just been published by Gina Pera and Arthur Robin, PhD (see Resources).

VOCATIONAL ASSESSMENT AND COUNSELING

When young adults are first starting to think about a career, those with ADHD would be wise to seek out a thorough vocational assessment first. This evaluation should be done by a professional who is knowledgeable about adult ADHD. By combining their expertise on vocational assessment and counseling along with specific knowledge of the problems inherent in ADHD, such counselors can suggest appropriate ADHD-friendly educational options and career paths (see Chapter 7). Even if such a counselor is not well aware of ADHD in adults, he or she can collaborate with those professionals more traditionally trained in the disorder. The latter include such professionals as clinical psychologists, psychiatrists, and clinical social workers who can help adapt the results of the vocational assessment to the particular symptoms and characteristics of your loved one with adult ADHD.

TECHNOLOGY

Dr. Kevin Murphy recommends that adults with ADHD be aware of the tools technology may offer to assist them in coping with their executive deficits. As he noted,

> A variety of tools and devices can help greatly in communication, writing, spelling, keeping track of time, and the like. . . . [Computers], smartphones, tablets, and PDAs offer a wide range of components including an electronic address book, a planner/calendar, "to do" list, and notepad. Smartphones and text messaging make communication easier, more spontaneous, and faster. Many software programs are available to assist with [word processing], personal finances, and taxes. Websites devoted to organizational skills, time management, and just about any

> other relevant topic are immediately available on the Internet. Electronic banking offers online bill paying, including setting up automatic payments at regular intervals to protect against delinquent payments and late fees. Books on tape and voice-activated word-processing programs can assist in learning and writing. Live Scribe Pens can greatly assist students in note taking and recording classroom lectures. These sorts of devices and interventions should be used whenever appropriate, but will require time, practice, and persistence to master. (p. 754)[4]

For instance, a major problem area for adults with ADHD is to remember to pay bills on time and then to actually pay them. You can help them by sitting down with them at their computer, going to each website for the monthly bills they must pay (loans with banks, credit cards, utilities, etc.), and setting up the autopay option at each website. The bills can then be automatically deducted from their checking account each month, billed to one credit card that is then autopaid each month, or set up so that an e-mail is sent to them to tell them to go now and pay the amount due. Obviously, given the forgetfulness associated with ADHD, the autopay option is best. Combine this with automatic payroll depositing of their paycheck into that checking account, and be sure the bills are autopaid a few days after the paycheck is typically to be autodeposited.

ROUTINE PHYSICAL EXERCISE

Although routine physical exercise is recommended for all adults, research suggests that it may be especially beneficial for people with ADHD. It seems to temporarily reduce the symptoms and/or help the adult to better cope with them. It can also help to address their

[4]Murphy, K. R. (2015). Psychological counseling of adults with ADHD. In R. A. Barkley (Ed.), *Attention-deficit hyperactivity disorder: A handbook for diagnosis and treatment* (4th ed., pp. 741–756). New York, NY: Guilford Press.

propensity toward obesity. Recent studies with children with ADHD even suggest that just allowing some movement or fidgeting while working can help those with ADHD to concentrate better and improve their performance of mental work. So your loved one with ADHD might wish to think about how to incorporate some repetitive movement into the work they have to do. Understand, of course, that exercise comes with its own risks, particularly for injuries. But done properly, moderately, and carefully, routine physical exercise may well prove to reduce symptoms, improve self-regulation, and help with weight management for adults with ADHD, given that it provides such benefits in studies of general population adults. No one particular form of sport or exercise has shown itself to be superior to others. Therefore, your loved one with ADHD should be encouraged to identify a method of exercise that interests them, for which they may have some aptitude and which they are most likely to incorporate routinely and easily into their daily schedule.

KEY POINTS TO REMEMBER

Adult ADHD is best treated through a combination of psychological, medical, and other interventions. Regardless of the type of intervention, some valuable general strategies and principles are involved in its effective management, which I discussed here as big-picture ideas to help an adult with ADHD. By understanding the big picture about ADHD and that it is a disorder of self-control and EF, one can see more clearly the critical principles that need to be followed in helping your loved one to better cope with and manage their ADHD. Psychological and other nonmedical therapies with some value, such as general counseling, CBT targeting adult ADHD executive deficits, marital/couples counseling, vocational assessment and counseling, ADHD coaching, routine physical exercise, and the use of some smart technologies, were also discussed here.

CHAPTER 12

MEDICATIONS FOR MANAGING ADULT ADHD

> My son just turned 20. He has complicated attention-deficit/hyperactivity disorder (ADHD). I say this because it shows up in so many ways that they (professionals) don't know what is ADHD, what is organic, and what is learned behaviors. He is hyperactive, and shows the attention deficits also. But he also exhibits aggression and defiance. I'll be honest with you. He is taking 30 mg of Vyvanse each day at breakfast. I have been following this prescription to the letter for the past month. I have noticed a completely different, "normal" young man. He became conscientious, helpful, empathetic, able to participate in warm two-way conversations rather than just being one-sided and selfish, happy to do housework and read books, cooperative and relaxed. In other words, he was able to exhibit higher order cognitive skills going way beyond rudimentary increases in attention or decreases in hyperactivity.

ADHD medications are the most effective treatments currently available for managing ADHD. Period. No other approach to managing ADHD in adults results in as much control of the symptoms and executive deficits, as much improvement in the adverse impact of ADHD on major life activities, for as many people and in such a cost-effective way as medication management of ADHD. So if your loved one opts not to use medication to master their ADHD for whatever reason, understand that they have just declined the most effective treatment currently available to deal with the disorder. It is a choice that is equivalent to a Type 1 diabetic choosing not to use insulin while trying to make a go of it in dealing with their diabetes strictly through diet, more exercise, and better hygiene. Maybe that will work, but it is much less likely to do so than would medication. And it will result in far less control of the disorder than using medication to manage it.

In my experience and that of many of my expert colleagues, adults with ADHD who choose not to try medication following their diagnosis typically return within 3 to 6 months asking to go on it. That is because by then they realize that all of the other options are not addressing their problems very well. I am not saying here that some adults with ADHD cannot manage their disorder without medication. Some can. This is likely the case for those adults who have marginal or mild symptoms of ADHD; have no other psychological disorders; are otherwise healthy; maintain good nutrition; avoid abusing nicotine, alcohol, and other drugs; exercise regularly; and have made a number of lifestyle modifications to permit them to function satisfactorily despite their ADHD symptoms. These adults may be able to get by without medication. I applaud them for doing so. But understand that these people are not representative of most adults with the disorder.

Although I recommend medication, I certainly do not advocate using medication as the only treatment approach. You can use many other methods to assist loved ones in mastering their ADHD, such as those in Chapter 11. I describe many more specific behavioral suggestions in Chapter 13. But for the majority of adults with ADHD, especially those with moderate to severe symptoms, medication management should be the core component around which to build the other treatments—just like in managing diabetes. Those other treatment methods will be designed to address what the medications are unable to change or improve sufficiently to reduce your loved one's ADHD-related impairment in any particular area of their life. But those treatments can rarely do it alone, however, without being combined with ADHD medications.

The other reason that medications are so important for managing ADHD—other than just the practical fact that they work and work well for most people with the disorder—is that over the past decade, research has shown that the medications actually help to either correct or compensate for the underlying neurological problems that are likely contributing to the ADHD. Indeed, in children who remain on the medications for several years, brain regions may develop closer to those of their peers without ADHD.[1,2] The medications control the symptoms only temporarily. That control lasts only as long as these medicines are in the bloodstream and hence in the brain of the adult with ADHD—but they do it. We now know that ADHD medications can normalize the behavior of 50% to 65% of those with ADHD. And they result in substantial improvements, if not normalization, in another 20% to 30% of people with the disorder. In other words, fewer than 10% of people with ADHD will not have a positive response to at least one or more of the ADHD medications currently available in the United States. When the medicines work, they can result in substantial improvements

[1]Frodl, T., & Skokauskas, N. (2012). Meta-analysis of structural MRI studies in children and adults with attention deficit hyperactivity disorder indicates treatment effects. *Acta Psychiatrica Scandinavica, 125*, 114–126. http://dx.doi.org/10.1111/j.1600-0447.2011.01786.x

[2]Spencer, T. J., Brown, A., Seidman, L. J., Valera, E. M., Makris, N., Lomedico, A., . . . Biederman, J. (2013). Effect of psychostimulants on brain structure and function in ADHD: A qualitative review of magnetic resonance imaging-based neuroimaging studies. *Journal of Clinical Psychiatry, 74*, 902–917. http://dx.doi.org/10.4088/JCP.12r08287

in the symptoms of ADHD. Those improvements are, on average, often 2 to 3 times greater than that seen with any other psychiatric medications used to treat other psychiatric disorders, such as antidepressants and anti-anxiety medications. And that improvement in ADHD symptoms is likely to lead to significant improvements in the downstream impairments in major life domains that are due to those symptoms.

Even though far more research needs to be done to fully illuminate the neurological and genetic bases of ADHD and the manner in which the ADHD medications work, enough is currently known, in my opinion, to conclude that ADHD medications are forms of *neurogenetic therapy.* These medicines are not simply masking or covering up the symptoms of ADHD instead of addressing the "real" underlying problems of the disorder, as some critics in the popular media have contended. They are in fact serving to directly correct or compensate for the underlying neurological and genetic factors in the brain that give rise to ADHD. They only do so temporarily while the medication remains in the bloodstream and especially the brain. Yet these medicines are not mere "band aids," nor are they chemical "billyclubs," "chemical straitjackets," or simply "mothers' little helpers," as they have sometimes been portrayed in antimedication propaganda or even the mainstream media. Therefore, a second reason for your loved one to seriously consider medication as part of his or her efforts to master ADHD is because, unlike any other treatments currently available, it has the greatest potential to temporarily improve the neurogenetic basis for this disorder.

> I first heard of ADHD when I moved to the United States 3 years ago to take a job in sports TV production with a major network. I, like a significant proportion of the population, believed it to be little more than an imagined diagnosis designed to abrogate the responsibilities of parents of brattish children. Seven days ago, at age 29, and after at least a

decade of gradual realization that many aspects of my behavior, mental faculties, and life history seemed entirely abnormal, perhaps even alien, as it were, in comparison to my peers, I was myself diagnosed with ADHD. In hindsight, I ought to have looked for help sooner. At any rate, I am now taking medication. The phenomenal efficacy of my medication gave me an immediate and startling insight into what the human condition entails for those without the disorder. In a sense, it feels as if a kind of mental shackle has been removed. It already seems that I no longer pathologically avoid any kind of activity requiring the sustained use of my intellect, and I can finally direct my attention in the same way that apparently comes so naturally to the majority of humanity. I find that I now spend my time living instead of compensating.

STIMULANTS

Table 12.1 lists medications approved by the Food and Drug Administration (FDA) for use for adult ADHD in the United States. That table also provides information about their dosing as described in a chapter by Dr. Jefferson Prince and colleagues at Massachusetts General Hospital from my professional handbook on ADHD.[3]

The two basic categories of ADHD medicines that are approved by the FDA for use with adults are *stimulants* and *nonstimulants*. Both have to be taken daily to be effective. They all control the symptoms of ADHD only as long as your loved one takes the medications. They produce no enduring positive effects on your loved one's ADHD once you stop them. Ceasing the use of medication often results in a return of the ADHD symptoms back to their pretreatment levels.

[3]Prince, J. B., Wilens, T. E., Spencer, T. J., & Biederman, J. (2015). Pharmacotherapy of ADHD in adults. In R. A. Barkley (Ed.) *Attention-deficit hyperactivity disorder: A handbook for diagnosis and treatment* (4th ed., pp. 826–860). New York, NY: Guilford Press.

TABLE 12.1. Available Food and Drug Administration (FDA)–Approved Treatments for ADHD

Generic Name (Brand Name)	Formulation and Mechanism	Duration of Activity	How Supplied	Usual Absolute and (Weight-Based) Dosing Range	FDA-Approved Maximum Dose for ADHD
MPH (Ritalin)[a]	Tablet of 50:50 racemic mixture d,l-threo-MPH	3–4 hr	5-, 10-, and 20-mg tablets	(0.3–2 mg/kg/day)	60 mg/day
Dex-MPH (Focalin)[a]	Tablet of d-threo-MPH	3–5 hr	2.5-, 5-, and 10-mg tablets (2.5-mg Focalin equivalent to 5-mg Ritalin)	(0.15–1 mg/kg/day)	20 mg/day
MPH (Methylin)[a]	Tablet of 50:50 racemic mixture d,l-threo-MPH	3–4 hr	5-, 10-, and 20-mg tablets	(0.3–2 mg/kg/day)	60 mg/day

MPH-SR (Ritalin-SR)[a]	Wax-based matrix tablet of 50:50 racemic mixture d,l-threo-MPH	3–8 hr variable	20-mg tablets (amount absorbed appears to vary)	(0.3–2 mg/kg/day)	60 mg/day
MPH (Metadate ER)[a]	Wax-based matrix tablet of 50:50 racemic mixture d,l-threo-MPH	3–8 hr variable	10- and 20-mg tablets (amount absorbed appears to vary)	(0.3–2 mg/kg/day)	60 mg/day
MPH (Methylin ER)[a]	Hydroxypropyl methylcellulose base tablet of 50:50 racemic mixture d,l-threo-MPH; no preservatives	8 hr	10- and 20-mg tablets 2.5-, 5-, and 10-mg chewable tablets 5-mg/5-ml and 10-mg/5-ml oral solution	(0.3–2 mg/kg/day)	60 mg/day

(continues)

TABLE 12.1. Available Food and Drug Administration (FDA)–Approved Treatments for ADHD (*Continued*)

Generic Name (Brand Name)	Formulation and Mechanism	Duration of Activity	How Supplied	Usual Absolute and (Weight-Based) Dosing Range	FDA-Approved Maximum Dose for ADHD
MPH (Ritalin LA)[a]	Two types of beads give bimodal delivery (50% immediate-release and 50% delayed-release) of 50:50 racemic mixture d,l-threo-MPH	8 hr	20-, 30-, and 40-mg capsules; can be sprinkled	(0.3–2 mg/kg/day)	60 mg/day
D-MPH (Focalin XR)[c]	Two types of beads give bimodal delivery (50% immediate-release and 50% delayed-release) of d-threo-MPH	12 hr	5-, 10-, 15-, 20-, 25-, 30-, 35-, and 40-mg capsules	0.15–1 mg/kg/day	30 mg/day in youth; 40 mg/day in adults

MPH (Metadate CD)[a]	Two types of beads give bimodal delivery (30% immediate-release and 70% delayed-release) of 50:50 racemic mixture d,l-threo-MPH	8 hr	20-mg capsule; can be sprinkled	(0.3–2 mg/kg/day)	60 mg/day
MPH (Daytrana)[a]	MPH transdermal system	12 hr (patch worn for 9 hours)	10-, 15-, 20-, and 30-mg patches	0.3–2 mg/kg/day	30 mg/day
MPH (Concerta)[a,c]	Osmotic pressure system delivers 50:50 racemic mixture d, l-threo-MPH	12 hr	18-, 27-, 36-, and 54-mg caplets	(0.3–2 mg/kg/day)	72 mg/day

(continues)

TABLE 12.1. Available Food and Drug Administration (FDA)–Approved Treatments for ADHD (*Continued*)

Generic Name (Brand Name)	Formulation and Mechanism	Duration of Activity	How Supplied	Usual Absolute and (Weight-Based) Dosing Range	FDA-Approved Maximum Dose for ADHD
MPH (Quillivant XR)	Extended-release liquid	12 hr	25 mg/5 mL	(0.3–2 mg/kg/day)	60 mg/day
AMP (Dexedrine Tablets)[b]	d-AMP tablet	4–5 hr	5-mg tablets	(0.15–1 mg/kg/day)	40 mg/day
AMP (Dextrostat)[b]	d-AMP tablet	4–5 hr	5- and 10-mg tablets	(0.15–1 mg/kg/day)	40 mg/day
AMP (Dexedrine Spansules)[b]	Two types of beads in a 50:50 mixture short and delayed-absorption of d-AMP	8 hr	5-, 10-, and 15-mg capsules	(0.15–1 mg/kg/day)	40 mg/day

Mixed salts of AMP (Adderall)[b]	Tablet of d-l-AMP isomers (75% d-AMP and 25% l-AMP)	4–6 hr	5-, 7.5-, 10-, 12.5-, 15-, 20-, and 30-mg tablets	(0.15–1 mg/kg/day)	40 mg/day
Mixed salts of AMP (Adderall-XR)[a,c]	Two types of beads give bimodal delivery (50% immediate-release and 50% delayed-release) of 75:25 racemic mixture d,l-AMP	At least 8 hr (but appears to last much longer in certain patients)	5-, 10-, 15-, 20-, 25-, and 30-mg capsules; can be sprinkled	(0.15–1 mg/kg/day)	30 mg/day in children Recommended dose is 20 mg/day in adults
Lisdexamfetamine (Vyvanse)[a,c]	Tablets of dextro-amphetamine and L-lysine	12 hr	30-, 50-, and 70-mg tablets		70 mg/day

(continues)

TABLE 12.1. Available Food and Drug Administration (FDA)–Approved Treatments for ADHD (*Continued*)

Generic Name (Brand Name)	Formulation and Mechanism	Duration of Activity	How Supplied	Usual Absolute and (Weight-Based) Dosing Range	FDA-Approved Maximum Dose for ADHD
Atomoxetine (Strattera)[a,c]	Capsule of atomoxetine	5-hr plasma half-life but CNS effects appear to last much longer	10-, 18-, 25-, 40-, 60-, and 80-mg capsules	1.2 mg/kg/day	1.4 mg/kg/day or 100 mg
Guanfacine ER (Intuniv)[d]	Extended-release tablet of guanfacine	Labelled for once-daily dosing	1-, 2-, 3-, and 4-mg tablets	Up to 4 mg per day	Up to 4 mg per day
Clonidine ER (Kapvay)[d]	Extended-release tablet of clonidine	Labelled for twice-daily dosing	0.1-mg tablet	0.1–0.2 mg twice daily	Up to 0.4 mg daily

Note. FDA = Food and Drug Administration; ADHD = attention-deficit/hyperactivity disorder; MPH = methylphenidate; SR = slow release; D-MPH = dexmethylphenidate; MPH = amphetamine; ER = extended release; CNS = central nervous system. From "Pharmacotherapy of ADHD in Adults," by J. B. Prince, T. E. Wilens, T. J. Spencer, and J. Biederman. In R. A. Barkley (Ed.), *Attention-Deficit Hyperactivity Disorder: A Handbook for Diagnosis and Treatment* (4th ed., pp. 828–829), 2015, New York, NY: Guilford Press. Copyright 2015 by Guilford Press. Reprinted with permission.

[a]Approved to treat ADHD age 6 years and older. [b]Approved to treat ADHD age 3 years and older. [c]Specifically approved for treatment of ADHD in adults. [d]Approved to treat ADHD in youth 6 to 17 years old as monotherapy or as adjunctive treatment with stimulant.

Both types of ADHD medications typically work by increasing the amount of two (or more) chemicals in the brain known as neurotransmitters: dopamine and norepinephrine. Those chemicals are involved in permitting nerve cells to communicate with each other so the brain can function effectively. More specifically, these drugs increase just how much of these chemicals are residing outside of the nerve cells. That can increase the activity of adjacent nerve cells. By causing nerve cells to express more of these neurochemicals, or by keeping the nerve cells from pulling these chemicals back into the cell once they have been released, the drugs increase the communication that occurs between nerve cells in regions of the brain that are related to directly causing ADHD. In short, increasing these brain chemicals in these regions lets that brain area function better and sometimes normally.

Types and Actions

The two basic types of stimulants currently marketed in the United States are methylphenidate (MPH) and amphetamine (AMP). These stimulants act in the brain mainly to increase the amount of dopamine available for use outside the nerve cells. Yet they can, to a smaller extent, increase the amount of norepinephrine outside the nerve cells as well. AMP does this mainly by increasing the amount of dopamine that is expressed from the nerve cell when it is activated. To a lesser extent, it may also block the transport system by which the dopamine is normally reabsorbed into that nerve cell after being released. That can result in more dopamine being left outside the cell to continue to function. MPH mainly acts mostly by preventing this reabsorption of dopamine. That is why it is known as a transport, or reuptake, blocker.

Both AMP and MPH have the potential to be abused because they increase dopamine in regions of the brain known as "reward centers." Stimulating those centers can lead to an increased likelihood of addiction to drugs that do so. But ADHD medications are very unlikely to do this when taken by mouth and swallowed, as prescribed. They certainly can do so when they are sniffed through the nose as a powder or injected into a blood vein in a solution, such as when mixed with water. Because of this potential for drug abuse, the Drug Enforcement Administration in the United States has classified the stimulants as Schedule II controlled substances, along with other potentially addictive drugs. This classification places limits on how much drug can be produced annually, how the drug is to be prescribed, how it is to be stored in pharmacies, and how it is to be dispensed and otherwise monitored in the United States.

The five different methods by which these two drugs are delivered into the body are described in the following box. The methods also differ in how long they maintain the blood levels of the drug in the body, and so in the brain. There are hundreds of studies on the safety and effectiveness of these stimulants and delivery systems.

The Five Stimulant Delivery Systems

The five different delivery systems are the 5 *Ps*—*pills, pumps, pellets, patches,* and *pro-drug*. The various brand names of attention-deficit/hyperactivity disorder (ADHD) stimulant medicines you will hear about are either one form or another of methylphenidate (MPH) or amphetamine (AMP) and involve one of these delivery systems:

- *Pills.* These are the original versions of these medicines that have been available for many decades. The first versions of AMP were discovered in the 1930s, and the first version of MPH was discovered in the 1950s. In pill form, these medications are absorbed quickly, usually within 15 to 20 minutes, after being taken by mouth and swallowed. They can reach their peak level in the blood (and so in the brain) in 60 to 90 minutes,

The Five Stimulant Delivery Systems (*Continued*)

usually, and may last 3 to 5 hours in controlling the symptoms of ADHD in most people. That was their problem: If you wanted to control the symptoms of ADHD across the waking day of, say, 14 to 16 hours, for most adults, you had to give these medications two to four times per day, or more often. The inconvenience that posed to people having to take these drugs is obvious, not to mention the fact that many had to remember to take these drugs so often and frequently forgot to do so. These and other problems with these immediate-release pills led pharmaceutical companies to explore better ways to get the medicines into the body and keep them active there longer. The brand names you are likely to hear about for these pills are Ritalin (MPH, a mixture of d-MPH and l-MPH), Focalin (just d-MPH), Dexedrine (d-AMP), Benzedrine (l-AMP), and Adderall (a mixture of the d- and l-AMP forms or salts).

- *The Pump.* Then came the invention of an ingenious water-pump system for delivering these drugs into the body and keeping them in the bloodstream longer. The brand name for this system is Concerta, and it contains MPH. It is a capsule-appearing container with a small laser-drilled hole on one of its long ends. Inside, there are two chambers. One chamber contains a paste-like sludge of MPH, and the other chamber is empty. Powdered MPH coats the outside of the capsule. Now here is the neat part: When you swallow the capsule, the powder goes right to work just as it would in the pill form of MPH described above (i.e., Ritalin). That gives just enough time for the capsule to start to absorb water from your stomach (and later your intestines). The water is absorbed through the wall of the pump in a continuous, even flow into the empty chamber. As that chamber fills up, it presses against the other chamber that contains the MPH paste. That pressure then squeezes the MPH paste out of the hole in the capsule. It is designed to do that continuously for 8 to 12 hours or more. The end result is that many people, especially children, only need to take one capsule a day, and not the usual two or three (or more) they would have to take using the regular pills discussed above. The capsules come in various

(*continues*)

The Five Stimulant Delivery Systems (*Continued*)

size doses, of course, so that physicians can adjust the dose to better suit the individual needs and responses of their ADHD patients. One problem, though, is that some older children and teens, and especially adults, may need a longer course of medication each day than what this provides. To deal with that issue, some physicians use the pills of MPH or AMP toward the end of the day. They do this to get an extra 3 to 5 hours of treatment with medication after the Concerta may be losing its beneficial control of ADHD symptoms. Even so, you just have to love the human ingenuity that led to the development of this delivery system.

- *The Pellets.* At around the same time as the water-pump method was being invented, chemical (pharmacological) engineers were modifying a method that uses time-release pellets to create a way to keep medicines in the body and bloodstream longer than the pills. This method had been used for years with some cold medicines, like the old Contac brand. But the system had to be modified in various ways for use with MPH and AMP. Now, we have time-release pellets for both of these stimulants. Little beads of the drug are coated in such a way that some dissolve immediately after being swallowed, others dissolve in 1, 2, 3, or more hours later. This means that the drug can be more gradually activated and absorbed into the bloodstream across 8 to 12 hours, for most people. Here is another ingenious delivery system. It has the added advantage that if someone simply cannot or does not want to swallow the capsule that contains these pellets, they can open the capsule (pull it apart) and sprinkle it on a teaspoon of applesauce, yogurt, or other food and swallow it that way. It does not change the way the drug will work in the body, typically. You may have heard of these delivery systems by the brand names Ritalin LA (MPH), Focalin XR (d-MPH), Metadate CD (MPH), and Adderall XR (AMP) in the United States. Again, there are different sizes (doses) to these capsules to permit a physician to adjust the dose for each individual to their optimum level. Similar to the water-pump method above, these time-release pellet

The Five Stimulant Delivery Systems (*Continued*)

systems sometimes have to be supplemented late in the day with a regular or immediate-release pill version of the same drug. That permits even longer symptom control if necessary. Some research exists that shows that this pellet system gives a little better control of ADHD symptoms in the morning than afternoon hours. In contrast, the pump system above provides a bit better control in the afternoon than morning hours. Both delivery systems provide good control of ADHD symptoms across the day but not at exactly the same hours of the day. This can be an issue sometimes in deciding which delivery system may be better for someone depending on when they need the greatest control of their ADHD symptoms during the day.

- *The Patch.* The next invention of a delivery system for the stimulants was FDA approved just a few years after the two above (pump and pellet). It is a patch with an adhesive coating that is applied directly to the skin, such as on the back of the shoulder or on the buttocks. The patch contains MPH. When applied to the skin, the MPH is absorbed through the skin and gets into the bloodstream. So long as you wear the patch, MPH is being delivered into the body for as many hours during the day as one needs. Because the stimulants can cause insomnia or trouble falling asleep, the patch needs to be removed several hours before bedtime to permit the drug left in the body to be broken down and removed without adversely affecting your sleep onset. This delivery system used to go by the brand name Daytrana (MPH), but the patent on the device is up for sale and may be purchased by another company and renamed in the future. Here is another clever invention for getting the stimulants into the bloodstream and keeping them there for a sufficient time to control the symptoms of ADHD across most of the waking day. It has the advantages of not needing to be swallowed and of delivering the medicine into the bloodstream as long as you are wearing the patch for that day. Of course, the disadvantage is that you have to remember to take the patch off well before you want to go to sleep. Another problem is that 15% to 20%

(continues)

The Five Stimulant Delivery Systems (*Continued*)

of people experience a skin rash at the site of the patch and may need to stop using the patch for this reason. As with the drugs discussed above, the patch comes in different doses to better adjust the amount of the drug to each individual.

- *The Pro-Drug.* In 2008, another delivery system received FDA approval for use with adults with ADHD, and that system goes by the brand name Vyvanse (a form of AMP). Here is yet a further example of human inventiveness. One of the problems with the immediate-release pills, as well as the pellet systems discussed above, is that they have the potential to be abused. That is usually done by crushing and inhaling the powder from the pills or the crushed beads from the pellet systems. That powder can also be mixed with water and injected into a vein. Whether snorted through the nose or injected into a vein, the stimulants get into the blood very quickly and so into the brain very rapidly. It is this rapid invasion of the brain by the drug and nearly as rapid decrease in certain brain regions that creates the "rush," or euphoria, that people can experience with stimulants delivered in this fashion. This does not occur from the oral ingestion of the drug. This problem led a small biotech company near Albany, NY, to invent a method in which the AMP (d-AMP) is locked up so that it cannot be activated unless it is in the human stomach or intestines. They achieved this by bonding a lysine compound to the d-AMP. This bonding of an active drug to another compound alters its typical pattern of activation and is called a "pro-drug" by the FDA. In this form, the AMP is inactive and will remain so until it is swallowed. Then, in the stomach and intestine and its blood supply, there is a chemical that naturally occurs there that splits the lysine from the d-AMP, and now the d-AMP can go to work and be absorbed into the bloodstream. The drug is designed in such a way that the d-AMP lasts 10 to 14 hours, typically. This delivery system greatly reduces the abuse potential of this version of AMP while providing for the desired longer time course of action from a single dose.

Sometimes these ADHD medications can also help to treat that other attention disorder (sluggish cognitive tempo or concentration deficit disorder) I described in Chapter 3.

Side Effects

The most common side effects people experience when taking a stimulant (MPH or AMP) are listed in their descending order of likely occurrence:

- insomnia, or trouble falling asleep;
- loss of appetite, especially for the midday meal (some adults perceive this as a benefit if they are trying to lose weight);
- weight loss (again, some adults do not see this as an adverse effect but positive effect if they are trying to lose weight);
- headaches;
- nausea, upset stomach, or stomachache;
- anxiety (the research is somewhat mixed on whether stimulants worsen anxiety but enough studies have found this to be the case, particularly with children with ADHD, that it should continue to be listed as a possible adverse effect);
- irritability, or being easily upset, angered, or prone to outbursts (but just as often or more often, managing the ADHD can actually reduce problems with controlling one's emotion; as I discussed earlier, problems with regulating one's emotions actually goes with ADHD so treating the ADHD can often make this area of functioning better, not worse);
- motor tics (stimulants may not cause these outright in patients unless they have a family history for tic disorders and thus are somewhat more vulnerable to develop a tic than are others without such a history; if tics are already present, they can be worsened in up to one third of such cases, but in the remainder the tics remain unchanged or may even be improved); and

- increased muscle tension (although this is not very common, some people report sensations like they may have if they drink too much caffeine, such as tenseness of or frequent clenching of the jaw, muscle tension in the forehead, or generally feeling more taut in their posture).

The stimulants also increase heart rate and blood pressure slightly but generally no more so, and often less, than if you had just climbed a half-flight of stairs. You may have heard claims that these drugs increase the sensitivity to, or risk for, abusing other drugs, especially other stimulants, but the vast majority of research does not support this claim. People who have taken ADHD stimulant medications for years, including children who had grown up with ADHD, were found to be no more likely to abuse drugs than were those not being treated.[4] In fact, in a few studies they were found to be less likely to do so, probably because the ADHD medication was controlling their impulsiveness.[5]

You may have also heard that these drugs, especially the stimulants, might increase the likelihood of sudden death, usually from heart block (heart stops beating). In rare cases, strokes have occurred in people on these drugs. Although some people have died

---

[4]Biederman, J., Monuteaux, M. C., Spencer, T., Wilens, T. E., MacPherson, H. A., & Faraone, S. V. (2008). Stimulant therapy and risk for subsequent substance use disorders in male adults with ADHD: A naturalistic controlled 10-year follow-up study. *American Journal of Psychiatry*, *165*, 597–603. http://dx.doi.org/10.1176/appi.ajp.2007.07091486

[5]Groenman, A. P., Oosterlaan, J., Rommelse, N. N. J., Franke, B., Greven, C. U., Hoekstra, P. J., . . . Faraone, S. V. (2013). Stimulant treatment for attention-deficit hyperactivity disorder and risk of developing substance use disorder. *British Journal of Psychiatry*, *203*, 112–119. http://dx.doi.org/10.1192/bjp.bp.112.124784

while taking a stimulant, these cases always involve other extenuating factors that alone can account for the sudden death. Those reasons include things like a history of structural heart defects, a family history of sudden death, or engaging in excessively vigorous exercise just preceding the death. The available evidence actually shows that people on stimulants have a somewhat lower likelihood of sudden death than the general population (which is one to seven people per every 100,000 people per year, depending on age). This is probably because physicians routinely screen for heart problems before starting people on stimulants. And, if one is discovered, physicians usually do not prescribe these medications. So those with the greatest likelihood of having heart problems if they took a stimulant are not prescribed them. Even so, physicians have been cautioned not to put people on stimulants if they have a history of sudden death in their family or a history of structural heart abnormalities, major arrhythmias, or other major cardiac problems. It also makes sense not to treat people with clinically or morbidly high blood pressure with a stimulant for the obvious reason that it can make the situation even more risky for them. The risk to otherwise healthy adults with ADHD is not significant, if there is any increased risk at all.

NONSTIMULANTS

Atomoxetine

In 2003, the FDA approved the first nonstimulant drug for the management of child, teen, and adult ADHD, and the first new drug for ADHD in more than 25 years: atomoxetine, under the brand name Strattera. This was the most-studied ADHD drug before receiving FDA approval that has ever been brought to market. Randomized and double-blinded studies were done involving more than 6,000 patients worldwide to thoroughly study the effectiveness, side effects, and safety of this medication. Now, similar to the stimulants, this medication is taken by millions of people worldwide for management of their ADHD.

ATX differs from the stimulants in that it does not affect the brain centers that are likely to be related to drug addiction or abuse. It increases amounts of norepinephrine in the brain by blocking the reuptake of this chemical once it is released from a nerve cell. And it does so in some parts of the brain where stimulants may not be acting. For instance, this drug does not activate the brain's reward center and so does not lead to risk for addiction. And that is also why it is not classified as a controlled substance in the United States. Research shows that the drug has a very low potential for abuse. The different means by which it acts in the brain can result in a different profile of potential side effects (adverse reactions) and possibly somewhat different benefits from this drug than what one sees with the stimulants.

ATX is nearly as effective for managing ADHD symptoms as are the stimulants, but not quite. The same percentage of patients appear to positively respond to both these classes of drugs (stimulants, nonstimulants), averaging about 75% of people responding. However, some studies suggest that although 50% of people respond positively to both types of medications, 25% may respond better to a stimulant than to ATX. However, the remaining 25% may respond better to ATX than to one of the stimulants. In other words, some people are unique responders who do better on one type of ADHD drug than on another. Some studies suggest that ATX may not produce quite as much improvement in ADHD symptoms as do the stimulants. But for some adults, the degree of improvement is sufficient to effectively manage their disorder while not necessarily producing the same types of side effects that one might get with a stimulant.

The issue that physicians face in daily practice with ADHD patients is therefore not which drug works better but which drug is best suited to which individual patient, given their unique profile of characteristics. Having many different drugs, just like having many different delivery systems, lets physicians better tailor their treatment to the uniqueness of each patient. Your loved one can expect, however, that ATX will take longer to adjust to find the right dose than is the case with a stimulant. That is because it takes longer for the body to adjust to the side effects of drugs like ATX. And that is why physicians like to leave patients on a particular dose a bit longer than they might do with a stimulant before adjusting the dose upward.

Atomoxetine Side Effects

The most common side effects of ATX are nausea or vomiting, dry mouth, dizziness or light-headedness, constipation, sweating, decreased libido (sex drive) or erectile dysfunction, sweating, insomnia (far less common than with the stimulants), and possibly irritability. Although ATX can also increase heart rate and blood pressure, it does so less than the stimulants. There is an exceptionally rare chance of liver complications that occurred once in every million people treated as originally reported (four cases out of 4.5 million treated to date). This seems to result from a very rare autoimmune reaction to the drug in which the body's immune system attacks and inflames the outer layers of the liver. More recently, two of these cases were discounted as being due to other factors not related to the drug. So the risk for this side effect is now about one in every 2 to 3 million people being treated. But to be safe, people with a history of liver damage or other liver problems may want to avoid using ATX.

The package insert for ATX contains a warning of a possibility of increased suicidal thinking from this drug, but not suicide attempts, and only in children. This side effect is highly questionable given the lack of rigor with which the information on which it is based was collected in the initial clinical trials for this drug. This problem of increased suicidal thinking was not found for teens and adults with ADHD taking ATX, even though they, not children, are the most likely to manifest that problem. Also, recent research has found that people with ADHD who are off medication have a far higher rate of suicidal thinking and attempts than do those who are taking either ATX or a stimulant medication. These findings suggest that taking these medicines for ADHD may actually reduce the risk for suicidal thinking and attempts.

Bupropion

Another nonstimulant, bupropion, is sometimes used for treating adults with ADHD, but it is not FDA approved for doing so. The drug is sold under the brand name Wellbutrin in the United States. Although it also increases norepinephrine in the brain by a mechanism similar to that of ATX, it also affects other brain chemicals. That can be an advantage if a physician is trying to treat ADHD and another disorder that responds to bupropion at the same time, such as anxiety or mild depression. But it can also produce unwanted side effects. It also may not work as well as the stimulants if all one is trying to change is ADHD symptoms. It has not been studied as extensively as ATX and so its value in managing ADHD is less well established. Even so, some physicians can still use this drug for treating ADHD if they choose to do so, a practice known as "off-label use." More often, the drug has been used to manage a coexisting anxiety disorder or mild depression in patients who also have ADHD.

Other nonstimulants have also been used off-label to treat adult ADHD, such as antidepressants, antianxiety drugs, and even some mood stabilizers or antipsychotic drugs. None of these are especially effective for managing ADHD or have as extensive a research background as the FDA-approved medicines discussed here. Often they are used to manage another coexisting disorder and may even be combined with the ADHD drugs discussed here. The antinarcoleptic drug modafinil (Provigil) has shown some promising results as a treatment for ADHD symptoms in children. Yet, even then the results have not always been replicated in other studies. No research, as of this writing, has focused on using this drug with adults with ADHD. The drug increases wakefulness and arousal and sometimes has been used to treat sleep apnea (disrupted breathing while asleep). But the drug has not received FDA approval for ADHD.

ANTIHYPERTENSIVE DRUGS

Two other medicines are sometimes used to treat adult ADHD, but they should be considered last-choice medicines to be used only if the other ADHD medicines are not proving satisfactory. Both originated as drugs used to treat high blood pressure, called antihypertensive drugs. One is clonidine, and works as an alpha-adrenergic enhancer. Some nerve cells in the brain have little portholes on them called alpha-2 receptors. These drugs seem to act to reduce or close off these portholes, and that results in stronger or more effective nerve signals in those cells. At low doses, this drug appears to stimulate inhibitory systems in the brain. The FDA approved an extended-release version of clonidine, clonidine ER (Kapvay), in 2010 as a treatment for ADHD in children ages 6 to 17 years. However, physicians can use it off-label outside of this age range, such as for adults with ADHD. It can be used alone or combined with stimulants. The drug is not as effective as the other ADHD medicines discussed earlier, in my opinion. So it is sometimes used to treat ADHD when it co-exists with another disorder, such as conduct or antisocial problems or irritability and anger. It can also treat tic disorders and sleep disturbances, and it may reduce anxiety. Regular clonidine does not last as long as the more recently approved extended-release version for the management of ADHD symptoms.

The most common side effect of clonidine is sedation, which tends to subside with continued treatment. It can also result in reduced blood pressure, called hypotension, and sometimes results in complaints of dry mouth, light-headedness, dizziness, possible fainting, vivid dreams, depression, and confusion. Unlike other ADHD medicines, this one cannot be stopped abruptly. Clonidine requires slow tapering over several days to weeks. The drug should not be used if your loved one is taking beta blockers or calcium channel blockers. Experts recommend that anyone using these drugs for treating ADHD have their blood pressure monitored when starting or when tapering off clonidine and when doses are being increased.

Another antihypertensive drug used for ADHD management is guanfacine. In 2009, the FDA approved an extended-release version, guanfacine ER (Intuniv), for the treatment of ADHD in people who are 6 to 17 years old. Again, physicians can use it with adults off-label if they think it essential to do so. The drug can be given alone or in combination with either of the stimulant medicines discussed earlier. Guanfacine may have some advantages of over clonidine, including less sedation, a longer duration of action, and less risk of cardiovascular problems.

These drugs can result in minor decreases in blood pressure and pulse rate. Other side effects include sedation, irritability, and depression. Again, this medication probably is not as effective as the stimulants or ATX. Its benefit may be in helping to treat coexisting disorders with ADHD, such as anger and aggression, and in reducing highly impulsive or hyperactive behavior.

You and your loved one should be aware that very little research has focused on using these two antihypertensive drugs to treat ADHD in adults. That is why the FDA approved them mainly for children, on whom more research was available. Again, because of the lack of research, these drugs are considered last-choice options for managing adult ADHD. The other ADHD medicines should be tried first.

WHAT TO EXPECT FROM MEDICATION TREATMENT

> I am 27 years old and come from East Asia. I recently was diagnosed with ADHD and recurring depression. Surprisingly, I felt extremely happy and relieved after the diagnosis because the old dejecting question, "Why am I such a loser who never succeeds in tenaciously sticking onto something and achieving it?" which used to pop up often in my mind, finally has an answer. It was very soothing and elating to know that all these traits of mine that had been mistakenly viewed, often by me and by others, such as extreme lethargy, carelessness, and a lack of genuine interest now had a way to be understood through psychiatry. Playing music is my passion. I morbidly love music. I am learning the piano, which demands hours of mindful and persistent practice for years, as you may know. Fortunately, I was born into a lineage of an elite class of musicians and so I literally lived in music since my infancy. My doctor says that I am a person with a lot of potential that remains underutilized because of ADHD. He tells me that I can surely make it with the help of proper medication and support. I am always grateful to him for his kind words. I started to follow the medication he prescribed to me, and it made a huge difference. Now I can sit and practice on the piano for 7 to 10 hours a day without any restlessness or boredom. I don't think I've spent at least one mindful hour on anything in my whole life before now.

Most adults with ADHD experience a significant improvement in their symptoms on these medications once a therapeutic dose has been found for them. A minority of patients reported such remarkable improvements that they were functionally normal. If so, they may be joyful or near tears over just how well they are able to function now that they have been treated. For some people, the medication is the only treatment they may require to address their ADHD-related concerns.

Most people report that their symptoms are improved substantially. They are (a) more productive at work, (b) more attentive while engaged in various tasks, (c) less impulsive and more thoughtful about what they are doing, (d) less scattered or distractible in their ability to focus on tasks and complete them, (e) less forgetful, (f) better able to organize their thoughts, (g) better able to carry on conversations with others, (h) able to compose written projects like business letters or reports faster and more coherently, (i) more persistent in following through on promises to others or activities, and (j) better emotionally controlled or stable.

Not infrequently, adults with ADHD often say that they finally know what it is like to feel or behave like a "normal" person or at least nearly so. But don't expect that all of your loved one's symptoms or concerns will be miraculously solved with medication. Troubles at work, in relationships, in school, or elsewhere can arise from other sources besides ADHD. Consequently, treating the ADHD does not always eliminate these other problems or unresolved issues. As I said earlier, most people with ADHD have at least one other disorder, and many have two other disorders. Those other disorders are not likely to be spontaneously cured by effectively treating their ADHD. Other treatments will be needed to address them.

The doses needed to treat ADHD vary substantially across people, with some requiring very small doses, equal to those used with children. Others need substantially higher doses, well above the average. Expect your loved one's physician to try a range of doses. The doctor will start with a low dose and increase it every week until a good response is obtained or your loved one reports such annoying side effects that make going to an even higher dose no longer an option. Your loved one has a 75% chance of responding to whatever ADHD drug is tried first. But he needs to be patient (not a strong suit of most adults with ADHD), as it can sometimes take 2 to 3 weeks or even 1 to 2 months to find the best dose for his needs. Your loved one has a 10% to 25% chance of not responding to the first drug tried, and a 3% to 10% chance of not being able to tolerate the drug at all. Be sure that the physician is getting information from others who know your loved one well, such as yourself or anyone he may be living with at the time. Sometimes these drugs can be improving his ADHD symptoms, but the adult with ADHD seems less aware of that change than do those around them.

If the first drug tried does not work or does not work as well as your loved one and the doctor would like, don't worry. One of several other options may well be the right ones for her. Your loved one should keep trying other ADHD medicines and delivery systems even if she didn't respond to the first one tried. These drugs are among the safest and best tested in all of psychiatry. Therefore, it pays for your loved one and her doctor to experiment with different drugs, doses, and delivery systems so as to find what is right for her. A physician should only go off-label and use a non-FDA approved drug for your loved one's ADHD if she has not shown a positive response to any of the ADHD medications or there is a very good reason not to start her on an ADHD drug first.

COMMON QUESTIONS ABOUT ADHD MEDICATIONS

Is there any scientific evidence to suggest that ADHD medications are either safe or unsafe during pregnancy? There is little evidence concerning the effects of any ADHD medications on pregnant mothers or their babies. One large study reported in 2013 found that women with ADHD who took their stimulant medications while pregnant did not have a higher risk of having babies born with any obvious malformations. This suggests that the drugs may be safe to take when pregnant. But one study is not definitive on this point. So at this time, all companies recommend that women discontinue their ADHD medications should they become pregnant. Of course, the woman and her doctor must weigh the disadvantages of stopping medication because it will result in an increase in their ADHD symptoms and all the attendant risks that go with that, like driving risks, financial management problems, marital and relationship stress, more problems with child rearing if they already have other children, not to mention more work and educational problems.

Is the effectiveness of medication likely to be influenced by any major changes in the body, like major weight gain or weight loss, hormonal changes (monthly menses, perimenopause, menopause, etc.)? Some people, particularly growing children, do find that their dose must be adjusted with time. This is likely due to weight gain and other changes with maturation. These are less likely to be issues in adults, but some adults have reported changes in the effectiveness of their medication with weight changes. So doses may need to be adjusted from time to time, although less often than in children. We have no evidence about the impact of perimenopause or even monthly menstrual cycles on medication effectiveness so this is an issue that remains unanswered at this time.

Is it possible to build tolerance to stimulant medicines, and if so, how should it be handled? How can someone either avoid building tolerance or deal with it once he or she is experiencing tolerance? Actual physical tolerance seems unlikely with the current ADHD medications. But some individuals report that their medication seems less effective about 3 to 6 months after starting their treatment. This usually requires adjusting the dose or, sometimes, changing to a different delivery system or even a different medication. Clinically, we sometimes see people complaining that their medicine isn't working as well. However, further information shows them going through an unusually stressful or demanding period in their life that may exacerbate their ADHD symptoms and make it more difficult for their usual dose to provide adequate treatment. Temporary dose changes or addressing the source of the stress may be needed at these times.

Can the generic medications be less effective than the brand name drugs? Perhaps. The generic medications appear not to be manufactured with the same degree of rigor as the brand name medications. The generics have been associated with numerous reports of greater variability in controlling the ADHD symptoms on a day-to-day basis or have been reported to overall produce less success in managing those symptoms. Should that occur, have your loved one ask their doctor to transfer them back to the brand name medicine.

Can my loved one become addicted to the ADHD stimulant medications? What if she or he has a history of drug abuse/addiction? Research shows that there is no real risk of addiction to ADHD medications when they are taken as prescribed. Problems can occur if a person tries to use a different route of administration with the medicine, like crushing the medication tablets into a powder and then snorting it into the nose like cocaine. Or if they abuse it by making it into a solution with water and injecting it intravenously. Then, yes, these drugs could become addictive. There is always a possibility that someone can develop a dependency on the medicine; overrelying on it to try and solve all their problems or to help them through a situation. Those problems often include some not really linked to having ADHD. They may simply be trying to stay awake longer than is typical in special situations, such as when they are studying for tests at college or driving long distances while avoiding sleep. If your loved one has a history of nicotine, alcohol, or marijuana abuse, then it seems perfectly safe for him to take ADHD medications while he is trying to detox from these other drugs. Indeed, controlling the ADHD symptoms with ADHD medications may help him to be better able to come off of other drugs because it can boost his self-control. But if your loved one has a history of abusing stimulants, such as cocaine or methamphetamine, then it is advisable that he take one of the nonstimulant ADHD medications, which pose no risk of contributing to further stimulant abuse.

KEY POINTS TO REMEMBER

Two types of FDA-approved medications were discussed here for the effective management of adult ADHD: stimulants and nonstimulants. Most patients respond positively to these medications, but up to 10% to 15% may not respond to any of them. Trying each drug and each delivery system can help improve the chances of finding the right one. Each drug also has its own unique profile of benefits and side effects, yet all are considered reasonably safe for use in managing adult ADHD. Two other drugs, both of which are antihypertensive medications, may also help to treat ADHD. These are FDA approved for use only in children because little or no research exists on their use to treat adults with ADHD. Even so, doctors can use them off-label to treat adults if they deem it appropriate to do so. These unapproved medicines may not be as effective as those approved for managing adult ADHD, such as MPH, AMP, and ATX. Although those medicines are quite effective, there are various reasons your loved one may not comply with taking them, not persist in doing so, or wish to cease taking them.

If your loved one is not currently taking medication, and his ADHD symptoms are at least of moderate or greater severity and frequency, and those symptoms are currently causing problems with functioning effectively in one or more major life activities, then you may want to talk with him about medication as a treatment option. In that case, encourage him to read this chapter about the medications or the comparable chapter in my other book, *Taking Charge of Adult ADHD* (see the Resources section). Then encourage him to speak with his physician about these medications. Of course, if your loved one has not yet been diagnosed professionally as having ADHD, then speaking with him about getting that evaluation is a necessary first step to going on the ADHD medications.

When your loved one is about to go on medication, you can suggest that she take stock of the degree of her ADHD symptoms the day before starting medication. You can do this using The Symptoms of ADHD checklist in Chapter 1. You might want to complete your own version of this scale about her symptoms as well so you have two baseline evaluations against which to judge how well the medication may work to treat her ADHD symptoms. A week or so after she is on medication, you can then have her complete this checklist for a second time. You may wish to do the same. You can both then compare these ratings with the initial ones completed before starting medication to gauge how well the medication may be working. You can do this again a week after each increase in her dose of medication to evaluate how well the new dose may be working to manage her ADHD symptoms.

Of course, if your loved one experiences significant and very annoying side effects that might cause him to quit taking the medication, have him discuss those with the prescribing physician right away. Otherwise, the minor side effects can be discussed at the next scheduled appointment with the doctor. Keep in mind that some minor side effects, such as insomnia or loss of appetite, may develop during the first week but decline in severity or even dissipate within the first week or two of treatment, as the body acclimates to the medication. If you have your own questions and concerns about the medication, or if you believe it is not effective for your loved one, ask him if he would mind if you go with him to his next appointment to get your questions answered. But by no means should you demand to do so or otherwise pressure your loved one into letting you do this if he is opposed to the idea. In that case, your own questions or concerns might be addressed by simply reading more about these medications at respected websites on the Internet (see the Resources section at the end of this book).

CHAPTER 13

HELPING YOUR LOVED ONE STAY ON MEDICATION

One of the greatest difficulties with attention-deficit/hyperactivity disorder (ADHD) medications for adults is not that they do not work—clearly, they do—it is that adults with ADHD are less and less likely to stay on them over the first few years of being treated. This can be hard for some people to understand. After all, if medications are effective, then why wouldn't someone want to remain on them to get the most benefit from their treatment plan? Because other issues cause noncompliance with medication even if it is effective at managing a disorder. This nonadherence to medical advice is not just a problem in the area of adult ADHD. It can be seen across most chronic conditions, including high blood pressure, high cholesterol, diabetes, epilepsy, and others. People simply don't always do what is best for them, for various reasons.

The first thing you can do to facilitate your loved one's staying on medication is to tell them how much improvement you are noticing in their symptoms and functioning. Sometimes adults with ADHD are less aware of how well their medication is working than are those around them who see them frequently, such as yourself. So be sure to let them know of any positive signs you see that the medication may be helping them to deal with their ADHD and the impairments in life activities those may be causing. If your loved one still seems uncertain about using the medication, then consider some of the following reasons that adults with ADHD may cease their medication even if it is effective. Along with these issues, I suggest some things you can do to address them.

NOT WANTING TO TAKE MEDICATION CAN BE DUE TO ADHD

Having ADHD can further contribute to the more typical problems with adhering to medical advice. That is because ADHD creates problems with self-regulation, which is one of the mental abilities (the executive functions) we use to do what is best for us over the long term. It makes perfect sense that people who have a disorder of self-control have difficulty properly controlling the management of their medicine. That is because ADHD involves the following challenges:

- *Poor time management.* Your loved one may not take his medications in a timely and consistent manner, may miss appointments with physicians to get refills, might fail to get to the pharmacy on time to get the refill, may miss the deadline to file for a renewal if it is via a mail-order prescription service, and so on.
- *Poor working memory, self-organization, and problem solving.* This can lead your loved one to not always remember to take her medications as prescribed, to not refill them when needed, to not deal with the problems that can be posed by insurance companies or others that are covering part or all of the medication costs, to forget to schedule the doctor's appointment to get a refill on their prescription or go to the pharmacy to fill it.
- *Deficient self-restraint.* This deficit often leads adults with ADHD to impulsively quit the medication if there are annoying or unpleasant side effects. Or they may impulsively stop if

the cost doesn't seem worth the benefits to them, if they fear being stigmatized if others know they take such medication, or if they come to believe that the medications are dangerous and they can get by with natural remedies or healthier food, for instance.

- *Low self-motivation.* If this occurs, it can lead an adult with ADHD to do all of the above as well as to not even bother trying to make regular doctor's appointments, take medication regularly, refill prescriptions, and so on, all of which take not only time but extra effort.
- *Poor emotion regulation.* Many adults with ADHD have this problem. If so, it can lead them to become angry and quit the medical system when frustrated by waiting lists to get seen or have a prescription filled. Or they may get into arguments with family members if you bug them too much about taking the medicine, getting appropriate dosage adjustments, having patience while the medications take effect, and so on.
- *Diminished self-awareness.* Many adults with ADHD are not as aware of the positive reductions in their symptoms and better functioning as those around them are.
- *Positive illusory bias.* This refers to viewing problems and deficits as not as bad as others see them or evidence proves them to be, or denying that a problem exists at all. Positive illusory bias can lead your loved one to simply not see the problem area in the first place or to underappreciate its seriousness.

Another problem is that the effects of many of these medications, especially the stimulants, last only 3 to 12 hours, depending on the type of medication and the delivery system used (see Chapter 12 for more details). This means that there will be times, especially in the early morning before the medication is taken or at night when it has worn off, that the medicine is not working at all because it is largely out of the bloodstream. Here again, the problems with ADHD symptoms and executive deficits can now interfere with complying with medical advice.

WHAT YOU CAN DO TO HELP

Go back and review some of the big-picture recommendations I made in Chapter 11. You can use these ideas to help your loved one cope with some of his executive deficits related to working memory, time management, organization, and so on. When applied to helping him to remember to take his medications, keep doctor's appointments, deal with pharmacies, and so on, those suggestions might just help. Using a pill organizer that groups medicines by days of the week can help. Try placing this container right beside the bathroom sink, where he can see it every morning when he brushes his teeth. These steps may help him remember to take his pills, but he still may need reminding each week to refill the organizer.

Having your loved one write down appointments in her calendar or schedule on her computer or smartphone may help with appointment keeping. So might placing these items in your own calendar so you can offer reminders. Many smartphones have a shared-calendar function so that two or more users may enter appointments and have them appear on each other's calendars automatically.

To aid with self-awareness and positive illusory bias, talk with your loved one periodically about the benefits of medication that you may be seeing both in his behavior and in the results (better school performance, better work participation, more responsible at home, better management of money, etc.). Encourage others who care about him to do the same. This is so your loved one gets someone else's perspective and does not base his decision to stay on or go off medication on his own subjective view. As with losing weight, there is nothing like hearing from others how much you

have improved to keep someone motivated to stay in treatment. What else you do here to help really depends on which of the ADHD symptoms are contributing most to your loved one's trouble adhering to the medication plan.

OTHER COMMON REASONS ADULTS DON'T WANT TO TAKE MEDICINE FOR CHRONIC CONDITIONS

Dr. Cynthia Last noted in her book for families of patients with bipolar disorder that there can be reasons other than their disorder for why a loved one may not comply with taking recommended medications.[1] To her list I have added some others from my own clinical experience with ADHD. Understanding her reasons for nonadherence can help you strategize how you may be able to help your loved one stick with her medication treatment plan.

I Really Don't Have ADHD, so Why Am I Taking These Medications?

This problem goes all the way back to the one of not accepting the diagnosis. So you may need to reread the suggestions I offered in Chapter 10 for how to help deal with denial. You can also go back and review how to approach your loved one when he is at an early stage of readiness to change in which he has not fully accepted the diagnosis.

I Don't Like the Idea of Taking "Drugs."

Unfortunately, the popular media has contributed to this perception that ADHD medications are the same as taking abusable "drugs"

[1]Last, C. G. (2009). *When someone you love is bipolar: Help and support for you and your partner.* New York, NY: Guilford Press.

like some junkie. Consequently, these medications have an unnecessary stigma and misperception attached to them that may not be the case with medications used for other medical conditions, like high cholesterol. Yes, as I said in Chapter 12, these medications do have some small abuse potential, but they are not being prescribed to make someone a drug addict, and they are not addictive when taken as prescribed. They are also not increasing any future risk of being dependent on or abusing these or any other drugs. Explain this to your loved one.

Let's also realize that a large segment of our society wishes to be on presumably healthier and more natural or organic diets or adopt vegetarian or vegan approaches to nutrition. Taking medications is often seen as contradictory to these and other "healthy" approaches to nutrition specifically and lifestyle more generally. To counteract such views in your loved one, you can talk about the fact that all food involves chemistry that affects the body. Some natural chemicals are actually deadly, especially if taken in large quantities. Thus, the distinction between natural chemicals as being healthier for you than artificial chemicals doesn't really hold up on close examination. If your loved one drinks coffee or uses alcohol, these are both chemicals that are natural but can be harmful when used to excess. They are often used for the changes they create in our mental functioning and not just our physical functioning. You can also discuss the fact that if your loved one had diabetes or epilepsy, they would not likely be against using medications to treat these life-debilitating or even life-threatening conditions. ADHD, as you have learned, is no different. It is both debilitating and potentially life threatening (accidents, injuries, poor health, cardiovascular disease, etc.) if not treated consistently and persistently.

Also, try to show understanding and empathy with your loved one around taking medicine. Tell her that you realize that no one really likes to take medications for a chronic problem, especially for managing behavior rather than physical functioning. Just as I don't like taking medication routinely to reduce my high cholesterol and others don't like taking medications for high blood pressure, your loved one may not like the idea of using medicines for the rest of their life. Moreover, this example can be used to educate your loved one that many, many people are taking various medications daily for chronic medical, as well as psychiatric, problems (think of arthritis, hypothyroid, pain, headache, etc., not to mention vitamins and nutritional supplements like fish oils, ginkgo biloba, garlic, etc.). Therefore, your loved one is not alone in needing to do so.

If your loved one's resistance to taking the medications stems from other concerns, such as fearing a risk for later substance abuse or heart attacks, you can assuage those fears with what you know. You can back up your opinions by directing them to books on adult ADHD that have chapters on these medications, such as this chapter or the one in my book *Taking Charge of Adult ADHD*. You can also send your loved one to the reputable websites on ADHD that I list at the back of this book (Resources) and so refute these misconceptions.

I Am Doing Well Now, so I Don't Need the Medicine any Longer.

This is a paradox that often occurs with psychiatric medications, including those used for other disorders, like bipolar disorder. When the drugs are effective, they can so reduce the patient's symptoms and so improve their daily functioning that the person comes to see themselves as relatively normal. When this effect goes on for a while, the person may even come to believe that many of the improvements are not the result of the medication but of their other efforts to manage their condition or of just "trying harder." Or they may come to think that since they are better, they never had a serious case of ADHD to begin with. Because the medication has reduced the very need to take it (serious symptoms), then those symptoms no longer exist to give one the motivation to have them treated. Such circular thinking can lead the person to believe he doesn't need the medication any longer to function well, so he stops. This is clearly a misunderstanding.

Fortunately for the ADHD medications, such as the stimulants in particular, the drugs do not need to be taken for long periods before an initial effect is evident (minutes) or before a downstream effect on daily functioning shows up (days) from using the medications. Most of the medicines for ADHD can also be stopped abruptly without causing harm. That is because most, like the stimulants, are washing out of the body within 24 hours anyway, so your loved one is having a drug washout period almost daily.

All this means that if your loved one doubts the benefits of medication or her continuing need for it, then there is really little harm in having her stop her medication for a day or a weekend so she and you can see what happens. However, be sure that your loved one discusses this with her doctor before doing so, just to be sure it is safe. Typically within 1 to 3 days after quitting the medicine, a difference becomes evident and convinces her to return to taking medication. If it does not do so, then have your loved one speak with the prescribing doctor about the results of this brief trial. A change in dose may be needed. Just be sure that stopping the medicine occurs at a time that won't pose undue risks. Remember that being off the ADHD medicine results in a return of the risks ADHD can pose, such as accidental injury, driving problems, diminished child care ability, and poor work performance, among others.

I Don't Think the Medicine Is Doing Me any Good.

This complaint can be a little different from the prior one as here your loved one is continuing to have problematic ADHD symptoms and is not impressed that the drug is helping him. If you agree with him that no improvements are evident, then encourage him to talk with the doctor about changing the dose or the type of medication. Your loved one could be right—perhaps this dose isn't working. But that doesn't mean that no dose will work or that no ADHD medicine type will help.

Sometimes the improvement your loved one is getting from the medicine is about as good as it may be for her on any type of medicine. If she has tried others and still finds this to be the case, then it may be helpful for her to her speak with a psychologist about adding the psychosocial treatments discussed in Chapter 11 to the medicine. In a minority of cases, combining different medicines may be the solution. These medicines each work differently in the brain, and thus combining them might provide wider improvements in symptom control than just one.

But as I said earlier, adults with ADHD often have less self-awareness. That means that you and others may perceive positive benefits from the medication that go unappreciated by your loved one. To address that, tell your loved one about the improvements you and others have seen. Also, ask him to discuss this with his doctor, as an increase in dose may be indicated if continuing problematic symptoms are driving this impression.

Sometimes the problems that are still evident to your loved one may be ones that ADHD medicines cannot treat. Symptoms of depression and anxiety or other mood disorders are typically not helped by ADHD medicines and may require separate treatments to be discussed with the prescribing physician. The problems in functioning in some domains may also not have much to do with ADHD, such as difficulties at work or in relationships with others or in school. The fact that these have not improved from taking medication might suggest they come from some other source, such as a difficult supervisor at work, jealousy in an intimate relationship, or a learning disability. These and other problems in functioning can arise from many other sources than just ADHD. Discuss this possibility with your loved one, if you can. Or have her discuss it with her physician so she can see more clearly what ADHD medicines can and cannot do for problems in daily functioning in certain domains.

I Am Not as (Creative, Fun, Spontaneous, Vibrant, etc.) as I Used to Be off the Medicine.

This can certainly be true. For instance, my colleagues and I have sometimes heard adults with ADHD who are poets, artists, musicians, or actors say that they find that they are not as creative in their work while on medicine as when off of it. Little or no scientific research has focused on the effects of these medicines on artistic creativity or expression. However, an indirect reason for this, at least in some people, is because lower levels of inhibition (up to a point) are related to higher levels of creativity. Being less inhibited contributes to thinking of more unusual ways to do things or making unusual connections among ideas. Inhibition enables us to suppress thinking of these more unusual ideas, largely because they may be distracting us from the work we may need to do and because they are not really relevant. But sometimes what can seem like an irrelevant idea can actually be a useful or brilliant way of seeing something. Because ADHD medicines increase inhibition, which is largely for the better, they might just be reducing this capacity to make linkages across seemingly irrelevant ideas. That could reduce someone's creativity, perhaps. At least this is theoretically possible, even if not documented in scientific research yet.

Where such reduced creativity is the case, speak with your loved one about possibly not taking his medication on those days or hours of the day when he is focusing on his creative work. One poet from my clinic did this. At other times or on other days when the more routine and even tedious aspects of life had to be dealt with, she went back on her medication. It is fortunate that most ADHD medications, like stimulants, dissipate from the body within 24 hours or less. One can stop and start them like this typically without significant harm. As always, make sure your loved one discusses this pattern of medication use with his doctor before trying it out.

As for the other concerns (less fun, vibrant, etc.), this may also be true. Adults with ADHD who are not on medication are certainly more talkative, emotional (including being humorous), demonstrative, active, and sometimes sensation seeking. All of these may be seen, at least in the short term, as making her more fun or interesting or adventurous. You can acknowledge this while pointing out that these features of her personality came with a price. These traits may have cost her jobs, friends, intimate partners, or other work and social opportunities because one person's "gregariousness" can be another person's "obnoxiousness" when carried on for too long. Moreover, that sensation seeking, thrilling, adventurousness could also have resulted in multiple accidents, property damage, injuries, higher insurance premiums or being uninsured, or it may have become intolerable to intimate partners when occurring on a chronic basis. You can't stay on a thrilling vacation for more than a few days if you expect others to stay on it with you. Doing so can wear people out, cause them undue chronic stress, and cost them financially as well. So be sure your loved one is appreciating the entire picture of costs and benefits from the medication should she wish to stop it for these reasons.

I Just Don't Like the Side Effects of This Medicine; They Are Really Annoying.

This can certainly be true: As you read in Chapter 12, the side effects of the various medications, while not life threatening, can be annoying. At times, these side effects may seem to be not worth the cost or the degree of benefits these medicines confer. For instance, stimulant medicines can create insomnia, loss of appetite, headaches, and stomachaches in some people. In rare cases, irritability, sadness, nervous mannerisms or even tics, staring, or emotional blandness may arise in response to the medicine. If these or other side effects are so prominent as to cause your loved one to question taking a medication, have him speak with his doctor right away. It may mean that a change in dose (usually downward), type of delivery system (long-acting ones might be better for some people than immediate-release ones), or type of ADHD medication (a nonstimulant, e.g., atomoxetine) is in order.

This Medicine Just Costs too Much.

This can be the case where your loved one has to pay for most or all of the costs of their prescription. It could also arise where she is taking one of the newer patented delivery systems rather than a generic form, or where her funds are so limited that even a small cost, like a copay, can be a burden on her finances. It can surely occur when the medicine is only partially effective and those benefits are perceived as not worth the cost. You can help your loved one address this issue by encouraging her to speak with her doctor about alternative, generic versions of the medication that may be less expensive. She can also talk with her doctor about programs the pharmaceutical company may have for providing reduced or free medication to people in financial need. Also have her ask her doctor about state-sponsored programs that can provide the medication to those low enough in income to qualify. Perhaps you may be able to help financially cover some of these costs or know of other family members who would be willing to help you do so.

CHAPTER 14

UNPROVEN TREATMENTS FOR ADULT ADHD

In this short chapter, I briefly mention various treatments available for adults with attention-deficit/hyperactivity disorder (ADHD) that have little, if any, convincing evidence to date for their effectiveness. Therefore, you should not encourage your loved one with adult ADHD to engage in these treatments unless or until they have used the treatments discussed earlier for which we have evidence for their effectiveness for ADHD. Even then, your loved one should never go into debt to engage in these treatments, given how little we know about their helpfulness.

MINDFULNESS MEDITATION

Several treatment approaches for adult ADHD are becoming more widely available, yet lack much of an evidence base in the scientific literature to determine whether they are actually effective with ADHD in adults. Mindfulness meditation is certainly a popular therapy modality. It is often suggested in the mainstream media as a self-help approach to coping with stress, anxiety, depression, and other emotional difficulties. It has also been recommended for coping with psychological problems that may be associated with chronic health disorders or even life-threatening disorders, such as cancer.

Although initial clinical reports suggest some promise for this approach to treating adult ADHD, those studies were not rigorously done. That leaves their results open to considerable debate and even doubt. The treatment has not been rigorously evaluated to date for use with adults who have ADHD. Until that type of research is done, mindfulness meditation is not recommended as a first-line treatment for ADHD as would be ADHD medications and cognitive behavior therapy (CBT) for adult ADHD. Dr. Mary Solanto and her student, Ayman Househam, from NYU Medical School recently reviewed the research to date on this treatment, concluding that the evidence has not yet proven its effectiveness for adult ADHD. But they believe that there is some promise to pursuing more and more rigorous research.[1] More information on this treatment can be found on the Internet.[2] Additional information is contained in the book by Lidia Zylowska, MD, *The Mindfulness Prescription for Adult ADHD* (see the Resources section of this book).

NEUROFEEDBACK (EEG BIOFEEDBACK)

Another experimental approach to treating ADHD is neurofeedback or EEG electroencephalogram (EEG) biofeedback. More than 30 years ago scientists began to test EEG biofeedback. Since then, some dramatic claims have been made for this kind of treatment. You may have seen advertisements stating that EEG biofeedback is

[1]Househam, A. M., & Solanto, M. V. (2016). Mindfulness as an intervention for ADHD. *The ADHD Report*, *23*(2), 1–9, 13. http://dx.doi.org/10.1521/adhd.2016.24.2.1

[2]See http://www.psychologytoday.com/blog/here-there-and-everywhere/201206/adhd-mindfulness-interview-lidia-zylowska-md, http://www.additudemag.com/adhd/article/1475.html, and http://psychcentral.com/lib/mindfulness-skills-useful-in-addressing-adhd/0004286.

an effective alternative to medication; that it results in permanent changes in the brain physiology underlying ADHD; that it improves IQ, social skills, and even learning disabilities; and that such improvements can last into adulthood in up to 80% of all treated cases of children. Those are fantastic claims for any treatment.

The term *biofeedback* means that a patient is given back information in some form (usually visual) about his biological functioning—in this case, his brain activity as measured by electrodes placed near or on the scalp. These sensors detect brain electrical waves and send them to a computer for averaging and display. The computer can then be used to show the person just how much or little brain activity is taking place. In this treatment, the computer can also reward him for practicing ways to increase that activity if it is unusually low. Over a great number of sessions, typically 40 to 80 sessions across 3 to 10 months or longer—at a cost of several thousand dollars ($100+ per session)—the patient supposedly learns to improve his brain activity. He does this through mental exercises and some form of signal from the biofeedback equipment. That signal tells him whether he has been successful at increasing the desired brain activity related to sustained attention and decreasing the undesired activity associated with daydreaming or distraction. He is then rewarded for doing so. In that sense, this treatment is a type of behavioral conditioning method that tries to increase some patient activity by rewarding it. The result, supposedly, is that the patient's inattention, hyperactivity, and impulsivity will then also improve.

Research does show that lower levels of brain activity are often associated with adult ADHD. So it makes some sense that trying to teach adults with ADHD to increase the brain electrical activity associated with paying attention might be beneficial for controlling those attention deficits. People can learn to change their brain activity, so that is not in dispute here. What is in question is whether such training produces results that last after the treatment session has ended; results in significant improvement in ADHD symptoms, such as inattention; and most important, whether those improvements generalize to their daily life activities. It is unfortunate that, to date, only a few well-controlled studies, mostly with children, have been conducted, and they are contradictory in their results. Indeed, among the better and more rigorous studies conducted, fewer benefits have been found, if any.

I believe biofeedback therapy at this time for adults with ADHD has considerable drawbacks. For one thing, little if any research has been done with this treatment using adults with ADHD. So it is not clear whether the treatment works on mature adult brain activity rather than maturing or developing child brain functioning. Also, the proponents of this treatment claim that it has no side effects or adverse consequences. But any treatment that is supposed to be this effective has to produce some side effects in a small percentage of people. That is because people can differ in their brain organization and also because clinicians may not always apply the treatment reliably or accurately. All effective treatments, including nonmedication ones, can produce side effects in some people. So it is quite surprising and a cause for skepticism that proponents claim that this one does not. Furthermore, the treatment is expensive, usually costing $100 per hour, and rarely covered by insurance—with the recommended 30 to 60 sessions, that's $3,000 to $6,000 out-of-pocket. An adult with ADHD could receive 12 years of ADHD medication, 3 years of weekly group therapy, nearly 3 years of twice-monthly individual therapy by a clinical psychologist, or almost 2 years of twice-weekly ADHD coaching for the cost of 6 months of this treatment, based on current average charges.

My advice, therefore, is to try the most effective and scientifically based treatments first (medication, CBT, counseling, etc.). Only then, if your loved one is not satisfied with their improvements, should they try neurofeedback. And it should be pursued only then if they have sufficient expendable income to cover the cost of treatment out-of-pocket. Do not encourage them to take on any debt to fund this treatment so long as its effectiveness remains unclear in the research literature.

NEUROCOGNITIVE TRAINING

Another form of psychological training, using computer games as mental exercises, is neurocognitive training. Typically, this involves people practicing mental exercises using games available on various computer software programs (BrainAge for Nintendo DS), websites (e.g., Lumosity.com), or separate hand-held devices (e.g., CogMed, which also involves consulting with a professional on a weekly basis). These games target mental functions, such as inhibition, resisting distractions, working memory, planning or anticipation, problem solving and mental flexibility, and other cognitive abilities. A person usually has to practice every day for about 30 to 45 minutes or more for most days of the week for benefits to accrue, if then. The costs can run from less than $10 per month for a subscription to the Internet websites that have such games available to $295 (or less) for a handheld Nintendo gaming device (the BrainAge software is often free and comes with the device), and on up to $1,200 to $1,500 for a hand-held device and associated professional consultation (CogMed). Some of the games can be fun, and others are entertaining initially but may become quite boring after a while.

The developers often claim that engaging in such mental exercise is like physical exercise in that it can increase your capacities in the cognitive domains being practiced (attention, impulse control, memory, etc.). But more recent research seems to show that although a person clearly improves in playing these games, the results do not generalize to everyday activities in which these mental abilities are involved. So people could get better at a game that involves remembering long strings of digits, yet this often does not mean they are any better in their memory during everyday routines that require good memory.

Much of the research on this treatment for ADHD has been done with children. Early studies by some of the game developers showed improvements in ADHD symptoms. However, later studies done by other researchers mostly did not show any benefits at school or even at home if the parents doing the reporting are not informed about the treatment versus placebo conditions. Yes, the children got better at playing the games. And yes, they were better at doing some lab tests that were quite similar to the games. But little benefit was observed outside the lab, and usually none at school, where such mental abilities are often critical to academic success. Once again, I do not recommend these treatments at this time unless other more effective treatments have been used first. The results to date are not convincing enough for recommending this training approach as a treatment for ADHD. I advise you and your loved one not to rely on them as a primary treatment of ADHD and to try them only if your loved one has expendable income to pay for these games out-of-pocket. Once again, as with neurofeedback, buyer beware.

DIET

Fish Oils

Many dietary supplements, such as omega-3/-6 fish oil supplements or antioxidants, such as Pycnogenol, have been proposed as beneficial for treating ADHD. But most have never been studied scientifically with adults with the disorder. And no studies to date have shown much, if any, benefit even when tested with children with ADHD using rigorous scientific methods. Some early clinical evidence was initially positive for the omega-3/-6 supplements. (When you see the words *clinical evidence*, it usually means case testimonials. The treatment was not studied very scientifically using randomized assignments to treatment or control groups. Instead, people took the medicine and reported that they seemed improved.) However, more recent randomized trials using larger samples, control groups, placebos, and blinded evaluations of improvement did not show much, if any, improvement from these oils. What little improvement that was found was limited to about 25% of the sample, mostly those who were just inattentive and not impulsive or hyperactive. Also, the degree of change in symptoms was rather modest.

A recent review combining all of the research results, called a meta-analysis, concluded that omega-3/-6 held no benefit for those having ADHD. That is why for now I do not recommend that adults with ADHD waste their limited financial resources on these supplements, or any others, until more research can be done on their effectiveness.

Elimination Diets

Another approach to managing ADHD, typically in children, that has been popular is removing certain substances from one's routine diet, such as eliminating or reducing sugar, food additives and preservatives, artificial flavors, and artificial coloring. One such approach started 30 years ago was the Feingold diet, which argued for eliminating most or all of these substances in children's daily diets. Another has been called the restrictive elimination diet, or RED. These treatments were supposed to cure 60% to 80% of all ADHD. When well-conducted scientific studies were done, the results did not support these claims. Some of the results in fact appear not to be credible at all.

No evidence currently suggests that sugar causes ADHD or that removing it benefits people with ADHD. The same is true so far for additives, preservatives, and flavorings. It is interesting to note that some research has suggested that food colorings or dyes are associated with small increases in ADHD symptoms in typical children, and small reductions in symptoms when the colors are removed. But the benefits are typically well below those seen with ADHD medications. Also, the research has been entirely done with children, not with adults with ADHD. Moreover, the more rigorous were the studies (using randomized assignment to groups, placebo controls, blinded conditions, etc.), the weaker were the results. These diets are also quite difficult to implement and, if focused mainly on organic foods, can be relatively expensive compared with typical grocery prices. I do not recommend such diets for adults with ADHD at this time.

CHIROPRACTIC HEAD MASSAGE

Some chiropractors use a treatment for ADHD and learning disorders that involves placing significant pressure at various points around the skull and even inside the mouth on the roof or palate. Known as scalp or skull massage or neurologic organization training, the therapy is based on a rather ridiculous idea. That idea behind the treatment is that nerve cells somehow became trapped in the wrong places during early brain development. Placing pressure on the skull over these points of entrapment supposedly causes the nerve cells trapped underneath to be released. That is supposed to enable the nerves to migrate to their appropriate destinations in the brain and spinal cord, and so function better, and thereby cure the problem. No evidence suggests that such manipulation or massage results in any improvement in ADHD symptoms or learning disorders.

CONCLUSION

This chapter has briefly discussed some of the alternative or complementary treatments for ADHD that are currently popular, especially at pop psychology Internet websites or websites that sell these products. Remember that the Internet is like an open-air market or rowdy, chaotic, unscreened, or unsupervised marketplace. Anything goes! Opinions abound! It is full of both true and false information. And much of what appears there about psychiatric disorders is unscientific. The websites of government mental health agencies, such as the National Institute of Mental Health, those of professional associations, such as the American Psychiatric Association or the American Psychological Association, and those of charities specializing in advocating for the disorder, such as Children and Adults with ADHD, are usually much better informed and contain more credible, science-based information than do commercial websites or those of political advocacy groups. If you want to read about scientific research on a treatment, then use Google Scholar as your web browser, as it will search just the science journals and medical literature.

CHAPTER 15

ROLES YOU CAN ADOPT TO BE OF HELP

You may have come to this book with the view that your loved one with attention-deficit/hyperactivity disorder (ADHD) had a motivational problem, a behavioral problem, a moral failing that they could readily change, or was willfully making bad lifestyle choices. You now know that none of this is true. This earlier frame of mind likely led you to think ill of your loved one, at least sometimes. Maybe you believed they could just change if they wanted to do so. Maybe you withheld your compassion for their plight because you thought that somehow they deserved what was happening to them since they "chose" to behave impulsively, emotionally, and inattentively. Maybe you thought that the natural consequences would teach them that they needed to change and act "normal." Or maybe you even criticized your loved one with ADHD for deciding to be "that way," viewing their actions as intentional misbehavior and irresponsibility. Perhaps you saw them as simply not wanting to "grow up."

All of these opinions stem from a faulty perspective about ADHD symptoms and those having them: that they could change and be normal if they wanted to, but since they don't want to, why should anyone try to help them? Doing so is just coddling them. It is protecting them from the consequences of their actions that were foreseeable to any normal person. It may even enable their ongoing irresponsible behavior or otherwise make excuses for them while not holding them accountable for what they have done. From this vantage point, helping someone with ADHD just encourages their inappropriate behavior.

But it doesn't. You know that now. By reframing your perspective on your loved one from the moralistic to the scientific one you have hopefully moved from seeing ADHD as a problem in the domain of moral choices to viewing it as a neurobiological (medical) disorder. That change usually brings with it not just a deeper understanding of what may be going wrong in your loved one with ADHD. Hopefully, it has led you to have a greater compassion for your loved one's plight and a greater willingness to assist him in managing this typically chronic disability.

In this chapter, I discuss some of the larger ways you can help your loved one with adult ADHD. I also talk about what things you can still do to be of help even if your loved one doesn't want any help or doesn't believe they have any disorder.

HELPFUL ROLES YOU CAN ASSUME IN YOUR LOVED ONE'S LIFE

Here, I am not referring to the larger social roles we all assume as an immediate family member, extended relative, spouse or partner, or close friend. Those are important, but you are engaged in one or more of those roles already just by virtue of your relationship with your loved one with adult ADHD. What other roles can you assume to best serve your loved one? That will depend on the type of relationship you already have with your loved one (parent, partner, sibling, friend, etc.). It will also depend on the current quality of that relationship, as will become obvious as you read about these potential roles.

Be an Acceptor and Good Listener

This is a starting position and takes the least effort. Yet, it can be quite valuable to your loved one with ADHD. That is not to say that even this starting role is an easy one to fulfill. Yes, it is a somewhat more passive one than the active ones I identify next. In various follow-up studies (including my own) of children with ADHD into adulthood, researchers working independently of each other discovered something: Adults with ADHD who felt they were doing pretty well always had someone who accepted them for who and what they were. That someone never abandoned them in times of trouble and listened to them when they needed to talk about their problems. This person may have been a parent, grandparent, or other relative; an understanding sibling or close friend; a teacher; or even a sports coach, camp counselor, scout leader, or good neighbor. The type of relationship did not seem as important as the nature of that relationship. This was their go-to person. When failure seemed imminent, when difficult times engulfed them, or when it seemed that other fair-weather friends or relations wanted little to do with them or even abandoned them, this was the person they always trusted to be there for them. Even if it was just to listen and relate to them in nonjudgmental ways, it was a valuable role nonetheless.

Being nonjudgmental does not mean you deny or make excuses for your loved one's inappropriate behavior or its consequences. The behavior and its consequences are facts whose existence cannot be denied. You can be a good listener and acceptor while still openly acknowledging the facts of a situation. You can tell someone you love that he has engaged in certain self-destructive behavior and identify the consequences of such behavior without insulting him or being otherwise condescending and staking out some morally superior position. You can be constructively critical without being morally judgmental. The former implies statements of fact—you can say, "Here are the things you did, this is what happened, now here is what you may need to do to deal with these problems." You can do all those things without castigating your loved one, denigrating his character, humiliating or insulting him, or diminishing his sense of self-worth.

Do you have the personal disposition and qualities to play such a role with your loved one with ADHD? That you are reading this book suggests that maybe you do or that you are at least willing to consider the role. If you do, you probably won't regret doing so, as you will be ensuring that you have a lifelong friend (a true loved one). This may also be a loved one who may be able to repay the favors and be of great assistance to you should your own life take a turn for the worse. If you don't, can't, or simply are unable to play this role for her, don't worry or feel guilty about it. Some people just aren't cut out to do this role with a loved one with adult ADHD. Sometimes even if you wanted to serve in this capacity, your loved one with ADHD may already have someone else who is doing so for her. This one person is enough for her for now. But that does not mean you cannot be ready to accept such a role if she turns to you in this capacity.

Be a Support Team Member

Adults with ADHD don't just need professionals to diagnose, treat, and otherwise support them through the difficulties they experience in trying to change themselves and their lives for the better. They also need loved ones around them who accept them for who they are, ADHD "warts" and all, and listen to them, as I mentioned earlier. They also need people who don't just understand they are struggling to cope with a neurodevelopmental disability but who also show some compassion for their struggles. That compassion should be expressed even if your loved one's attempts to change are not always successful.

But here I want to focus on a more active role than being a good listener or compassionate acceptor of your loved one with ADHD. That adult also needs someone who encourages him or actively assists him throughout this change process. Like a birthing coach or midwife, this role involves actively encouraging, supporting, and assisting your loved one through a passage to a new and better life.

This role may require you to take the initiative to contact and stay in periodic contact with your loved one as you encourage her in specific ways she is trying to change for the better. If you are so inclined, you can even be willing to help her with the changes she is trying to make. You can do that by assisting her with doing some of the things recommended in Chapters 11 and 13 as effective treatments. You can also help her do the more specific recommendations in Chapter 16, dealing with certain major life activities in which she may still have problems functioning. In short, you don't just "get it" about adult ADHD—you help her to "do it." You actively encourage and support your loved one as she strives to change.

Maybe you become someone who is like a more informal life coach or mentor: Someone to whom your loved one can make themselves periodically accountable for the goals he sets, changes he strives to make, professional treatments in which he must participate, and so on. As you may recall from some of the success stories discussed in Chapter 7, this is the sort of role that some of the mothers of those successful people with ADHD assumed so as to help their loved one. They assumed this role not just when their loved one was a child but also into adulthood. Again, don't feel guilty if you are not able to do this for some reason. These roles are suggestions for you, not compulsory ones.

Become an Advocate

Sometimes your loved one may need help in explaining what ADHD is to others in and outside your family. Or she could use your assistance in defending her against the callous or ignorant opinions of others. Your loved one could also use your help in encouraging others to accept and even make accommodations for her. This role is one of being an active advocate for an adult with ADHD. Not everyone is cut out to play such a role, so don't worry if you are not one of them. But if you are an outgoing, gregarious, assertive, or self-confident person, you may find this role to be an easy fit for you.

At times, when other relatives, friends, or social acquaintances make insensitive or otherwise critical statements about your loved one with ADHD, you can help change their minds. Those others may appear not to understand the nature of this disorder and may even hold the view you held about ADHD before reading this book. If so, you can diplomatically correct their misunderstanding. You can do so by briefly sharing what you know about ADHD with them. You can teach them how it is a neurobiological disorder, not a life choice or personal failing. This can help them understand why your loved one may sometimes behave in ways that are impulsive, immature, or just inappropriate for the situation that may have led to such criticisms. You can even suggest resources they can pursue to learn more about adult ADHD such as the websites and trade books on adult ADHD mentioned in prior chapters (and the Resources section).

Your job as an advocate is not to bite someone's head off in defense of your loved one when someone has spoken ill of him. Instead, your role here is that of a teacher, liaison, or diplomat who clarifies the true nature of your loved one's ADHD symptoms. Advocates, by their very name, are vocal protectors and even defenders of another, often a person with a disability. Advocates strive to help others gain a more accurate, better perspective about the person for whom they are advocating. Again, don't make excuses, deny, or cover up the wrongdoings of your loved one and the adverse consequences of his actions: Those are facts. But you can help others to understand what role ADHD may have played in such misconduct or mistakes.

You can make the case for why you are helping your loved one to correct for those mistakes. You can also help those who misunderstand your loved one to improve their understanding. That will help make it harder for these critics to cast moral aspersions and condescending judgments on your loved one with adult ADHD.

This role of advocate can be played not just with relatives, social acquaintances, and so on but also with people at government agencies, schools, or other organizations with which your loved one must deal when trying to obtain certain services or entitlements. Even just being with her in person when she is trying to negotiate with these bureaucracies can be of great help.

Become a Benefactor

This is not a role most relatives, partners, or close friends can play. Not because they don't want to do so but because they may not have the financial means to do so. It involves having sufficient excess financial resources to be able to step in when needed to help pay for constructive things that your loved one with adult ADHD wishes to do. It is not free money or anything goes. Rarely should it be cash and certainly not cash or credit given for self-destructive activities, such as using tobacco, alcohol, or drugs, or for merely entertaining activities, such as a new video game console or flat screen TV.

Assuming this role *can* mean paying for professional evaluations and treatments, school tuition and books, necessary college living expenses, such as meal plans, or hiring your loved one in a summer or part-time capacity if you have your own business. It could also involve supporting him during an unpaid internship with a business or in a new career field during or after college or technical training. It might mean paying his rent partly or wholly while he works his way up from a starting or below subsistence wage. As he earns raises in salary, you can reduce his support in equal measure.

Perhaps being a benefactor means you help to get your loved one preventive medical and dental care checkups, or cover the copays if she has insurance but can't afford those copays. This was one way I chose to help out my brother and nephew, who both had ADHD. It could even be helping her with transportation expenses like buying a used car. But you would do so only if she is going to school or working (not for just joyriding or social activities). It might entail paying for public transportation like subway or bus passes or fares, and so on. If you have the means and the idea seems good, you can even become an investor in her new self-employment enterprise or other entrepreneurial activity should she be looking to start a promising new business. If what you are buying are physical assets, like cars or business equipment, be sure to maintain your name on the deeds, titles, etc., as you may have to step in and sell these assets if the plan does not work out.

Notice that all of these things for which you are a benefactor have in common that they are for the support of constructive activities that offer a chance for improving your loved one's life. Continued support in any of these areas is contingent on your loved one's continued involvement in and reasonable progress through these constructive activities. It is certainly not carte blanche support for irresponsible behavior while he superficially engages in these constructive enterprises, such as partying frequently throughout a college semester while failing most classes. Such support also would not continue for using a car that was intended for work that is instead being used for joyriding, leisure travel, and so on, while routinely not reporting to work or attending classes. In this role, money isn't everything; problems can still occur. But what your financial support can do that the other roles cannot do so easily is to open doors of opportunity for self-improvement by your loved one. And that, as they say, can be "priceless."

Notice that your assumption of, and performance in, these various roles may not be constant or continuous. Instead, it can be episodic on the basis of the circumstances of your current relationship and your loved one's openness to your assuming any or all of these roles. That's OK. Do what you can, when you can, as your loved one is open to your constructive involvement in her life. If you are not ready to offer any direct support, then that is OK too. In can sometimes take a while before we fully appreciate the depth and nature of our loved one's ADHD and related problems. It can therefore take a while to reframe her condition as the neurodevelopmental disorder it is rather than as a lifestyle choice that could be readily changed if she were simply motivated enough to do so.

WHAT YOU CAN DO IF YOUR LOVED ONE DOESN'T WANT ANY HELP

Having a family member or other loved one with adult ADHD who is in denial about it, is not interested in getting diagnosed and treated, or participates in such treatment so inconsistently as to be of little value to managing his disorder can fray your nerves. I can speak from personal experience as to just how frustrating, disappointing, nerve wracking, and demoralizing this situation can be. It can cause you to run out of patience with him or even abandon him. There is absolutely no research on what helps people with ADHD when they deny they need help or reject help that is offered. So the simple advice I offer here is based on common sense. It is also based on my personal experience with my late twin brother who had ADHD, with others in my family who I know have the disorder yet go without treatment, and with my colleagues who have operated clinics for adults with ADHD for more than 20 years.

What options are left for us as family members, spouses, partners, or close friends when faced with an adult with ADHD who wants no help? We can and should, of course, continue to strongly encourage them to recognize that they have problems. We should find opportunities to nudge them to get diagnosed and treated and, if appropriate, to use the prescribed ADHD medications. Whenever an opportunity arises, we can work to move them from the precontemplation to at least the contemplation stage of being ready to change, or influence their progress through later stages (see Chapter 9 for more details on the stages of change). We can give them information about the risks untreated ADHD poses. All that, however, is easier said than done. Why is it so difficult to get our loved ones to accept their disorder and participate in professional treatment? The reasons are many, and if my own experience is worth anything, they are too complex to riddle out here. The bottom line is, you can do a few things when your loved one is in denial. Here is what I recommend.

First, *cease the moral interpretation of your loved one's misbehavior.* This is the mental reframing I discussed at the start of this chapter. It is brick number one in the path to having a better and hopefully more helpful and supportive relationship with your loved one, whether she acknowledges her own ADHD and gets treatment or not. The problems she is showing and the self-destructive behavior in which she engages are not merely the choices of someone wishing to be irresponsible. So you must not view the behavior as willful misconduct. As I keep hammering away in this book, ADHD is a neurogenetic disorder. Try to adopt a more humane and compassionate view of her, as you would anyone with a mental or developmental illness. She needs you even if she doesn't know it and even if she doesn't ask for your help or that of a professional.

Second, *recognize the practical limitations we all face yet rarely acknowledge as family members* trying to persuade mentally or developmentally disabled adults to get help. These limitations rest on the very limits of our powers of persuasion and social influence as family members. You can provide information on the risks of untreated ADHD all you want to an adult with ADHD. You can even arrange inducements and mild coercions in an effort to get your suggestions adopted. But at the end of the day, it is entirely the choice of the adult with ADHD to adopt or ignore that advice. And we all know that you cannot do a damned thing about it if he opts to continue in his self-destructive ways.

The limits of our social influence may be even greater between siblings because of a massive difference in the roles we may play inside versus outside our families. This was certainly the case for my brother and me. I may well be an international expert on ADHD outside my immediate family. But within it, and especially with my twin, I was just a brother—that's all. I was a brother with the history of affection, competition, regrets, and resentments that such a sibling relationship often entails. Yes, you can admonish, argue, threaten, and coerce your siblings, adult offspring, partners, and parents all you want, given your supposed expertise on a topic. However, the very real risk you run, and that I experienced, is that you will be ignored and eventually become estranged from your loved one, sometimes for years.

Nearly a decade before my brother died, I gave up the role of expert advice giver and moral judge that had led to our estrangement—after all, he was 50 years old by then. I realized that despite my best intentions, he was viewing my earlier efforts as nagging and unnecessary intrusions into the life he had chosen to live. From his view, I should butt out and mind my own business. So I did. I also sadly realized that my well-intentioned efforts in minding my own business were only serving to create an even larger wedge between us.

So I opted to redefine my relationship with Ron. I chose to play a supporting role when the consequences of his actions became dire (near homelessness, medical and dental crises, legal actions, etc.). It is a suggestion I have repeatedly made to families facing the same dilemmas with their own adult children with ADHD. When you hit the limits of your influence to change a loved one's adult life, what role do you assume then? Do we abandon them to the ruthless indifference of the world in hopes that our "tough love" will one day make them wake up and smell the coffee and opt to lead a normal life? Not likely. My own answer and the one I give to others in this same predicament is "No!": *Be a listener and benefactor or safety net, whenever you can.*

This is not enabling bad behavior. One is certainly not giving them money for drugs or directly encouraging or facilitating their carelessness. It is not serving as reinforcement for continuing that lifestyle. Being a safety net is different: It is facing and accepting the reality of having a family member who is mentally disabled. Ask yourself, seriously: Is it enabling misconduct to provide for the safety and care of adults who are seriously disabled, such as those with intellectual disabilities, autism, schizophrenia, bipolar disorder, and so on? Of course not! Those disorders and associated lifestyles and actions are a consequence, at least in part, of known genetic and neurological abnormalities. It is the same when families must do so for their adult members with serious ADHD. Indeed, we are compelled by moral force to help them.

Third, *recognize what research shows us: Adults with ADHD, like children with ADHD, do not evaluate their own behavior and performance deficits the same way as individuals who do not have ADHD.* They view themselves as functioning better than they actually may be doing in various tasks and major life activities. This is not to say they have an inflated or grandiose view of their functioning relative to the general population. Instead, they judge themselves as likely to be somewhat above average—the same as would an adult without ADHD. The difference between those with ADHD and others is in the disparity between these self-appraisals and their actual performance, which is often well below normal.

So adults with ADHD are therefore less likely to engage in any treatment for it. From their perspective, there is no problem here. Should that treatment be imposed on them, or should they be coerced into it, one can readily predict that high rates of noncompliance will ensue given their view that there is nothing wrong and thus there is no need to change. This was certainly the case with my brother. He did not see himself as different from other adults in his driving habits, yet he repeatedly failed to heed police citations for not wearing a seatbelt and for speeding. The first step in engaging treatment is acknowledging that a problem exists that requires treatment—it is a step that adults with ADHD may be less likely to take, if at all. When someone does not believe they have deficits or problems, they are obviously unlikely to be motivated to get any help for them.

Fourth, *understand that ADHD is not a disorder of knowing what to do but one of doing what one knows*. As I discussed in earlier chapters, the executive system enables one to take prior knowledge and use it to govern ongoing behavior and plan for future events. Given that ADHD disrupts that system, then many of the problems those with ADHD have are not merely due to deficient knowledge or skill. They are more likely due to an inability to apply that knowledge they already possess at crucial junctures in their natural life, where that knowledge would have been useful for greater social and personal effectiveness, if not safety. Thus, even if you tell someone with ADHD what they need to do by conveying information or skills, they are less likely to be able to use that information for their own self-improvement than is someone else without the disorder.

Where your loved one's voluntary engagement of professional care may fail, changes in the attitudes of family members or other loved ones wishing to help the adult with ADHD are essential. This is so that you do not abandon hope for and stop giving help to your uncooperative loved one.

KEY POINTS TO REMEMBER

Until your loved one with adult ADHD wants help and is willing to get it, consider trying these things, as discussed earlier:

- *Cease any moral interpretations of your loved one's behavior.* Accept his ADHD as a neurogenetic disorder (frontal lobe syndrome), and care for him as you would want anyone to do for someone with a serious mental or physical disorder.

- *Be a safety net.* Financial and otherwise, be a safety net whenever your resources permit.
  - This is not enabling misconduct; instead, you are keeping her from homelessness and worse.
  - Get her health maintenance, medical, and dental care if you can.
  - Get her food, clothing, housing, or other shelter when she needs it.
- *Be ready to support him in constructive life activities.* Do this at the first sign of any comments he makes about getting help or doing something constructive about his ADHD (give encouragement, get him therapy, get him medication, further his education, help with job retraining, locating employment, drug detox, etc.).
- *Stay involved in her life.* Estrangement won't help her.

CHAPTER 16

ADVICE FOR LIVING WITH AN ADULT WITH ADHD

Here, I describe some of the more specific things that you and your loved one may be able to do to help address common problem areas related to attention-deficit/hyperactivity disorder (ADHD) that you may encounter in living together. In the next three chapters, I target some specific domains of living with an adult with ADHD in which your loved one may be having problems and recommend some methods you can suggest to him for dealing with them. Think of these ideas as a buffet of possibly helpful things from among which you select those that seem the most suitable (and acceptable) to his difficulties.

HOME RESPONSIBILITIES AND ROUTINE TASKS

You may have noticed that your loved one with ADHD has problems managing her home life or dealing with the routine tasks of daily life. This might include such things as grocery shopping and meal preparations, doing laundry regularly, paying bills, handling yard work, or dealing with the demands of child rearing (bathing, children's chores, homework, general monitoring and supervision of your children, etc.). One way to begin to help improve the performance of these daily responsibilities of living together would be to formally sit down with your loved one and review them.

First, note which ones are handled well. You want to start such discussions on a positive note. Then get to which ones need some improvement. Ask your loved one to consider swapping or reassigning those responsibilities she has difficulty doing because of her ADHD symptoms with ones that you are already doing, if you live with her, or that her current partner with whom she is living may already be doing. In general, the more time sensitive a task happens to be (paying bills on time, getting children's homework or major school projects organized by deadlines, keeping children on regular bedtimes, etc.), the better off she will be if you or her cohabiting partner takes on these tasks. Then let your ADHD loved one take on the tasks that don't involve time, deadlines, or a lot of organization as critical elements (e.g., doing laundry, yard work, grocery shopping, bathing her young children).

In specific domains, your loved one's ADHD can sometimes pose safety issues for him or for others, such as his children. For instance, think about who does most of the driving when your loved one's children have to be taken to school or to other commitments (doctor's appointments, visiting their friends' houses, etc.). If your loved one is not taking medication for ADHD while driving, his ADHD can pose increased hazards for his children. Perhaps driving is a domain you or his partner are better off handling while reassigning one of your responsibilities that does not involve such safety issues to your loved one. In other words, try to make the more ADHD-friendly tasks the ones that you assign to your loved one while taking on those that are not so ADHD friendly. Even if the responsibilities you are considering are not ones that ADHD is likely to interfere with (getting children bathed and in bed each evening), it may be that your loved one finds these more stressful. Thus, these tasks are likely to prove more frustrating or anger inducing to him than some other tasks. Swap those tasks around for some of your own chores your loved one does not find so stressful.

If you or their live-in partner cannot assume such tasks on a routine or daily basis and reassign others to your loved one in their place, then consider sharing them. That is, consider alternating with her which days she is to handle this task and which days you do so. Consider the tasks of getting children bathed and in bed each night. This could be done by an approach that I call "shared parenting," which simply involves alternating which nights you handle this responsibility and which nights she does so. Just getting such periodic breaks from routine and routinely stressful tasks can facilitate her doing these tasks better on the days when it is her turn to do them.

MARITAL AND COHABITING RELATIONSHIP ADVICE

Perhaps you are living with or married to an adult with ADHD. Or maybe you just wish to help out your loved one with ADHD with problems he is having in such intimate relationships. Here are some things to consider doing.

Get more information about ADHD in adults and its impact on such close relationships. Consult some of the books listed in the Resources section at the end of this book; for instance, Gina Pera's book, *Is It You, Me, or Adult A.D.D.? Stopping the Roller Coaster When Someone You Love Has Attention Deficit Disorder.* Ms. Pera is not a mental health professional but a journalist with both a long-standing interest in adult ADHD in couples and the author of two books for assisting them, one with Dr. Arthur Robin (see Resources). She was the first to focus attention on the problems such couples may have, she created a website on the topic, she conducts periodic group discussions on her website, and she maintains a blog on the topic, among other activities. Melissa Orlov, a therapist who specializes in marital counseling at the Hallowell Center, Sudbury,

Massachusetts, has a similar book: *The ADHD Effect on Marriage: Understand and Rebuild Your Relationship in Six Steps.* These books provide detailed advice on cultivating empathy with your partner, dealing with emotions that can be obstacles to a better relationship, and focusing on the positives in the relationship. The books also address how to formally schedule time for emotionally connecting or for intimacy and learning more effective styles of communication and problem solving. Similar to the book you are presently reading, these others also encourage getting formal professional treatment for your partner with ADHD. They are also filled with numerous ways of addressing stress, conflict, or just imbalances in the relationship.

Just reframing your perspective on your loved one so that you come to understand that ADHD is a neurological (and genetic) disorder can help you here. As I said earlier, this altered viewpoint keeps you from not attributing your partner's problems to her not caring, being lazy, or having a personal or moral failing. Instead, you reframe some of her difficulties as arising from a disorder of brain functioning that predisposes her to act in certain ways you find problematic.

Have your ADHD partner join an adult ADHD support group. If such groups are available in your community or at a nearby mental health center, recommend to your partner with ADHD that he join. Your partner can gain support for his efforts to change and cope better with his ADHD from attending the monthly meetings. He will also be keeping up-to-date on information, learning what works for other adults with ADHD, and receiving routine support from others striving to cope better with his disorder. Can't find one near you? Encourage the professional who diagnosed your loved one to consider starting one. Or your partner and you can join online Internet support groups or periodically visit blogs about adult ADHD relationships and then discuss their advice, such as the website operated by Gina Pera (http://www.adultadhdrelationships.blogspot.com) or this website (http://www.totallyadd.com).

Join a group for partners of those with ADHD. If you are a spouse or partner of an adult with ADHD, do the same. If none exists in your area, consider helping to start one.

Help your partner get treatment with a long-acting ADHD medication. As I showed you in an earlier chapter, ADHD medications are typically the most effective treatments. Therefore, ensuring that those medicines are prescribed so that they work across much of the waking day can go a long way to helping with relationship problems that stem from ADHD symptoms.

Consider getting professional marital or relationship counseling. If the marriage or relationship seems in serious trouble and close to breaking up, consider getting counseling. But do so with a therapist that knows about ADHD in adults, understands its impact on relationships, and knows the treatments ADHD often requires, including medications. If, at your first meeting, the therapist seems to not know that adults can have ADHD, is antimedication, or even antiscience, don't go back. Find a more informed therapist with the help of the professional who made your loved one's diagnosis.

Help her to identify any counterproductive, mutually self-destructive, or otherwise bad relationships in which she may be involved. If you are not married or not living with someone with adult ADHD but are a parent, sibling, or friend to that adult, help them identify these relationships. The last thing an adult with ADHD needs is to be around another person who is even more impulsive, self-destructive, now-focused, disorganized, emotional, forgetful, and inattentive as she is. Just being around someone who denies the existence of ADHD and blames the adult with ADHD for every mistake or failing is destructive in the long run. If you think your loved one with ADHD is in such a relationship, have her strongly consider leaving it, if possible. If she is socializing with such "friends," talk to your loved one about "firing" those friends (essentially disconnecting from them) and finding better, more effective, productive, organized, and socially capable ones. Adults with ADHD do better when they are married to, live with, or otherwise socialize with adults who are more organized, long-range focused, emotionally stable, and more easily able to defer their gratification than they are. Of course, such people also have to be compassionate toward someone with a disability, while being helpful, constructive, optimistic about life, and willing to work with or otherwise assist a partner or friend with ADHD.

Take minivacations from your ADHD partner, and have him do the same from you. These are short periods in which each person does something that they find enjoyable and rejuvenating of their emotional batteries. Steven Covey called this "finding renewal" in his great book, *The 7 Habits of Highly Effective People.*[1] You can spend too much time together with a partner with adult ADHD. This may only cause further stress in your relationship or cause your partner's ADHD symptoms to wear you down. So give yourself and your ADHD partner a break periodically and take an evening, a day, or even two to go away, or have him go away, and do something he or you enjoy. Maybe it's a sports-focused or hobby-focused getaway (golfing, fishing, boating, sporting, quilting, or whatever weekend). Consider having either of you go to visit a long-time friend or a close relative. This intermission in the relationship might involve going to a spa, beauty, or artist retreat, or engaging in whatever recreational pursuits that person finds enjoyable (photographic safari, sightseeing, hiking, camping, etc.) and renewing one's emotional strength.

Keep these relationship minivacations brief, and stay in touch with your partner once daily while away just to keep the connection and the interest showing. Use these periods as a time not to just relax and have fun, which is important, but also to gain a broader

[1]Covey, S. R. (2004). *The 7 habits of highly effective people: Powerful lessons in personal change.* New York, NY: Free Press.

perspective on your life and relationship that cannot come as easily during day-to-day relations. Going away from your usual home life can help you both "widen the lens," so to speak, on your relationship; by that, I mean that it places that relationship in the larger context of the arc of your life. Do so and you each will typically find a renewed appreciation for each other.

This is not to be a deeply soul-searching weekend of introspection or therapeutic meditation on the relationship or your partner's personal failings—quite the opposite. It is to be a period of relaxation, enjoyment, and hence rejuvenation. Sprinkled throughout the year, these minivacations (rejuvenations) can save a relationship. As the country song says, "How can I miss you when you won't go away?"[2] Absence can and does make the heart grow fonder, as the old bromide goes. You can have too much togetherness and need a bit of a break from each other from time to time. Take it, and have your partner do the same. It also shows that you care about each other, the relationship, and your mental health, because this short separation is intended to renew the relationship on your return. This is in contrast to not taking such breaks and so martyring yourself to a relationship.

Neither of you should view the time apart as some form of loss of interest in the other person or as outright abandonment. Taking brief breaks away from a partner and the relationship is healthy and focuses on the long term. Such breaks are ways of acknowledging that all relationships are in need of periodic refueling and rejuvenation using short-term "time away" periods. The view that such breaks are forms of disinterest or abandonment takes the short-term perspective of "you owe me all your free time now," which will exhaust the fuel in the relationship, truly burning it out.

---

[2]Hicks, D. (2001). How can I miss you when you won't go away? [Recorded by Dan Hicks and His Hot Licks]. On *The Most of Dan Hicks and His Hot Licks* [record]. New York, NY: Epic Records.

When Your Intimate Partner Has ADHD: Problem-Solving Steps

Got an issue with an intimate partner who has ADHD? Try these problem-solving steps:

- Choose a time when you are both in a reasonable mood, perhaps right after when you have been dining at home together.
- Be sure in your mind that you have defined the problem in a specific way: What exactly is it that concerns you?
- Start by commenting on an earlier time when your loved one may have mentioned this problem, such as, "Remember when you said you thought you might have a problem with ________________. Well, I have been thinking about that issue as well and wondering if there are some things we could think of to try and make that situation better."
- Suggest that you write down the problem (have a sheet of paper handy).
- Now suggest that you both try to think of as many ways you can that might help address the issue. Be creative, even crazy and silly in your ideas. Just try to come up with as many solutions as you can. There should be no criticism or negativity expressed during this discussion.
- Then go down the list and briefly discuss how practical and how you feel about each suggestion. Have your partner do the same.
- By the time you have discussed each option, one or two are likely to stand out as the most practical to try.
- Draw a large circle around this one and suggest that you each try doing this for just the next week, like an experiment.
- Each of you should initial this paper like it is a contract, then tape it on the front of the refrigerator or some other convenient place as a reminder of what you are both going to try to do to improve this problem or issue.
- In a week, sit down during a calm moment and discuss how the contract is working. Make any revisions to it that may come to mind based on how things have gone with this issue the past week. Try this modified plan for another week.

MONEY MANAGEMENT

One of the most conflict-ridden areas of many married or cohabiting relationships is money. This problem area can be made much worse when you are in a close relationship with an adult with ADHD in which money plays a role, as between spouses, partners, and parents and their grown children. Adults with ADHD have far more financial problems than adults in the general (typical) population. If that sounds like your loved one with adult ADHD, then you may need to help her get control of her financial life, especially if you live with her and share such finances. You can do so by encouraging your loved one do the following and directly helping her do so as well if she is open to your involvement.

Budget! If he is not already doing so, encourage him to make a monthly budget sheet that shows all of his monthly expenses as well as one twelfth of his once-annual expenses (those that you may pay just once per year, for example, taxes, car insurance, housing insurance). Your loved one needs to have a monthly financial plan with all the bills listed so that he can see what is owed each month, to whom, and especially how much must be set aside (total bills). This budget needs to be less than what he makes per month. And the items on the budget are always to be paid first, before any money is used for entertainment or just discretionary spending, such as high-priced specialty coffees or teas on the way to work each day. Keep this budget out on a desk at home where your loved one does paperwork or on a dresser so he can refer to it often.

Merely spending as you go each month is a recipe for disaster, such as having the utilities turned off or your car repossessed. Software programs and smartphone apps are available to help with budgeting. But I think it's just as easy or easier, and surely cheaper, to do it with good old-fashioned, low-tech, pencil and paper. That doesn't require buying a computer or smartphone, keeping it charged, opening the app when you need to enter financial information, and so on. Each of these becomes yet another obstacle to doing routine budgeting and so another excuse not to do so.

Get control of the credit cards! Have your loved one get rid of all store credit cards, keep one general card like Master Card or Visa, and put a sticker on it that reads "For Emergency Use Only." Suggest that she transfer all unpaid balances on store cards to this single card and work to pay off the balance as soon as she possibly can. In the United States, credit card companies' monthly statements must, by law, include information on how long it will take to pay off the bill and the total cost to the consumer as a result of paying only the minimum amount due. Statements also include how much the consumer should pay each month to pay the bill off in 3 years versus 10 years, the total cost to the consumer in doing so, and the savings compared with paying only the minimum payment.[3] Although this information is helpful to people who are already on top of their credit cards, it's unlikely to help someone who chronically doesn't pay attention to his finances. Still, it might help start a conversation about the consequences of making only minimum payments if you can point to the information in black and white, right there on the statement. Many adults, even those who don't have ADHD, fall prey to predatory consumer credit card practices. And so in 2009, the government passed new legislation requiring greater transparency in credit card interest rates, fees, and other practices for new contracts issued after February 2010. The law has a number of safeguards to help protect consumers who have credit cards, many of which may be helpful to adults with ADHD, who may be more likely not to manage their credit cards and balances very well.

---

[3]Credit Card Accountability Responsibility and Disclosure Act of 2009, 15 U.S.C. § 1601 (2009).

Summarizing from the White House Press Office's fact sheet,[4] the key provisions include:

> (1) Giving consumers enough time to pay their bills. Credit card companies have to give consumers at least 21 days to pay from the time the bill is mailed. Credit card companies cannot "trap" consumers by setting payment deadlines on the weekend or in the middle of the day, or changing their payment deadlines each month. (2) No retroactive rate increases. Credit card companies must give consumers at least 45 days' notice if their rates are about to go up, and cannot change any terms of the contract within a year. Low introductory rates must last at least six months. (3) Easier to pay down debt. Credit card companies must apply payments to a consumer's highest interest rate balances first. Statements must show consumers how long it would take to pay off their existing balance if the consumer made only the minimum payment, and must show the payment amount and total interest cost to pay off the entire balance in 36 months. (4) Eliminates "fee harvester cards." The act restricts fees on low-balance cards sold to cardholders with bad credit. For many of these cards, the up-front fees charged exceeded the remaining credit.[4] The act also restricts the fees that can be charged for gift cards and other prepaid cards. (5) Eliminates excessive marketing to young people. Consumers under the age of 21 must prove that they have an independent income or get a co-signer before applying for a credit card. The Act also prevents credit card companies from mailing offers to consumers under 21 unless they "opt in," and prohibits companies from wooing students with T-shirts, free pizza and other free gifts at university-sponsored events.[5]

[4]See https://www.whitehouse.gov/the-press-office/fact-sheet-reforms-protect-american-credit-card-holders

[5]See https://en.wikipedia.org/wiki/Credit_CARD_Act_of_2009

Set up a checking account. If your loved one has not done so already, help him set up a checking account, then have him pay himself first out of it. By that, I mean that he should have his employer put 10% of the pretax earnings into a retirement plan (tax deferred) such as a 401k, 403b, Keogh, or IRA. Then have the after-tax paycheck direct deposited into that checking account. Once it is there, have his bank move 10% of it into a savings account automatically each month. The less your loved one can see of cash, the less he can spend it impulsively. Your loved one also needs an emergency savings account or emergency fund. It is to be for those unexpected expenses (car repairs, medical bills) that if not planned for can devastate a budget. And that can lead to increasing amounts going on credit cards with little idea of how the balances will get paid off. If creating that savings account does not leave your loved one enough for the usual monthly expenses, then he is obviously living beyond his means. That is a recipe for financial disaster. Instead, he must cut down on those expenses somewhere. Your loved one can and must find 10% fat in this budget to get rid of so he can start saving—both for emergency expenses as well as his future retirement. As financial planners say, if you can't save for retirement, you are having it now and won't have any later.

Balance the checkbook monthly. Don't just let your loved one wing it, guesstimate, or otherwise have little idea of how much money she has at any one time in her account(s). And don't have her live on her debit card while also not keeping track of her expenses and balances in that account. This failure to do regular monthly checkbook balancing can be one of the biggest causes of bounced checks, credit card overuse, and debt accumulation. That occurs because your loved one keeps getting caught with less money than she thought would be needed and so she borrows off credit cards to make up the shortfall. And then hidden penalty fees will be charged for not keeping an appropriate balance, overdrawing the account, and for the bounced checks. As for debit cards, because they may not come with the same fraud protection guarantees, suggest that she only use them at ATM machines to get cash. Otherwise, leave them alone or at home when shopping.

Take out cash from the checking account only when it is absolutely needed. Ask him to carry as little cash as possible. This way, he is not tempted to spend it impulsively on stuff that is not really needed.

Don't let your loved one lend anyone other than her children any money. Period. And even those children are not a good bet to repay the loan. So keep those loans limited to educational expenses or necessities, not clothing, entertainment, and so on. Odds are if your loved one loans money to others, she will not see that money again. Therefore, if your loved one gives money to someone else, you both had better view it as the gift it most likely will be, not as a loan.

If you are married or living with someone with adult ADHD (and assuming you do not have ADHD as well), you should likely handle bill paying and budgeting. I am assuming here that you are more organized and timely in your management of money than your loved one happens to be.

Your loved one should never borrow money for something he will consume, wear, or use for entertainment. These items include flat screen TVs, smartphones, and so on. He should borrow just for buying a home, getting a car (maybe), or a reasonable investment. If the value goes down right after your loved one buys it, then he should buy it only if it's a necessity and not on credit, unless it is a car or house.

If your loved one must carry a cell phone, make it the cheapest model out there and the cheapest calling plan that still meets their needs. Of course, this assumes it is not provided by her employer. Does she really need a camera or Internet, e-mail, or Twitter access everywhere she goes? Perhaps she does as an aid to her memory difficulties, as she can use the camera to take pictures of lists, tasks, or other things she needs to attend to later. She might want to use some of the numerous apps that can help with time management, scheduling, reminders, and so on. If so, then a smartphone may make sense. At least get the least expensive phone and data plan she may need for such purposes. But if it is merely to be trendy or for purely social purposes, then talk to her and see if your loved one can stop or reduce her use of her smartphone as an entertainment and social networking device. Help her to start using it as a practical tool to call or hear back from the people she must and nothing more. Or consider a far cheaper "dumb" phone that has a camera, slide-out keyboard for texting, and phone, but no Internet capabilities. To really go cut rate, check out options like Jitterbug or one of the discount calling plans like those sold at Walmart. Your loved one does not need a smartphone unless her employer is paying for it, the apps on it are essential for her work or for managing her ADHD, and she is wealthy enough to easily handle the monthly fees.

Live within his means. Speak to your loved one about not spending more each month than he earns, which leads to using credit cards, loans, or other means of borrowing to get through the month.

Encourage her to get free credit counseling from a bank or credit union. Do this if a loved one is massively in debt and it seems hopeless or she is thinking of bankruptcy. Bankruptcies can ruin a credit score and result in no ability to borrow for years afterwards. Credit counseling companies can often help reorganize a person's finances, consolidate debt, and renegotiate unusually high interest rates. They can also meet with your loved one monthly to keep her and her budget in check and accountable to someone else. Some smaller banks, credit unions, or even state or county agencies may be available to do this for her. Search around your area for these services, as you can bet your loved one is not the only one who needs such help.

Try to get your loved one health and disability insurance through his employer. If your loved one doesn't have it, try to help him find a similar job that does. Under the Affordable Care Act, health insurance may be easier to come by for your loved one. However, what his premiums may be and what government assistance with those premiums is available vary widely across the states. If he can't get such employment with fringe benefits, encourage him to consider working for the local, state, or federal government that nearly always provides these as fringe benefits. Unexpected medical costs are one of the biggest sources of surprise expenses, large debts, and even financial bankruptcy.

Advise your loved one to keep all receipts as she gets them. Put the receipts in a wallet. Each night when your loved one takes her wallet out while undressing, remind her to take these receipts and put them in a file. You and your loved one can use this file to help keep track of what she is spending and to keep those receipts that will be very useful when preparing taxes and getting the most out of available deductions.

Remind your loved one not to go to a mall or department store as entertainment. Remind her of this when she is bored if there is nothing that she needs to buy—and I mean needs, not wants, to buy. The last place a person with ADHD needs to be is in a store or mall with all those attractive goodies crying out, "Buy me!" So, the simplest solution is, don't go. If your loved one finds it hard to stop shopping and spending on things she does not need, have her get professional help from a psychologist or financial counselor.

Tell your loved one to stay away from casinos. They always win. Impulsive people are prone to gambling (and often losing). Your loved one with ADHD should not put himself in situations such as being at casinos, where it is too easy to bet. He should not play cards for money, and if he must play at all, certainly play for no more than pennies a hand. Your loved one is way too impulsive to be around gambling activities, so, as with shopping, suggest that he avoid such places where impulsive spending can get the best of him.

Never, ever, ever should your loved one take out a payday loan from one of those companies. The interest rates are so high, she will never be able to get out of debt. This is legalized loan-sharking, so have your loved one stay away from it. Period.

Help your loved one to get on and stay on an ADHD medication. This will help to control his ADHD-related impulsivity (including around money matters) and to keep him better organized around finances. For more great advice, read Sarkis and Klein's *ADD and Your Money* (see the Resources section of this book).

PARENTING

Adults with ADHD need to understand that their children are likely to have an increased risk of ADHD and related disorders. Those childhood disorders and more general psychological problems are likely to require separate evaluation and management from the problems posed by ADHD in the parent. So, if your loved one has children and those children have ADHD or other concerns in their psychological development, get them evaluated and treated by an appropriate mental health professional. Having an undiagnosed and untreated parent with ADHD raising an undiagnosed and untreated child with the disorder is a recipe for chronic conflict and other psychological disasters. My advice here is simple and straightforward.

1. *Push to get your loved one's ADHD evaluated and treated.* If it is moderate to severe, recommend that she get on an ADHD medication. She cannot raise children well if she is out of control with her own ADHD.

2. *Strongly urge that the children of your loved one be evaluated for possible ADHD and related disorders if all the signs are there and get them treated as well.*
3. *Suggest that your loved one take a behavioral parent training class.* These should be available at a nearby mental health clinic, medical school, university, hospital, or county mental health center. Most large metropolitan areas have such resources. If your loved one lives in a rural area lacking such services or cannot find such a parenting class, consider getting him my book, *Your Defiant Child*,[6] or any other on this topic. He can learn more about parenting methods that can be very helpful in raising a child with ADHD. For teens, see *Your Defiant Teen*.[7] Both are available through Internet booksellers as well, such as amazon.com and barnesandnoble.com. Parents with ADHD do not do well in these classes if their own ADHD is not being treated. That means you should suggest that your loved one get his ADHD treated first before starting in one of these classes.
4. *Suggest that the parent without ADHD handle school homework.* This is important especially if your loved one's ADHD is untreated. Most parents are not good tutors to their children, so you can bet that one with ADHD may not be good at it either, if not worse.
5. *Suggest that your loved one alternate child care nights with his partner.* Each parent can take turns managing the children every other night, especially if that child has ADHD.

---

[6]Barkley, R. A., & Benton, C. M. (2013). *Your defiant child: 8 steps to better behavior* (2nd ed.). New York, NY: Guilford Press.

[7]Barkley, R. A., & Robin, A. L. (with Benton, C. M.). (2014). *Your defiant teen: 10 steps to resolve conflict and rebuild your relationship* (2nd ed.). New York, NY: Guilford Press.

This is done so that no parent carries the entire or most of the burden of supervising and caring for the children throughout the day or after school and across an entire week.

6. *Advise your loved one to let the parent without ADHD handle time-sensitive events related to the children.* For instance, let that parent handle medical and school appointments or deadlines for school projects. That is because the adult with ADHD is likely to have serious problems with time management and deadlines, as you learned earlier in this book. The parent with ADHD can make up for it with her spouse or partner by taking on tasks that are not time sensitive (doing the washing, cleaning up the house, doing home and car maintenance, yard care, bathing the children, etc.).
7. *Advise your loved one to put himself in time-out (a quiet room) if he is feeling overwhelmed or stressed by his children.* Taking a self-imposed time-out is a great technique for any parent who needs a moment to calm down. Because ADHD can affect the brain's emotional centers, however, it's especially important for parents with ADHD to have a simple protocol planned ahead of time when such stress arises. They can also model this healthy practice for their children.
8. *Suggest to your loved one with ADHD that she discuss major child disciplinary actions she wants to take with her spouse or partner before implementing them.* This is done so that she avoids impulsively and perhaps excessively disciplining her children because of their ADHD-related symptoms.
9. *The adult without ADHD should drive the kids to their activities.* As I noted earlier, this is important, and the other parent should be the driver whenever possible (unless the parent with ADHD is medicated).
10. *Remind your loved one to stop what he is doing and monitor the children's activities or whereabouts.* If it is after school,

a weekend, summer vacation, or any other time your loved one's children are home or in the yard, and he is responsible for their supervision, recommend that he set an external timer (like the timer on an oven or microwave or smartphone) to frequent intervals, such as every 15 to 20 minutes, as a reminder. This is even more important if the children also have ADHD.

11. *Encourage your loved one to build in weekly respites from her kids.* This is particularly important if she does not work outside the home and bears the brunt of being the stay-at-home parent. Help her to find some hobby, activity, club, organization, project, or just recreational activity that she loves, that renews her emotionally, that de-stresses her, or in other ways gives your loved one time to recharge her "parental batteries." Every parent needs some time away from their children (and spouse) each week to regroup and otherwise renew themselves emotionally. That is especially true for a parent with ADHD who is raising their children. So, encourage your loved one with adult ADHD to find renewal—have her do it weekly or more often if need be.

CHAPTER 17

ADVICE FOR WORK AND EDUCATION SETTINGS

As you learned from earlier chapters, the vast majority of adults with attention-deficit/hyperactivity disorder (ADHD) experienced problems in their educational history. They are likely to still do so if they are pursuing adult education classes or workplace educational programs. If your loved one is a young adult who is in college or technical training, then she will likely require certain accommodations to help succeed. She is entitled to reasonable adjustments to both her educational activities as well as in the workplace as provided under the Americans With Disabilities Act (ADA),[1] discussed in Chapter 7. You may want to become familiar with the requirements for documenting a diagnosis of ADHD, as this will have to be provided to the college or employer if your loved one wishes to take advantage of these reasonable accommodations. I have provided the titles of several books in the Resources section that can better explain to your loved one the protections provided under this act. Those books also explain the documentation needed to access such protections and accommodations, and the sorts of reasonable adjustments to

[1]Americans With Disabilities Act of 1990, Pub. L. No. 101-336, § 2, 104 Stat. 328 (1991).

the school or workplace setting that may be required to assist your loved one with adult ADHD. Where they are already available in the workplace to provide assistance, using administrative assistants and office managers to help with goal setting and accountability for progress, among other forms of help, can be valuable accommodations for adults with ADHD.

Besides recommending they take medication, I list a variety of strategies your loved one can use in the school or workplace environments to help compensate for his ADHD. This assumes, of course, that these strategies are feasible to implement in those settings.

Find a coach or mentor. Find someone to whom your loved one can make herself accountable every day for the work that needs to get done that day. This can be a teacher, professor, roommate, classmate, more senior student, or someone in the special student services office. At work, it can be a coworker, friend, or supportive supervisor. If possible, your loved one should meet with this person two to three times each weekday for 5 minutes each. Use the first meeting, usually in the morning, to review her to-do list or goals for that day. Then she should meet with that person again at midday (lunchtime, perhaps) and again late in the day to show the mentor what has been accomplished on that list. One surefire way to help your loved one stay focused and on task in pursuing goals and work is to have her be accountable publicly to someone else and meet with that person frequently.

Identify the ADHD specialist if your loved one is in a college setting or the disability specialist in human resources in the workplace. This is usually the person to whom your loved one must declare that he has ADHD and provide to them the documentation (prior evaluations) that proves it. At colleges, ADHD specialists are usually in student special or disability services. That specialist will then explain to him the types of curriculum adjustments and other accommodations typically provided to students with ADHD in that college or workplace adjustments to see which ones he may need. They will also work with the teachers (or supervisors, if at work) to see that he gets those accommodations. And they can often link him up with psychologists, counselors, and physicians (usually psychiatrists) that work at the student counseling center or that have contracts with the employer for providing employee mental health services should he require therapy or medication.

Encourage your loved one to use a daily assignment calendar and a journal. The calendar is for setting goals for that day and tracking appointments. Typically, it shows the entire week at a glance, broken down into 1-hour segments. This can be very useful not only for tracking appointments but also for writing in the time one will use to handle a project or smaller steps in a more complex, longer term project. The journal is simply a book with blank pages into which they can write any promises, deadlines, assignments from others, and so forth. Later, some of these can be transferred into the calendar. These two books are what she will review with the coach during the meetings discussed earlier. She should keep both in a visible spot in the workspace so she can see them often and help be reminded to stay focused on goals and appointments for that day. Writing everything down can help compensate for a poor working memory. Your loved one can use a journal for anything of the slightest importance that should be written here to make up for his working memory deficits. Yes, one can use computers, tablets, or smartphones to take such notes—and this may be preferable if he has trouble with handwriting (see next paragraph). But I find that, generally, low-tech paper journals and calendars are better, as they are always visible and available for writing. The similar apps on smartphones or iPads disappear from view when the device is closed, and thus become out of sight, out of mind. Suggest that your loved one review this journal several times a day to make sure he is doing the things recorded here.

Use word processing on a computer rather than handwriting lengthy assignments. People with ADHD often have motor coordination or other handwriting problems that make them write more slowly and less legibly. Whenever possible, she should use a laptop computer or other means to type her work. In college, your loved one may also use the word processor for easier note taking. She can also record some of the assignments this way. Computers with cameras can also be used to create an audio CD or media file as an alternative to a written report if she has a history of significant writing problems. The special student services counselor mentioned earlier can get her this type of curriculum adjustment if she requires it. Or many recent-generation computers, smartphones, and tablets have voice recognition software built into them that allows users to dictate assignment answers or lengthier reports that are then automatically transcribed into print. Those passages can then be further edited before being printed out on paper as her report.

Digitally record important lectures or meetings or use continuous note taking. Record using the Smart Pen digital recorder (http://www.livescribe.com), or if handwriting is not a problem, use continuous note taking to boost concentration in classes or meetings. One way to stay awake, alert, and focused is to be doing something more active while you have to pay attention. If your loved one has to write down the gist of what is being said in the lecture or meeting, he is more likely to stay awake, alert, and focused than if he is just sitting and observing the person giving the lecture. He should keep the hand moving, then, and take notes even if he doesn't really need to write down the information.

Get any extracurricular materials teachers may have available. Get extra materials, including those that have been reserved at the library especially for these classes. These may be videos that supplement what is being taught in class, additional notes or articles that further explain the topics that are being covered in class, and so on. Some adults with ADHD in college settings have been able to get assistance with note taking in class if their writing problems are particularly severe. In the workplace, your loved one should check to see whether there is a library or information center that contains resources for further learning on the job.

Get your loved one a notebook organizing system. Visit the local bookstore or office supply store to help him get and stay organized. Having separate colored folders for each school class or project at work can be very helpful. This is where he keeps completed assignments to ensure that they can be easily found and so turned in on time. It is not unusual for adults with ADHD in college settings or at work to do assignments and then misplace their work, subsequently missing the due date for a report work project. Because many people now store their work on computers in digital files, encourage your loved one (or assist them directly) to better organize these files for easier access, relocating them when needed, and backing them up to cloud storage facilities for safe keeping such as with Dropbox, iCloud, and so on.

Suggest that your loved one schedule harder classes/meetings/work in her peak-performance time slot each day. Most people likely work best in the mid-morning or early afternoon, but people vary in the time each day they are most alert. By now, your loved one should know when these peak hours of alertness and concentration are likely to occur each day. Some research shows that adults with ADHD find afternoons or even evening hours to be their best time to focus and concentrate, which is a few hours later than adults in the general population are likely to report as their peak performance time. In any case, encourage your loved one to identify her daily cycle of arousal and alertness and use that knowledge to better schedule those tasks that require more concentration and effort into that time slot.

Your loved one should alternate required or harder courses with elective or fun classes. During the day or across the weekly schedule of classes, your loved one should alternate classes in this way. Don't let him stack all the hard classes up on a single day or during the first few days of the week, as this can overtax him. It can also make him too tired to do well in these classes, lose interest or motivation part of the way through them, and ruin his attitude toward school. So suggest that he intermingle the hard stuff with classes or activities he finds more interesting or entertaining. That way, he is never faced with too many classes or projects that demand lots of effort that are too close together. You can suggest that he do this at work as well by arranging the work that day so that he alternates difficult/demanding with easy/interesting tasks.

Should your loved one request extra time on timed tests in college or at work? Request test settings that are free of distractions. Many young adults with ADHD in college settings believe or have heard from others that this may be a useful accommodation to request. But what little research there is on the subject is not that clear-cut. Everyone, regardless of whether they have a disability, seems to benefit from some extra time to take timed tests; usually about 20 minutes more is sufficient. But that does not mean it will necessarily help compensate for ADHD or solve other problems with taking these tests.

More recent opinion suggests that your loved one is better off using a method called "time off the clock." This involves using a stopwatch to take these timed tests. Your loved one will not get any more "face time" with the test using this stopwatch to take the test than do other students. But what she will be allowed to do is to stop the watch anytime as often as she likes to take a short break of a minute or two. Use this time to stand up, stretch, walk about the room or into the hallway, get a drink of water, use the bathroom, then return to the test and restart the stopwatch. When she has used up the test time on the stopwatch, then the test is done.

Yes, this will result in taking more time than others to complete the test, but that is not the point. The strategy that one is using here is the important thing: breaking up the test into smaller work quotas and having frequent breaks to briefly refresh her mental focus and concentration. If she is required to periodically take timed examinations as part of her work, she should try to get this type of accommodation on the tests by using the human resources department that is responsible for getting ADA accommodations in that work setting. Whether or not a time-off-the-clock approach is allowed for your loved one, encourage him to request test settings that are free of distractions or offer greatly reduced chances of being distracted.

Encourage your loved one to exercise before exams, boring classes, extended meetings at work, or protracted work periods. Routine aerobic exercise improves a person's ability to concentrate for up to 45 to 60 minutes more than usual. He should learn to build in brief exercise breaks throughout the day but use them especially before he has to do something that is difficult to concentrate on or pay attention to during that day. Although I also encourage adults with ADHD to routinely engage in more extensive workouts regularly throughout a typical week, that is not what is being suggested here. Here I am encouraging much briefer exercise periods—just 2 to 5 minutes of exercise may be enough to help your loved one concentrate better if done just before he enters a boring or demanding class or exam. If the class, meeting, or work project is long enough that he is being given beverage or restroom breaks, suggest that he use those breaks to do some quick aerobic exercise. This can be helpful even if it is just faster-than-normal walking outside the building, walking in a hallway near the work area, or walking up and down stairs in a nearby stairwell.

While in settings where staying seated is required, suggest that your loved one stay restless and active in small ways. I mentioned this earlier, but people with ADHD are able to concentrate better and do mental work better if they are allowed to move around a bit while working. This movement can be simple things, such as squeezing a rubber ball in her left hand while writing with her right hand; crossing her legs and moving one of them rhythmically while listening or taking notes; doodling with a pencil on scratch paper while listening to a lecture or discussion; or even chewing gum while working, thinking, or listening to someone else. She needs to keep moving to keep focused.

Wear a tactile cuing device to frequently prompt self-awareness and focus on goals or the work at hand. For a small amount, your loved one can buy "The MotivAider" on the Internet (http://www.addwarehouse.com). This is a small plastic box about the size of a cell phone that contains a vibrator inside and a digital clock. The clock can be set for any intervals one may wish or the random setting can be chosen. When the interval expires, the device vibrates (or will do so at unpredictable intervals if they chose the random option). This tactile cue can serve to remind your loved one to stay alert and focused on what she is doing.

If your loved one has lots of reading to do for school or work, encourage him to learn to use the SQ4R method. Use this method for improving his reading comprehension if that is a problem. Read Exhibit 17.1 to see how it works.

Try some peer/coworker tutoring. It may help your loved one if a fellow student (or coworker) study together and alternate teaching each other the material. One of them is the instructor, the other the student. Then reverse these roles with each tutoring session. Having to teach someone new material is a surefire way to learn and retain such information compared with just routine independent study.

Suggest that your loved one work as a team with a more organized person. Working around or with others who do not have ADHD can serve to keep her better focused on the work that is to be done. It also makes her more publicly accountable for doing that work than if she goes solo and does the work in isolation.

Find a fallback college classmate or coworker. Your loved one is going to use this person in any instances in which he is outside of

EXHIBIT 17.1. Improving Reading Comprehension—The SQ4R System

1. *Survey* the material to be read—just leaf through it quickly to get some idea of how much is to be read, how it is broken up, and so forth.
2. Draft some *questions* that need to be answered from what you are to read. Often these are at the end of the chapter to be read or have been given to you by your teacher or workplace supervisor.
3. Now use the *4Rs:* read just one paragraph, recite out loud in a soft voice or whisper what was important in that material, write that material down in your notebook, then review what you just wrote.
4. Do this for each paragraph. This not only makes one review what one is reading four times per paragraph (read, recite, write, review) but it gives one frequent mental breaks at the end of each paragraph. That can happen as the reader shifts their concentration from reading, to reciting, to writing, to reviewing across the assignment. As your loved one gets good at this, she or he can read longer passages, such as two paragraphs at a time or an entire page before engaging in the recite, write, and review steps. This is a great strategy for people with working memory problems.

school classes or away from work and finds that he has forgotten an assignment or other important information. So suggest that he swap contact information with this other person. That way, both people can get the lost or missing assignments or information quickly when either one finds they have this problem.

Attend after-class (or after-work) help sessions whenever they are given. Many teachers in college or instructors in workplace educational settings are willing to set aside extra time to help people who need more instructor assistance in learning a topic. If that is available at your loved one's college or worksite, then recommend that she use it to the hilt. Even if she doesn't really need the assistance, the extra review will help with forgetfulness. It will also show her to be a motivated student or employee and hence make a better impression with instructors.

Your loved one should schedule faculty or supervisor review meetings often—every 3 to 6 weeks. These meetings should be more frequent than just at the end of the grading period or the annual workplace formal performance review meeting. Remember that the more often your loved one is held accountable for his work, the better he will do. So, in addition to using the previous coaching suggestion each day, suggest that he schedule more frequent and informal reviews with the people actually responsible for grading or evaluating his work at school or on the job. This lets him get more frequent feedback more quickly on just how well he is doing.

Gently prompt your loved one to watch, limit, or eliminate caffeine, nicotine, alcohol, or marijuana use. Adults with ADHD are more prone to use these substances and become dependent on them. And they sometimes try to self-medicate their own disorder using readily available caffeine-containing beverages or tobacco products. Yes, caffeine and nicotine are stimulants and they can help people be more alert, though nowhere near as well as the ADHD medications can do. But caffeine especially works on the wrong brain neurochemicals for people with ADHD and it can, in moderate or high doses, be counterproductive. That is because it makes your loved one less focused, more jumpy and jittery, more nervous, and more likely to frequently need to urinate. She is better off using a prescription ADHD drug than trying to use substances containing caffeine or over-the-counter pills that contain caffeine. And although nicotine may benefit ADHD symptoms to some degree, she is using a highly addictive drug to self-medicate. Doing so is only going to increase the risk of addiction to this chemical, not to mention increase her risk for pulmonary and heart disease and cancer. Again, using a prescription ADHD drug instead does not carry such risks and works even better.

Help your loved one manage her Internet use. The Internet can become a big source of wasted time or an incredible distraction from work or home tasks, even for typical people. But for adults with ADHD who already have significant problems with self-control, having Internet access readily available at home or work can pose far worse problems. Research shows that teens and adults with ADHD spend far more time on the Internet, whether surfing various websites or gaming, than do typical people of the same age. They are also far more likely to have problems disengaging from the Internet or gaming when the situation demands that they shift to other more important things that need to get done. And 15% to 20% of young adults with ADHD can be said to be Internet addicted, showing all the typical signs of dependence or addiction often used to diagnose more common alcohol and drug addictions. Whether at work or home, you can advise your loved one with adult ADHD to do a few different things if the Internet is proving to be a big time-suck for them and interfering with other more important demands. If you or your loved one are not sure just how much time is being wasted on the Internet, get a software program like RescueTime (http://www.rescuetime.com) installed on that computer. It will track each Internet page that was opened; how much time was spent on that website; and even send you or your loved one a report broken down by categories, including the websites he is browsing the most. What else can you do to help?

At home, place the computer and Internet access in a space set aside for working, such as a home office. Don't just leave computers, iPads, and other Internet-enabled devices in bedrooms, family rooms, and kitchens where they will tend to capture the ADHD adult's attention so readily during times when they should be busy doing more important tasks or projects. Advise your loved one to have a room for computers and their access and only use these rooms when computer work is to be done, while otherwise keeping the computer out of sight (and so out of mind) when tasks are being done that don't require the use of computers or the Internet. When in the workspace, your loved one could keep the door closed and wear headphones or use a white-noise machine if necessary to cut down on distractions occurring elsewhere in the home (or office) that might distract them one from their work.

Better yet, set up two different computers—one for work only and the other for play. Your loved one can use a desktop or laptop computer for their work and another for nonwork activities.[2] This computer is only to have programs on it that are critical to the type of work that they need to do. This device is to have just one browser and also one of the following programs that can be set for limiting Internet access or access to certain play related websites. Keep the work e-mail program closed until certain times of the day set aside for doing work e-mails. And keep the instant messaging program closed as well. If your loved one must instant message someone, open the program for just that short query and close it when they have gotten the reply. Don't leave this program in the active mode while working. Software for gaming, social media, or other such time wasters is not to be installed on this computer. Instead, your loved one can use a tablet or even another laptop as their "play" machine. On this computer is to be installed all those entertainment and social media software your loved one wishes to use, but it is to have no work-related programs or work e-mail. By setting up two different systems, it becomes easier when using the work device to not be distracted by the availability of play, gaming, or other social media programs or personal e-mail accounts. Advise your loved one

[2]See Mike Elgan's article on this method on the following website: http://www.computerworld.com/article/2507281/web-apps/elgan—how-to-overcome-internet-distraction-disorder.html.

to never play on their work computer and never work on their play computer.

Install Internet time management software on the home and workplace computers. Several software programs can be added on to Internet browsers that can be programmed to restrict Internet access or block access to websites that are for sheer entertainment and to which your loved one is likely to go that can interfere with work.[3] Programs, such as StayFocused and Chrome Nanny for Google Chrome, WasteNoTime for Chrome and Safari, or Leech Block for Firefox, can be set to allow fixed times and durations for accessing certain websites, after which the sites will be blocked. They can be programmed to limit access to certain times during work or business hours and for specified durations. Some of these add-on programs can also be set up so that they cannot be disabled and so that any changes the adult tries to make to alter the settings don't take effect until the next day, both of which can serve to block impulsive use of the Internet for entertainment or distraction when other work needs to be done. Some of these only work on a specific browser so they won't prevent your loved one from getting out on the Internet using another browser.

If your loved one has a Mac computer, then programs such as Self-Control and Anti-Social can be set up to manage Internet or website access or even block it on any browsers on that computer. So can the program FocalFilter. On that type of computer, the program Time Out can be installed and programmed to give gentle reminders to take a break at specified intervals while an individual is on the Internet. The program Freedom can be used on both Mac and PC computers to shut down Internet access on that computer for specified time periods. Of course, you can also use the Parental Controls setting to have your

[3]My thanks go to David Cravens, Application Developer at Palmetto Health IT, for sharing some of these suggestions with me.

loved one give control of website access to another caring adult, such as yourself or a friend, who can serve this parental role in blocking or unblocking Internet or website access. Such software programs and settings are designed to protect your loved one from getting distracted by the Internet and wasting incredible amounts of time on it, especially when doing so is interfering with necessary tasks. If the problem is Internet access from a cell phone, look at programs like Tasker and Do Not Disturb as possible ways to limit or block Internet access to keep your loved one from using it to waste time.

Of course, all of these can be overcome with workarounds if an adult with ADHD really, really tries hard enough to circumvent them. But their goal is really to put enough initial obstacles in the way of access or lengthy Internet use to cause your loved one to have second thoughts about this impulsive desire to get on the Internet and hence restrain himself from doing so.

With your loved one's permission, monitor her Internet use and gently remind her when the time on the computer has become excessive or is interfering with other work. She can tell you in advance how long she wants to use the Internet, when she wants access, and when it needs to be terminated to do other things. This is similar to the software programs discussed earlier in this chapter that can do the same sorts of things, but with this kind of monitoring you or others serve that supervisory and restrictive role, diplomatically of course. This method can be quite effective because, as noted earlier, it is a means of making us accountable to others—a strategy that is far more likely to succeed than if a person just tries to manage such self-change on their own.

CHAPTER 18

ADVICE FOR ADDRESSING HEALTH RISKS

Adults with attention-deficit/hyperactivity disorder (ADHD) need to pay careful attention to the health and lifestyle risks likely to come with their disorder. Those risks were discussed in Chapter 5. Many health habits and lifestyle activities that adults with ADHD have are prone to put them at greater risk for coronary heart disease and cancer, among other medical and dental problems (more dental cavities, possibly more mouth infections). Add to this their greater risk for accidental injuries, and you have a recipe for a life filled with preventable misfortunes. So your loved one with ADHD is going to need more assistance from medical and health professionals who are expert in the management of these health risks and lifestyle problem areas, such as smoking cessation programs, dietary management, exercise regimens, and so on.

Don't let your loved one's ADHD shorten her life expectancy because of its association with these risk factors. This means not only helping your loved one to get her ADHD under control as much as possible but also encouraging her to pay attention to those lifestyle, nutrition, and other choices that may leave her at greater risk of a shortened life.

ADVICE FOR HEALTH MAINTENANCE

Here are some reminders to pass along to your loved one to help get started. Choose from among them those that seem best suited to the problems your loved one may be experiencing.

Develop regular weekly exercise patterns. Your loved one should exercise three or more times per week for increased attention, better health, stress management, and so on. As you have already heard, regular routine physical exercise done three to four times per week even for just 20 to 30 minutes each time is good for health. But it also seems to be of particular benefit for further controlling or compensating for ADHD symptoms. Regular exercise can also help fend off the risk for obesity that comes with this disorder. So whether it's running, biking, weight training, dance classes, using one's favorite gym equipment (treadmills, elliptical trainers, stair-climbers, etc.), or some mixture of various types of exercise, the adult with ADHD, more than most people, needs to be doing routine physical exercise.

Encourage your loved one to make an appointment for a physical exam if he has not had one in a while or has never had one as an adult. This is a status check to see what problems or issues are developing and to try to head them off early with better preventive medical care. If he doesn't have insurance or the money needed to do so, maybe you, a parent, sibling, or relative could cover this cost. If that is not possible, check with the local county or city hospital about getting such a physical through them at the county or state's expense under such programs as Medicare or Medicaid if your loved one falls below the poverty line in income. Call the local department of social services to see whether they can direct you to free care clinics. Your loved one avoids medical care at his own long-term risk, and maybe yours, too. Don't play the odds thinking that because he feels well or has no obvious current medical problems some are not festering unseen or undetected. Help him to get a baseline physical and follow the advice of the doctor. Other things that you and your loved one may wish to discuss with the physician are outlined here.

- If your loved one smokes tobacco and/or marijuana, get the doctor to recommend a smoking cessation program to help him stop.
- If your loved one drinks to excess or may have alcoholism, ask the doctor to enroll him in a nearby alcohol rehabilitation program and Alcoholics Anonymous (AA) group or other such ongoing support program for recovering alcoholics.
- If your loved one has a drug problem, ask the doctor to enroll him in a drug detox clinic or other local program.

Facilitate a consult with a local dentist for your loved one. Consult with a local dentist to catch any developing dental problems or diseases your loved one may have. If left unchecked, these could cause her to lose some or all of her teeth, require a partial or full set of dentures, lead to more extensive dental or gum surgery, or possibly even abscessed teeth. The latter has the potential to be lethal if that infection happens to enter the bloodstream and attack the heart.

Again, strongly encourage your loved one, if appropriate, to go on medication to treat his ADHD. Often the medical and dental risks we have identified in our research on adults with ADHD stems from their unmanaged ADHD and the disorganizing effects it has on their life. Getting your loved one's ADHD under control with medication can enable him to engage these other medical, dental, and health related activities with a greater chance of success. One side effect of those medicines is that they can often result in weight loss. For an adult who is already overweight, this is not actually a side effect but a side benefit of taking these medications for managing ADHD.

DRIVING

As my twin brother learned all too well, driving is a serious and potentially life-threatening area of impairment for adults with ADHD. Here I list some specific recommendations regarding driving.

Have your loved one use an ADHD medication whenever operating a motor vehicle or heavy equipment. If your loved one's ADHD is moderate to severe, I strongly urge you to have her use an ADHD medication whenever operating a motor vehicle or heavy equipment. Here I provide some more recommendations for things you can have her do to improve this domain.

Make sure the medication covers as much of the waking day as possible. What is important here is greater attention to the timing of when your loved one takes his medication relative to when he is most likely to be driving. That is because you want to ensure that your loved one has adequate levels of medication in the bloodstream at those hours, such as morning and evening commuting, late night driving for work or social occasions, and so on. It is possible that earlier doses, even of extended release medicines, may have worn off to a degree that he is no longer adequately treated with medicine at these peak driving times.

If your loved one is not taking medication, or refuses to, suggest that the spouse or partner who does not have ADHD drive the children to their various activities. The same applies when she is out with a partner, spouse, family member, or other loved one in the same vehicle and your loved one is not medicated. Forget her pride—let someone else drive.

Strongly advise your loved one that absolutely no alcohol be consumed when he plans to operate a motor vehicle. Period. So ask your loved one to please "stay off the sauce" if he plans to be driving.

SUBSTANCE ABUSE

At least one in four adults with ADHD are likely to have a problem with excessive use, dependence or abuse of one or more substances. As I discussed in Chapter 5, the most common substances an adult with ADHD may overuse or abuse are nicotine, alcohol, and marijuana, and sometimes all three. A lesser percentage of adults are likely to be using or abusing hard drugs, such as cocaine, heroin, methamphetamine, and so on, or illegally using prescription drugs. Sometimes your loved one's excessive drug use or abuse is obvious; you likely have witnessed his use, dependence, or abuse. Or perhaps you have found drug paraphernalia, such as marijuana pipes, cigarette wrappers, baggies with some seeds in them, needles, or empty prescription bottles lying about his living space.

Other times, you suspect your loved one may be using substances inappropriately or excessively but aren't sure. Some signs of drug abuse are typically associated with abrupt changes in her mood, behavior, or physical appearance for which there is no obvious explanation. Several examples follow.

- If your loved one is showing excess drowsiness, slurred speech, glassy eyes, slowed reaction time, poor motor coordination and imbalance, or even depression, you might suspect he is abusing alcohol or prescription sedatives, such as Valium, Librium, and Seconal.
- In contrast, is your loved one excessively alert, has narrowed pupils, shows more energy than usual, or seems high or manic? Or does he seem more restless, nervous, or fidgety more than usual? Does he show excessive talking with pressured speech (words rush out like a fountain), have disjointed thinking, or even seem to be paranoid or hallucinating? Then consider that

he may be abusing a stimulant. These include cocaine or crack, speed or methamphetamine, as well as prescription stimulants such as the kind used to treat adult ADHD. Those drugs can be abused by crushing the tablets and snorting them nasally, mixing them with water and injecting them, or even by taking prescription medication in doses far larger than prescribed.

- Are you seeing signs of mild euphoria, an excessively laid-back or unconcerned attitude, or is she overly relaxed? Does she show racing or paranoid thoughts? Does she report odd perceptual distortions (vivid colors, acute hearing of soft sounds, etc.)? Do you see her engaging in unusual smiling as if everything seems mildly ironic or funny? Then she may be abusing marijuana, hash, or THC (the main abusable ingredient in both), or heroin, morphine, or codeine.

Another sign a loved one with adult ADHD may be abusing drugs is an abrupt change in his daily life functioning. This can include unexpected and unexplained changes in his finances, where money you thought he had is now gone. Or maybe money you had in your wallet or purse is missing. Has he asked to borrow money from you for vague expenses or ones that don't make much sense? Have you found bills you thought were paid that really were not, utilities threatened to be turned off, or that he is suddenly overextended on his credit cards (from taking cash advances)? Look for changes in his work life, such as being repeatedly late for work when he previously was not, because of oversleeping or a sudden loss of motivation to work. Or you notice he is getting calls from employers about being absent or for inappropriate things that have happened at work; perhaps he has even been fired. A sudden change from his normal driving patterns, increased negative consequences of driving (speeding tickets, etc.), or using his car at inappropriate times such as very late at night to meet "friends" unknown to you.

Sudden declines in educational performance can also be evidence of this. Yes, as I said earlier, adults with ADHD may have trouble in these domains anyway, even without abusing substances. That is why I have emphasized here that you look for sudden changes from his usual level of functioning as a potential sign of drug use or abuse.

If your loved one has such problems with excessive drug use or even abuse, she will find it harder than others to quit using or abusing them. That is because ADHD creates a problem with self-control. It requires substantial self-control to detox from a substance on which someone is dependent or to which she is addicted. So even if your loved one with adult ADHD is interested in discontinuing her abuse of a substance, it can prove quite difficult. That means she is going to need all of the support she can get from others who care about her, such as you. And it also means that she may need to have her ADHD treated to help boost her self-control.

The approach you should take to helping your loved one with a drug use problem is similar to the way you approached him about having adult ADHD—it depends on which stage of readiness to change he is currently in (you may need to review Chapter 9). Some are in denial. Others understand they have a problem but are not sure how bad it is or what to do about it. Still others are further along and ready to make a commitment to change and get the professional help they require. What you do to help him hinges on where he is along this spectrum and so how best to keep him moving along to the next stages.

One thing has become reasonably clear in research on adults with ADHD who carry a dual diagnosis of a substance use problem: They do better in drug rehabilitation if their adult ADHD is already being treated. Otherwise, their untreated adult ADHD causes them problems with self-control, and that leads to problems with adhering to their drug treatment program. Once their ADHD is being reasonably managed, usually through medication and counseling, then they may be ready to tackle their drug use problems. These in fact may already be declining due to the degree of success they are having managing their adult ADHD.

What else can you suggest to help? Once again, this may depend on whether you are living with your loved one with adult ADHD or see her frequently enough to actually be of some assistance. If you do live with or interact with your loved one frequently, then you can consider some of the methods I describe here to get her further help.

Help your loved one monitor how often he is consuming that substance. If your loved one with adult ADHD isn't sure that he has a drug use problem, an initial step to consider is to help him to monitor how often he is consuming that substance. This might be done by just keeping a calendar on which you and he record the frequency of these instances. Several questions should be asked as you review this tool. Is he using alcohol (or other substances) far more than is typical for most adults? Is this use occurring in an uncontrolled fashion across various settings and times of the day? Is he binge drinking or binge consuming that substance? Is his behavior or daily functioning being adversely affected? Have others commented to him about his excess substance use? Watch to see whether he is dependent on use of the substance to get through stressful situations.

If you live together, can you remove the substance from the home without provoking serious problems with withdrawal? If she is an alcoholic, daily user of tobacco, or of marijuana, or is clearly addicted to harder drugs, then you may not be able to eliminate the substances from her living space so easily. She may need some medical assistance to help treat her withdrawal symptoms.

Encourage your loved one to get professional assistance with his substance use problem. Follow the same steps suggested earlier for finding an expert on adult ADHD to diagnose and treat your loved one. Except this time, focus more on the expertise of the professional in treating substance abuse disorders. You can probably start by asking or having your loved one ask the professional who diagnosed him with adult ADHD to see whether they also treat substance use problems. If not, ask who they would recommend. If that is not possible, then check with your loved one's primary care provider or your own to see whether they know of such resources. You can call the state psychiatric or psychological associations or visit their websites to learn which professionals in your region provide such services for substance use disorders.

If the problem is with nicotine, then primary care physicians are usually knowledgeable about area programs for quitting smoking. They may also be able to deliver some limited programs themselves. They or those programs can provide nicotine alternatives to ease withdrawal while your loved one steps down from using tobacco or goes cold turkey.

If your loved one has an alcohol use problem, then primary care doctors usually know the regional resources for treating alcoholism. Your loved one may benefit from AA or other forms of group and individual therapy. Again, she may need certain medications to help her quit (e.g., Antabuse) or to help her cope with her symptoms of withdrawal. Sometimes the alcoholism is sufficiently severe to warrant a short-term (1- to 2-month) stay in a residential treatment center for alcoholism or other drug use disorders. If that is the case, be sure the center staff understands that your loved one also has a dual diagnosis of adult ADHD and is knowledgeable about treating the drug use disorder in that context. The presence of both disorders usually complicates the otherwise routine treatment plan for drug abuse.

If your loved one has a problem with marijuana use or abuse, then the same sorts of steps may also help you identify the resources he needs. Although there are not as many resources for dealing with this type of dependency or abuse as there are for alcoholism, you may find them by following the same advice given: Speak with your primary care doctor, call the state psychological and psychiatric associations, call university medical school psychiatry departments or university clinical psychology programs, check with county mental health centers, and use the Internet to search for resources.

If your loved one is dependent on, or addicted to, other, harder drugs than these, then inpatient hospitalization may be needed. Inpatient hospitalization may be necessary to help acutely treat his problem. This hospitalization can be followed by a short-term stay in a residential facility that focuses on treating his type of drug use. To identify such resources, again follow the steps just listed to see whether they can reveal any specific professionals or clinics that can help your loved one. Most individuals who are using substances excessively or abusing them often have more than one psychiatric disorder besides the drug use problem. Many have several, including adult ADHD. Disorders such as anxiety, depression, bipolar disorder, personality disorders, and so on, often coexist with drug use disorders. So don't be surprised if your loved one winds up being treated for these additional disorders alongside his treatment for his drug use and even for adult ADHD.

CHAPTER 19

GOVERNMENT PROGRAMS RELEVANT TO ADULT ADHD

It is important for you and your loved one with adult ADHD to know that laws and government regulations in the United States protect people with disabilities from discrimination or limited access to various domains of life. Those domains include education, work, housing, medical care and insurance, and access to public places, among others. These regulations have been extended to adults with mental, not just physical, disabilities. In rare cases, adults with ADHD may have such a severe degree of impairment that they need to substantially limit working, stop working altogether, or even refrain from entering the workforce. For these individuals, government assistance in the form of income supplements are available.

LEGAL PROTECTIONS AND THE AMERICANS WITH DISABILITIES ACT

The most widely known legal protection for adults with ADHD is the Americans With Disabilities Act (ADA)[1] implemented in 1990 and its more recent 2008 amendments. Adult ADHD is covered under this act and its interpretive regulations.

[1]Americans With Disabilities Act of 1990, Pub. L. No. 101-336, § 2, 104 Stat. 328 (1991).

Drs. Gordon, Lewandowski, and Lovett have written extensively on this topic, and much of what appears in the following is adapted from their work.[2] It is important for you and your loved one with ADHD to realize that this legislation is not intended to provide someone with treatment for a disability, it is instead a form of civil rights legislation that is intended to protect people with disabilities from discrimination or unfair practices used against them because of their disability.

To gain these protections and accommodations, the individual with the disability must ask for them. In so doing, he or she must disclose that disability to the employer, college, or other setting in which they are seeking protections and accommodations for their disability. This disclosure typically includes providing written documentation of that disability from an appropriate professional who routinely evaluates and treats that type of disability. In the case of an adult with ADHD, that evaluation and documentation would most likely come from a clinical psychologist or psychiatrist or other medical specialist having demonstrated competence in diagnosing adult ADHD (such as a neurologist or a family practitioner).

Here are a few things to bear in mind about this legislation.

- First, a disability is not simply a diagnosis. It is possible to get a professional diagnosis of adult ADHD but not be considered to have a disability under the ADA. That is because a *disability*

[2]Gordon, M., Lewandowski, L. J., & Lovett, B. J. (2015). Assessment and management of ADHD in educational and workplace settings in the context of ADA accommodations. In R. A. Barkley (Ed.), *Attention-deficit hyperactivity disorder: A handbook for diagnosis and treatment* (4th ed., pp. 774–794). New York, NY: Guilford Press.

is defined as a physical or mental impairment that substantially limits functioning in a major life activity. That substantial limitation to a major life activity cannot be temporary but must be recurring or permanent.

- Second, the standard or comparison group for judging someone to be functionally impaired in that major life activity is the average person, not some highly intelligent, highly educated, or high-functioning special peer group, such as other law or medical school students.
- Third, the determination of a disability is done on a case-by-case basis using the totality of evidence available and is not guaranteed simply because someone carries a diagnosis of adult ADHD or believes themselves to be impaired in a major life activity. Such documentation must be thorough and convincing and not just based on personal self-reports by the adult with ADHD. The more diverse the documentation of persistent impairment, the more likely it is that the person will be deemed to have a disability and entitled to protections and accommodations.
- Finally, the determination of the presence of a disability must be done, in most circumstances, without regard to the effects of treatment or other mitigating measures that may reduce the impact of the disability. The fact that an adult with ADHD is taking medication that reduces their symptoms does not disqualify them from their being judged to have a disability.

This protection against discrimination for a mental disorder sounds fine in theory, but the impact of a disability can be difficult to prove in reality. An adult with ADHD, for example, can still be dismissed from a job or not granted admission to or accommodations in college so long as the reasons for these refusals are not related to the person's disability. An adult with ADHD who manifests poor hygiene, dresses badly for their workplace and job, uses illegal drugs that affect workplace performance, and fails to show up for work repeatedly can still be fired, because none of these can be construed as being a direct feature of their disability. But an adult with ADHD who is incredibly distractible may be allowed to have a quieter location to do their work, to wear noise reduction headphones if it doesn't interfere with their work, or to take a standardized test for licensing within their profession in a quiet room with extra time (or "time off the clock," as described in Chapter 17).

Although the law does not entitle a person with a disability to treatment, it does require that those in charge of these important major life activities, such as employers, make "reasonable accommodations" (in the workplace) for an individual's disability. What is a reasonable accommodation? Generally, it means making existing facilities used by employees readily accessible to, and usable by, persons with disabilities. It can also include job restructuring, modifying work schedules, or reassignment to a vacant position. Employers may also be required to obtain or modify equipment or devices, adjust or modify examinations, training materials, or policies and provide qualified readers or interpreters.[3] In short, the law is about protecting reasonable access to major life activities. It does not guarantee success in major life activities. Moreover, as the ADA describes, an employer does not have to provide even a reasonable accommodation if it imposes an "undue hardship" to the employer: "an action requiring significant difficulty or expense when considered in light of factors such as an employer's size, financial resources, and the nature and structure of its operations."

[3]See http://www1.eeoc.gov//eeoc/publications/

Any adjustments to the workplace or nature of the work that are being requested as an accommodation must be

- directly related to the nature of the person's disability;
- targeted to the deficits associated with that disability;
- have some evidence that the accommodations are likely to help correct for the impact of their disability in their work; and
- considered reasonable—that is to say, the accommodations must not be significantly cumbersome or exorbitantly expensive (pose an undue burden) for the employer, college, building owner, and so on, to implement.

Therefore, an adult with ADHD is not likely to be entitled to whatever they want, such as a corner office (to reduce distractions from coworkers), a parking spot adjacent to the front door, an assistant who routinely takes notes for them in various meetings, and so on, or multiple forms of expensive smart technologies, such as smartphones, iPads, and so on, even though these may be helpful in their work. That is because these requests are either not directly related to their disorder or are unreasonable (unduly burdensome) accommodations.

Furthermore, the accommodations being requested cannot so radically alter the nature of the work being done that the person is now no longer performing the core nature, features, or purpose of the task. Moreover, the courts have ruled that the person with a disability must be receiving routine or typical medical or mental health treatment for their disability, if available, in order to compel the employer to make these reasonable accommodations for them. For instance, an employer is not required to make accommodations for a person's poor vision or visual acuity if the person with such a disability refuses to wear glasses. Likewise, an employer may not necessarily be compelled to make adjustments to work for someone's adult ADHD if they refuse to take any of the medications approved by the Food and Drug Administration for its management or if they refuse to engage in any of the treatments recommended.

Employers, schools or colleges, and others are usually well aware of the requirements under the ADA and the protections the law affords. However, occasionally acts of discrimination do occur. If your loved one has experienced such discrimination as a direct result of their having adult ADHD, then you may wish to have them contact legal counsel or the U.S. Office of Civil Rights for further guidance on addressing their complaint.

SOCIAL SECURITY DISABILITY INSURANCE AND SUPPLEMENTAL SECURITY INCOME

If your loved one has severe ADHD, he might be eligible for financial assistance under two federal programs. One is the Social Security Disability Insurance program, or SSDI. This applies to individuals who have worked a significant amount of time in the past and so have contributed money into Social Security. But because of his ADHD, that adult is now unable to work and will be so for at least the next year. This financial assistance can be provided to people even if they have other sources of income (not work related).

In contrast, Supplemental Security Income (SSI) is available to people who have never worked in the past or have worked for only a short period of time. The program provides them with financial assistance. But the eligibility for that assistance is limited by any other income your loved one may receive or assets they possess, all of which must not exceed a certain amount as specified under current SSI regulations. The bar for obtaining such assistance is relatively high in terms of the severity of the mental disorder, its impact on working, and the documentation that must be provided so as to be granted these forms of assistance. For more information on these programs, visit the website for the U.S. Social Security Administration (http://www.ssa.gov/disability/ or http://www.ssa.gov/ssi/) or go to a nearby office of this agency and speak with one of their counselors.

CONCLUSION

I hope that this book has taught you much about the nature of adult ADHD, its causes, and its life course risks. I have also discussed the types of nonmedical and medical treatments often used to treat adult ADHD. I have tried to explain the kinds of roles you can play to help your loved one with adult ADHD, and I have made some general recommendations for mastering the executive deficits associated with it. And I have provided a wealth of specific recommendations you can consider suggesting to your loved one with adult ADHD on how to deal with problems in various specific domains of life, such as work, education, money management, driving, child care, and so on.

In closing, remember that although adult ADHD is a serious disorder, it is also one that is highly treatable using a variety of science-based interventions that can reduce the symptoms and greatly improve daily functioning. As illustrated by the success stories I shared in Chapter 7, adult ADHD does not have to prevent one from pursuing one's dreams and becoming a successful, happy, well-adjusted adult, provided the disorder is properly diagnosed and treated. And that success also depends in no small degree on the support that adults with ADHD receive from loved ones like you. Please accept my very best wishes on your journey.

APPENDIX

DSM–5 Criteria for Diagnosing ADHD (Including *ICD–10* Billing Codes)

A. A persistent pattern of inattention and/or hyperactivity-impulsivity that interferes with functioning or development, as characterized by (1) and/or (2):

1. Inattention: Six (or more) of the following symptoms have persisted for at least 6 months to a degree that is inconsistent with developmental level and that negatively impacts directly on social and academic/occupational activities:

Note: The symptoms are not solely a manifestation of oppositional behavior, defiance, hostility, or failure to understand task instructions. For older adolescents and adults (age 17 and older), at least five symptoms are required.

(a) Often fails to give close attention to details or makes careless mistakes in schoolwork, at work, or during other activities (e.g., overlooks or misses details, work is inaccurate).

(b) Often has difficulty sustaining attention in tasks or play activities (e.g., has difficulty remaining focused during lectures, conversations, or lengthy reading).

(c) Often does not seem to listen when spoken to directly (e.g., mind seems elsewhere, even in the absence of any obvious distraction).

(*continues*)

DSM–5 Criteria for Diagnosing ADHD (Including *ICD–10* Billing Codes) (*Continued*)

(d) Often does not follow through on instructions and fails to finish schoolwork, chores, or duties in the workplace (e.g., starts tasks but quickly loses focus and is easily sidetracked).
(e) Often has difficulty organizing tasks and activities (e.g., difficulty managing sequential tasks; difficulty keeping materials and belongings in order; messy, disorganized work; has poor time management; fails to meet deadlines).
(f) Often avoids, dislikes, or is reluctant to engage in tasks that require sustained mental effort (e.g., schoolwork or homework; for older adolescents and adults, preparing reports, completing forms, reviewing lengthy papers).
(g) Often loses things necessary for tasks or activities (e.g., school materials, pencils, books, tools, wallets, keys, paperwork, eyeglasses, mobile telephones).
(h) Is often easily distracted by extraneous stimuli (for older adolescents and adults, may include unrelated thoughts).
(i) Is often forgetful in daily activities (e.g., doing chores, running errands; for older adolescents and adults, returning to class, paying bills, keeping appointments).

2. **Hyperactivity and impulsivity:** Six (or more) of the following symptoms have persisted for at least 6 months to a degree that is inconsistent with developmental level and that negatively impacts directly on social and academic/occupational activities:
   Note: The symptoms are not solely a manifestation of oppositional behavior, defiance, hostility, or failure to understand task instructions. For older adolescents and adults (age 17 and older), at least five symptoms are required.
   (a) Often fidgets with or taps hands or feet or squirms in seat.
   (b) Often leaves seat situations when remaining seated is expected (e.g., leaves his or her place in the classroom, in the office or other workplace, or in other situations that require remaining in place).

DSM–5 Criteria for Diagnosing ADHD (Including *ICD–10* Billing Codes) (*Continued*)

(c) Often runs about or climbs in situations where it is inappropriate. (Note: In adolescents or adults, may be limited to feeling restless.)

(d) Often unable to play or engage in leisure activities quietly.

(e) Is often "on the go," acting as if "driven by a motor" (e.g., is unable to be or uncomfortable being still for extended time, as in restaurants, meetings; may be experienced by others as being restless or difficult to keep up with).

(f) Often talks excessively.

(g) Often blurts out an answer before a question has been completed (e.g., completes people's sentences; cannot wait for turn in conversation).

(h) Often has difficulty waiting his or her turn (e.g., while waiting in line).

(i) Often interrupts or intrudes on others (e.g., butts into conversations, games, or activities; may start using other people's things without asking or receiving permission; for adolescents and adults, may intrude into or take over what others are doing).

B. Several inattentive or hyperactive–impulsive symptoms were present prior to age 12 years.

C. Several inattentive or hyperactive–impulsive symptoms are present in two or more settings (e.g., at home, school, or work; with friends or relatives; in other activities).

D. There is clear evidence that the symptoms interfere with, or reduce, the quality of social, academic, or occupational functioning.

E. The symptoms do not occur exclusively during the course of schizophrenia or another psychotic disorder and are not better explained by another mental disorder (e.g., mood disorder, anxiety disorder, dissociative disorder, personality disorder, substance intoxication or withdrawal).

(*continues*)

DSM–5 Criteria for Diagnosing ADHD (Including *ICD–10* Billing Codes) (*Continued*)

Specify whether:

314.01 (F90.2) Combined presentation: If both Criterion A1 (inattention) and Criterion A2 (hyperactivity-impulsivity) are met for the past 6 months.

314.00 (F90.0) Predominantly inattentive presentation: If Criterion A1 (inattention) is met but Criterion A2 (hyperactivity-impulsivity) is not met for the past 6 months.

314.01 (F90.1) Predominantly hyperactive/impulsive presentation: if Criterion A2 (hyperactivity-impulsivity) is met and Criterion A1 (inattention) is not met for the past 6 months.

Specify if:

In partial remission: When full criteria were met in the past, fewer than the full criteria have been met for the past 6 months, and the symptoms still result in impairment in social, academic, or occupational functioning.

Specify current severity:

Mild: Few, if any, symptoms in excess of those required to make the diagnosis are present, and symptoms result in no more than minor impairment in social or occupational functioning.

Moderate: Symptoms or functional impairment between "mild" and "severe" are present.

Severe: Many symptoms in excess of those required to make the diagnosis, or several symptoms that are particularly severe, are present, or the symptoms result in marked impairment in social or occupational functioning.

Note. From the diagnostic criteria for attention-deficit/hyperactivity disorder (ADHD) contained in the *Diagnostic and Statistical Manual for Mental Disorders* (5th ed., pp. 59–61), by the American Psychiatric Association, 2013, Washington, DC: Author.

RESOURCES

WEBSITES

Dr. Barkley: http://www.russellbarkley.org and http://www.adhdlectures.com

My personal website contains fact sheets on attention-deficit/hyperactivity disorder (ADHD), my speaking schedule, and information about my various books and newsletter. The site adhdlectures.com contains 10 hours of lectures for parents and 25 hours for professionals addressing various topics related to ADHD and its management, all of which can be viewed for free.

ADD Warehouse: http://www.addwarehouse.com

This site sells a variety of books, videos, and other products related to ADHD.

American Academy of Child and Adolescent Psychiatry: http://www.aacap.org

This is the official website for this organization, which also contains a separate directory of fact sheets on childhood and adolescent mental disorders.

American Academy of Pediatrics: http://www.aap.org

This is the official website for this organization, on which one can find some factual information about ADHD and other developmental disorders.

Attention Deficit Disorder Association (ADDA): http://www.add.org

This organization advocates for those with ADHD and has, over time, come to focus more on adults with the disorder.

ADHD coaching: http://www.adhdcoaches.org, http://www.totallyadd.com, and http://www.nancyratey.com

These three websites provide information on the ADHD coaching approach to treatment, several of which contain lists of coaching professionals by region.

http://www.adhdrollercoaster.org

This website was created by journalist Gina Pera, who also specializes in providing information on ADHD for adults, especially for couples in which one partner has adult ADHD.

Children and Adults With Attention-Deficit/Hyperactivity Disorder (CHADD): http://www.chadd.org

This U.S. national nonprofit organization is dedicated to advocating for children and adults with ADHD and their families. This website contains fact sheets on ADHD, a directory of state and local CHADD chapters, and information on its annual conferences.

http://www.everydayhealth.com/adhd/adult-adhd.aspx

Sponsored by Everyday Health Media, this web page has information on the symptoms and treatments for ADHD. The website does accept advertisements for products in the ADHD marketplace.

http://www.helpguide.org

This site bills itself as a trusted nonprofit guide to information on mental health and well-being created to the memory of Morgan Segal, whose suicide may have been prevented by having better, factual information on mental health disorders and their treatment. The website notes that it collaborates with the Harvard Medical School concerning information posted to the site.

National Institute of Mental Health: http://www.help4adhd.org

Cocreated with the CHADD organization (see earlier description), this website is sponsored by the U.S. federal government and offers informative and useful fact sheets about many aspects of ADHD in children and adults.

http://www.totallyadd.com

This website was cocreated by two Canadians, one a comedian with adult ADHD and the other a video producer with adult ADHD, who became well known for their independently produced program, "ADHD and Loving It," that aired on many PBS and CBC stations several years ago. It provides a positive, light-hearted, and sometimes humorous approach to understanding ADHD in adults.

http://www.webmd.com

This is a for-profit website providing information on many medical and mental health disorders, including ADHD.

BOOKS AND VIDEOS ON ADULT ADHD

This list is not intended to be comprehensive or exhaustive but notes those books that I believe offer useful and evidence-based information on adult ADHD.

Adler, L. (with M. Florence). (2006). *Scattered minds: Hope and help for adults with attention deficit hyperactivity disorder.* New York, NY: Putnam.

Bailey, E., & Haupt, D. (2010). *The complete idiot's guide to adult ADHD*. New York, NY: Alpha Books.

Barkley, R. A. (2001). *ADHD in adults* [DVD]. New York, NY: Guilford Press.

Barkley, R. A. (with Benton, C. M.). (2011). *Taking charge of adult ADHD*. New York, NY: Guilford Press.

Barkley, R. A. (Ed.). (2015). *Attention-deficit hyperactivity disorder: A handbook for diagnosis and treatment* (4th ed). New York, NY: Guilford Press.

Barkley, R. A., Murphy, K. R., & Fischer, M. (2008). *ADHD in adults: What the science says*. New York, NY: Guilford Press.

Bramer, J. S. (1996). *Succeeding in college with attention deficit hyperactivity disorders: Issues and strategies for students, counselors, and educators*. Plantation, FL: Specialty Press.

Brown, T. E. (2013). *A new understanding of ADHD in children and adults: Executive function impairments*. New York, NY: Routledge.

Brown, T. E. (2014). *Smart but stuck: Emotions in teens and adults with ADHD*. Hoboken, NJ: Jossey-Bass.

Children and Adults With Attention-Deficit/Hyperactivity Disorder. (2001). *The CHADD information and resource guide to AD/HD*. Landover, MD: Author.

Goldstein, S., & Teeter Ellison, A. (2002). *Clinician's guide to adult ADHD: Assessment and intervention*. New York, NY: Academic Press.

Gordon, M., & Keiser, S. (Eds.). (2000). *Accommodations in higher education under the Americans With Disabilities Act (ADA): A no-nonsense guide for clinicians, educators, administrators, and lawyers*. New York, NY: Guilford Press.

Gordon, M., Lewandowski, L. J., & Lovett, B. J. (2015). Assessment and management of ADHD in educational and workplace settings in the context of ADA accommodations. In R. A. Barkley (Ed.), *Attention-deficit hyperactivity disorder: A handbook for diagnosis and treatment* (4th ed., pp. 774–794). New York, NY: Guilford Press.

Gordon, M., & McClure, F. D. (2008). *The down and dirty guide to adult ADHD* (2nd ed.). DeWitt, NY: GSI.

Hallowell, E. M., & Ratey, J. J. (1994). *Driven to distraction: Recognizing and coping with attention deficit disorder from childhood through adulthood.* New York, NY: Pantheon.

Hallowell, E. M., & Ratey, J. J. (2005). *Delivered from distraction: Getting the most out of life with attention deficit disorder.* New York, NY: Ballantine Books.

Jacobs, C., & Wendel, I. (with Cerulli, T.). (2010). *The everything health guide to adult ADD/ADHD: Expert advice to find the right diagnosis, evaluation, and treatment.* Fairfield, OH: Adams Media.

Joffe, V., & Iachan, M. (2006). *A day in the life of an adult with ADHD.* Miami, FL: Author.

Kessler, Z., & Quinn, P. O. (2013). *ADHD according to Zoe: The real deal on relationships, finding your focus, and finding your keys.* Oakland, CA: New Harbinger.

Kohlberg, J., & Nadeau, K. (2002). *ADHD-friendly ways to organize your life.* New York, NY: Routledge.

Levrini, A., & Prevatt, F. (2012). *Succeeding with adult ADHD: Daily strategies to help you achieve your goals and manage your life.* Washington, DC: American Psychological Association.

Lovett, B. J., & Lewandowski, L. J. (2015). *Testing accommodations for students with disabilities: Research-based practice.* Washington, DC: American Psychological Association.

Matlin, T., & Solden, S. (2014). *The queen of distraction: How women with ADHD can conquer chaos, find focus, and get more done.* Oakland, CA: New Harbinger.

Nadeau, K. G. (1994). *Survival guide for college students with ADD or LD.* Washington, DC: American Psychological Association.

Nadeau, K. G., & Quinn, P. (2002). *Understanding women with AD/HD.* Silver Spring, MD: Advantage.

Orlov, M. (2010). *The ADHD effect on marriage: Understand and rebuild your relationship in six steps.* Plantation, FL: Specialty Press.

Orlov, M., & Kohlenberger, N. (2014). *The couple's guide to thriving with ADHD.* Plantation, FL: Specialty Press.

Pera, G. (2008). *Is it you, me, or adult A.D.D.? Stopping the roller coaster when someone you love has attention deficit disorder.* San Francisco, CA: 1201 Alarm Press.

Pera, G. A., & Robin, A. L. (Eds.). (2016). *Adult ADHD-focused couple therapy: Clinical interventions.* New York, NY: Routledge.

Puryear, D. A. (2012). *Your life can be better: Using strategies for adult ADD/ADHD.* Minneapolis, MN: Mill City Press.

Ramsay, J. R., & Rostain, A. L. (2014). *Cognitive-behavioral therapy for adult ADHD: An integrative psychosocial and medical approach* (2nd ed.). New York, NY: Routledge.

Ramsay, J. R., & Rostain, A. L. (2015). *The adult ADHD tool kit: Using CBT to facilitate coping inside and out.* New York, NY: Routledge.

Ratey, N. A. (2002). Life coaching for adult ADHD. In S. Goldstein & A. Teeter Ellison (Eds.), *Clinician's guide to adult ADHD: Assessment and intervention* (pp. 261–279). San Diego, CA: Academic Press.

Ratey, N. A. (2008). *The disorganized mind: Coaching your ADHD brain to take control of your time, tasks, and talents.* New York, NY: St. Martin's Press.

Safren, S. A., Otto, M., Sprich, S., Winett, C., Wilens, T., & Biederman, J. (2005). Cognitive-behavioral therapy for ADHD in medication-treated adults with continued symptoms. *Behavior Research and Therapy, 43,* 831–842.

Safren, S., Perlman, C., Sprich, S., & Otto, M. W. (2005). *Therapist guide to the mastery of your adult ADHD: A cognitive behav-*

ioral treatment program. New York, NY: Oxford University Press.

Sarkis, S. M. (2008). *Making the grade with ADD: A student's guide to succeeding in college with attention deficit disorder.* Oakland, CA: New Harbinger.

Sarkis, S. M. (2011). *Ten simple solutions to adult ADD: How to overcome chronic distraction and accomplish your goals.* Oakland, CA: New Harbinger.

Sarkis, S. M., & Klein, K. (2009). *ADD and your money: A guide to personal finance for adults with attention deficit disorder.* Oakland, CA: New Harbinger.

Sarkis, S., & Quinn, P. O. (2011). *Adult ADD: A guide for the newly diagnosed.* Oakland, CA: New Harbinger.

Solanto, M. V. (2013). *Cognitive-behavioral therapy for adult ADHD: Targeting executive dysfunction.* New York, NY: Guilford Press.

Solden, S. (2012). *Women with attention deficit disorder: Embrace your differences and transform your life* (2nd ed.). Nevada City, CA: Underwood Books.

Surman, C. (2012). *ADHD in adults: A practice guide to evaluation and management.* Totowa, NJ: Humana Press.

Surman, C., Bilkey, T., & Weintraub, K. (2014). *Fast minds: How to thrive if you have ADHD (or think you might).* New York, NY: Berkley Trade.

Thurlow, M. L., Elliott, J. L., & Ysseldyke, J. E. (2003). *Testing students with disabilities: Practical strategies for complying with district and state requirements.* Thousand Oaks, CA: Corwin Press.

Tuckman, A. (2007). *Integrative treatment for adult ADHD: A practical, easy-to-use guide for clinicians.* Oakland, CA: New Harbinger.

Tuckman, A. (2009). *More attention, less deficit: Success strategies for adults with ADHD.* Plantation, FL: Specialty Press.

Tuckman, A. (2012). *Understand your brain, get more done: The ADHD executive functions workbook*. Plantation, FL: Specialty Press.

Wasserstein, J., Wolf, L. E., & LeFever, F. F. (2001). Adult attention deficit disorder: Brain mechanisms and life outcomes. In J. Wasserstein, L. E. Wolf, & F. F. LeFever (Eds.) *Annals of the New York Academy of Sciences* (Vol. 931, pp. 104–118). New York, NY: New York Academy of Sciences.

Weiss, M., Hechtman, L., & Weiss, G. (1999). *ADHD in adulthood: A guide to current theory, diagnosis, and treatment*. Baltimore, MD: Johns Hopkins Press.

Young, J. (2007). *ADHD grown up: A guide to adolescent and adult ADHD*. New York, NY: Norton.

Zylowska, L., & Siefel, D. (2012). *The mindfulness prescription for adult ADHD: An 8-step program for strengthening attention, managing emotions, and achieving your goals*. Westville, South Africa: Trumpeter.

INDEX

ABOUT THE AUTHOR

Russell A. Barkley, PhD, is a clinical professor of psychiatry at the Medical University of South Carolina. He holds a diplomate (board certification) in three specialties: clinical psychology, clinical child and adolescent psychology, and clinical neuropsychology. Dr. Barkley is a clinical scientist, educator, and practitioner whose publications include 22 books, rating scales, and clinical manuals; seven award-winning DVDs; and more than 260 scientific articles and book chapters related to the nature, assessment, and treatment of attention-deficit/hyperactivity disorder (ADHD) and related disorders. He is also the founder and editor of the clinical newsletter *The ADHD Report*, now in its 24th year of publication. Dr. Barkley has presented more than 800 invited addresses internationally and has appeared on nationally televised programs, such as *60 Minutes, The Today Show, Good Morning America, CBS Sunday Morning, CNN*, and many other television and radio programs to disseminate the science about ADHD. He has received awards from the American Psychological Association, American Academy of Pediatrics, American Board of Professional Psychology, Association for the Advancement of Applied and Preventive Psychology, the Wisconsin Psychological Association, and Children and Adults

With ADHD for his career accomplishments, contributions to ADHD research and clinical practice, and dissemination of science about ADHD. For more information, visit his websites (http://www.russellbarkley.org and http://www.adhdlectures.com).